# Teaching and Learning in Higher Education

# Teaching and Learning in Higher Education

Barry Dart

and

Gillian Boulton-Lewis

First published 1998
by The Australian Council for Educational Research Ltd
19 Prospect Hill Road, Camberwell, Melbourne, Victoria, 3124

Edited by Mignon Turpin
Designed and formatted by Pages in Action
Cover designed by Pages in Action
Printed by Print Impressions Pty Ltd

National Library of Australia Cataloguing-in-Publication data:

Dart, Barry C.
Teaching and learning in higher education.

Bibliography.
Includes index.
ISBN 0 86431 234 2.

I. College teaching. I. Boulton-Lewis, Gillian M. (Gillian Marie), 1940-.
II. Australian Council for Educational Research. III. Title.

378.125

# Foreword

## A TRIBUTE TO JOHN BIGGS

This book cannot do full justice to the contribution of John Biggs to educational theory and research. It does not attempt to represent the breadth and depth of his work over almost 40 years as a first rate educational psychologist. What the book does achieve, however, is a welcome recognition of the contribution of Biggs to the understanding of learning and teaching in higher education contexts. That contribution has been enormous and deserves to be celebrated.

In my judgment, and given my interest in synthesising research in education, especially across seemingly impenetrable ideological boundaries, the biggest benefit of the work of Biggs is the demonstration by his colleagues and by him that key educational concepts, such as surface and deep approaches to learning, can be researched across paradigms. It is interesting that some of the leading advocates and practitioners of phenomenographic research on learning are contributors to this book. While the phenomenographic tradition of inquiry has dominated the work in this area over the last two decades, Biggs and his colleagues have succeeded in showing that quantitative psychological approaches can produce knowledge that is just as hard-won and possibly more applicable. This is probably not the best place to provoke debate on that issue. Nevertheless, it is gratifying to see that recognition of excellence can be secured across the paradigms.

A search of the Social Sciences Citation Index evidences the fact that John Biggs is among the world's leaders of research on learning and cognitive processes in institutional settings, as well as in the application of this research in the professional development of teachers, particularly at the tertiary level. Moreover, he is one of the very few scholars who have succeeded in researching these matters cross-culturally.

I met John in Armidale, NSW, in 1963 in rehearsals for a local musical society's production of *The White Horse Inn*. He was the male, romantic lead, with a fine tenor voice, and I was a member of the chorus. We were both young lecturers at the time. Since then our paths have crossed and re-crossed many times – in Sydney, Newcastle and Hong Kong. Our minds have come closer together over the decades and I was especially complimented when he modified a model of research on teaching that Bruce Biddle and I had developed to produce what he called the '3P model'. I am pleased to see its usefulness demonstrated in his work and I am pleased to join with the others who have contributed to this book in celebrating his excellent contribution over many years.

Michael J. Dunkin
*The University of Sydney*

# Contents

# Figures and Tables

# Preface

This book is organised around one of the frameworks which Professor John Biggs has elaborated and modified over the last 20 years, the '3P model' of learning. The 3P model includes presage, process and product factors related to the learning process. Presage factors include both student and situational variables influencing learning and teaching; process factors concern how students go about their learning; and product factors refer to student learning outcomes.

The 3P model as developed by Biggs (1993) is an adaptation of a linear model proposed by Dunkin and Biddle (1974), '... not only to aid understanding of the teaching process but also to enable a summary of research knowledge' (p. 48). The 3P model of Biggs in its current form is a fully interactive systems model (Biggs, 1993).

This model enables teachers to be action researchers as it allows them to monitor and modify their teaching in light of their students' learning. This is possible since the model builds on research in student learning to illustrate the relations between student characteristics and what they think and do; teacher characteristics and what they think and do; and the quality of learning outcomes.

This framework gives the chapters a sense of coherence so that they present as a book rather than a set of related papers. The book consists of 11 chapters organised into five Parts, three of which reflect the parts of the 3P model, the fourth which encompasses the whole model, and the fifth, the conclusion, which integrates the preceding chapters and highlights implications for teachers.

## Part One
This section contains three chapters. Chapters 1 and 2 consider teachers' beliefs about teaching and how these influence their curriculum design and teaching approaches and the impact these have on student approaches to learning. Chapter 3 considers the

problems associated with measuring and modelling student individual differences in learning.

**Part Two**
Chapters 4 and 5 consider how students approach their learning in relation to the assessment specified for the subject being studied, and Chapter 6 reviews the use and appropriateness of the Study Process Questionnaire by Biggs for cross-cultural research into how students approach their learning.

**Part Three**
Chapter 7 proposes the use of the SOLO model (Structure of Observed Learning Outcomes), as an alternative taxonomy to Bloom's model, as a basis for the technology of testing within learning theory. Chapter 8 addresses the issue of quality in higher education through exploring the nature of learning and research.

**Part Four**
Chapter 9 considers how the SOLO taxonomy can be used in higher education as a means of facilitating and assessing learning and Chapter 10 is a case study of teaching and learning in one subject and illustrates the interrelatedness of the 3 'P's in the model.

**Part Five**
The final chapter, 'Teaching in Higher Education', sums up and identifies implications in the preceding chapters.

We would like to acknowledge the assistance of Sheina Brunsmann in producing this book. She organised all of us and attempted unsuccessfully to help us meet deadlines. She also sorted out disks and e-mails and assisted with re-typing.

## References

Biggs, J. (1993). From theory to practice: A cognitive systems approach. Higher Education Research and Development, 12, 73–86.
Dunkin, M., & Biddle, B. (1974). *The study of teaching*. New York: Holt, Rinehart, Winston.

# Notes on Contributors

**Gillian Boulton-Lewis** BA, MEd, PhD, Fellow of the Australian College of Education.
Professor of Education and Head, School of Learning and Development, Faculty of Education, Queensland University of Technology.

Gillian is the author of many books and articles on student learning and development. Her main area of expertise and research is in the application of cognitive theories of learning to mathematics education and, more recently, to teaching and learning in higher education.

**Barry Dart** BEd, MEdSt.
Barry is recently retired from his position of Lecturer, School of Learning and Development, Faculty of Education, Queensland University of Technology.

His main area of expertise and research is in teaching and learning, with particular focus on teaching approaches that facilitate students adopting deep approaches to their learning. Barry has had several chapters in books and journal articles published on student learning and development.

**Noel Entwistle** BSc(Hons), PGCE, PhD, Fellow of the British Psychological Society, Honorary Doctorate, University of Gothenburg, Sweden.
Professor of Education, Centre for Research in Learning and Instruction, University of Edinburgh.

Noel is an experienced editor and member of editorial boards. He is currently editor of *Higher Education* and is on the Editorial Board of the South African *Journal of Higher Education*. He has written widely on student learning

**John Hattie** BA, MA(Hons), PhD.
Professor and Chair of Educational Research Methodology, University of North Carolina at Greensboro.

John has been an advisory consultant for 17 journals since 1989. He has had over 100 articles, conference papers and reports published, covering many areas of research in higher education. His current areas of research interest are measurement, self-concept, and models of teaching and learning.

**David Kember** BSc, GradDipDistEd, MSc, PhD.
Co-ordinator of the Action Learning Project, Hong Kong.

David's previous positions have been in the Educational Development Unit of The Hong Kong Polytechnic University and a variety of Australian and overseas institutions. Student learning, its improvement through action research, distance education and open learning are his areas of interest on which he has written numerous books and articles.

**Elaine Martin** MA, PhD.
Professor of Higher Education and Head, Curriculum and Academic Development Unit, Royal Melbourne Institute of Technology, Victoria.

Elaine is currently joint editor of *HERD*, the journal of The Higher Education and Development Association of Australasia. Her research interests are in the area of teaching and learning in higher education.

**Ference Marton** BA, PhD, DSc.
Professor of Education, Department of Education and Educational Research, University of Gothenburg, Sweden.

Ference is Founder of Phenomenography which has produced 1000 publications based on its research methodology. He is on the editorial board of several education publications and is Scandinavian editor of the *International Journal of Qualitative Studies in Education*. He is author of over 170 publications.

**J.H.F. (Erik) Meyer** BSc(Hons), MSc, PhD.
Professor, School of Education, University of Cape Town.

Erik was Foundation Director of the Student Learning Research Group, University of Cape Town. He is a member of both the Editorial Advisory Board, *Higher Education* and the Editorial Board, *International Journal of Engineering Education*. He has written numerous journal articles and books on student learning.

**Michael Prosser** Bsc, DipEd, BEd, MAppSc, PhD.
Professor and Director, Academic Development Unit, La Trobe University, Victoria.

Michael's previous appointments were at Curtin University, Griffith University and the University of Sydney. His major area of research interest is in teaching and learning in higher education, particularly the relationship between qualitative variation in teaching and qualitative variation in student learning. He has published widely the results of that research.

**Nola Purdie** BEd, MEd, DipPhysEd. PhD.
Lecturer in Educational Psychology, School of Learning and Development, Queensland University of Technology.

Prior to university teaching, Nola taught and researched in Western Australian schools. Her current research into aspects of student learning focuses on conceptions of learning, self-regulated learning, approaches to learning, study skills and cross-cultural learning. She is widely published in journals in these areas.

**Paul Ramsden** BSc, MPhil, PhD.
Professor of Higher Education and Deputy Dean, Faculty of Education, Griffith Institute for Higher Education, Griffith University, Queensland.

Paul is a member of the Australian Vice-Chancellor's Standing Committee on Education and Students, and of the Course Experience Questionnaire Advisory Committee. His recent research areas include academic leadership, organisational development and university management. His writings on higher education have been widely published.

**Catherine Tang** BAppSc, MSc, PhD.
Assistant Director, Educational Development Unit, The Hong Kong Polytechnic University.

Catherine has over 15 years of teaching experience in tertiary education. Her main interest is in student learning, with a particular focus on the role of assessment in teaching and learning, Chinese students' approaches to learning, and the implications for staff development. She has several publications in these areas.

**Keith Trigwell** BSc, PhD.
Director, Centre for Learning and Teaching, University of Technology, Sydney.

Keith's most recent research interests relate to studies of the variation in the quality of university teaching, the experience of teaching, and an exploration of what constitutes the outcome of teaching.

**David Watkins** BSc(Hons), MSc, PhD.
Reader in Education, University of Hong Kong.

David has been published widely in education and psychology journals. His fields of research interest are cross-cultural studies of student learning and self-conception.

## PART ONE

CHAPTER 1

# Teaching Beliefs and Their Impact on Students' Approach to Learning

*David Kember*

## INTRODUCTION

TEACHERS AND LECTURERS

In Hong Kong, the University Grants Committee funds the Action Learning Project to encourage and support academics to engage in action research projects taking as their theme some aspect of their teaching and learning. It is currently supporting over 50 projects in the seven universities in Hong Kong. These action research projects take as their subject teaching and learning issues which interest, or are the concern of, the participants. Many seek to introduce forms of teaching which are quite innovative for higher education in Hong Kong, and probably in most of the rest of the world. Examples include:

- games and simulations
- multimedia packages
- peer assessment
- problem based learning
- project work
- reflective journals

Most of the projects have already led to conference papers as the academics concerned realise that the rewards of academia go to the most prolific publishers. It should not be too hard for those involved to find journals to publish their work as initiatives like these constitute innovative teaching in universities. Earlier action research-type studies in the Hong Kong Polytechnic have already led to publications about learning activities and games (Sivan, Leung, Gow & Kember, 1991; Sivan & Kember, 1996), peer teaching and peer assessment (Conway, Kember, Sivan & Wu, 1993), project work (Conway & Kember, 1993), teaching through self-study packages (Jones & Kember, 1994), reflection upon learning approaches (Davies, Sivan & Kember, 1994) and other teaching initiatives.

Supporting action research projects like these has become a major facet of my academic career. Yet, when I come home from work at the end of the day and listen to my children's accounts of what they did at their junior school, the Australian International School in Hong Kong, I often wonder at the contrast between school and university. Teaching approaches which are considered novel and innovatory at universities are used on a daily basis in my children's school.

In my children's school, project work is common, with themes which can last for up to a term. The projects usually incorporate work on several subjects from the curriculum, to facilitate interdisciplinary connections. The eldest children, at least, become involved in peer teaching by sharing what they have learnt from their project with the rest of the class. Problem based learning is used, particularly in science and mathematics. Activities may be tackled as a class, in a small group or as individual self-paced work. In the group activities the children are encouraged to solve problems and teach each other. In one of her classes my eldest daughter wrote a reflective journal which the teacher wrote responses to.

The junior school classrooms look totally different from those I am used to in universities. The school classroom is a melange of colours, shapes and activities. The desks are formed into flexible clusters. The university classroom, by contrast, is a dull orderly arena with benches fixed in neat rows, often tiered around the sole focal point of the imposing lectern.

I cannot cite a list of publications to 'prove' these observations and assertions. School teachers' career prospects do not revolve around the number of their publications. My descriptions of the school's teaching approaches are drawn from observations on various visits to the school and conversations with teachers. They also draw upon conversations with my children which, under academic conventions, can presumably be cited as personal communications (Kember; Heather, Annelise and Neal, personal communications). If this evidence seems insubstantial by formal academic conventions, I suspect that it will not be problematic to most readers as they will readily accept that there can be a marked distinction between prevalent teaching approaches in junior schools and universities. Most will have spent sufficient time in school and university classrooms to accept that both the physical environment and what takes place can be very different.

## BELIEFS ABOUT TEACHING

Before going any further I must be careful to draw out the implication I wish to make from this contrast between school and university teaching. I am certainly not setting out a claim that school teaching is of a much higher standard than that in universities. Even from my own experiences as a school student, I know that there are teachers who do not reach the standards set in my children's school. I have also been privileged to collaborate with some superb university teachers in action research projects, and these are by no means the only good teachers in universities.

Nor am I asserting that school teaching is invariably more innovative than university teaching. My very narrow sphere of comparison is insufficient for such global generalisations, and I am unsure as to the utility of such a comparison.

What I do wish to contrast are the beliefs about teaching of the teachers in my children's school with those commonly found in university academics. I intend to make the case that it is these beliefs which underlie and explain many of the disparities noted above between observed school and university teacher behaviours.

## RESEARCH INTO BELIEFS ABOUT TEACHING

In the early 1990s several groups of researchers were working quite independently to examine the beliefs about teaching of university academics. Some of the groups had noted that research into student learning had established a relationship between student conceptions of learning, learning approaches and learning outcomes. The search for a parallel relationship between lecturers conceptions of teaching, teaching approaches and possibly student learning approaches and outcomes appeared to be a logical development. There had been earlier research into the beliefs of school teachers (see for reviews Clark & Peterson, 1986; Pajares, 1992) but, as the introduction suggests, many university lecturers consider themselves a breed apart from school teachers. Universities also operate under quite different value systems and traditions to schools. While some elements of the school based research was likely to be applicable to university beliefs, it was also probable that there would be dimensions which were not apparent in school teachers, and certainly in junior school teachers.

Papers from the various groups, researching into university academics beliefs about teaching, appeared in journals mostly in the period from 1992 to 1994. As the groups had worked independently, and taking into account the time scale for work to be refereed and then published, there was little opportunity for comparison of results in the published papers. It is now possible to compare the published outcomes to look for commonality.

Awareness of the literature came originally through contact with some of the other research groups, and a more systematic search was subsequently made through the ERIC index. Searches were made on terms such as *beliefs about teaching* and *conceptions of teaching*, usually combined with *higher education*. It is quite possible that there is other published material on this topic which has not been discovered. Educational researchers' use of terminology tends to be looser and less prescribed than in some other disciplines, so computer searches can never guarantee a complete return. The ERIC index, also, is not comprehensive so book chapters or conference papers, for example, might have been missed.

Efforts were made to track down what has been written, but if the odd article has been missed this is not seen as problematic. The aim was not to produce a comprehensive review of everything which has ever been written on this topic. It was rather to analyse and compare the outcomes of a substantial number of largely independent studies to see what commonality there was in the findings.

## THE STUDIES

The search located 14 studies, which are summarised in Table 1.1. All of the samples were drawn from university academics except

TABLE 1.1    Research into conceptions of teaching

| Author(s) | Date | Sample | Location | Comments |
|---|---|---|---|---|
| Dall'Alba | 1991 | 20 teachers in 4 subject areas | Australia(?) | |
| Dunkin | 1990 1991 | 55 new lecturers | Sydney | |
| Dunkin & Precians | 1992 | 12 award winners | Sydney | |
| Fox | 1983 | ? | Britain | Develops metaphors |
| Gow & Kember Kember & Gow | 1993 1994 | 39 lecturers | Hong Kong | Developed questionnaire for larger sample |
| Martin & Balla | 1991 | 13 staff enrolled in course for academics | Melbourne | |
| Martin & Ramsden | 1992 | 13 staff enrolled in course for academics | Melbourne | 5 case studies followed, 3 presented |
| Pratt | 1992 | 253 adults and teachers of adults | Canada, China, Hong Kong, Singapore, USA | Concentrates on adult education |
| Prosser et al. | 1994 | 24 teachers of 1st year physics and chemistry | Australia | Focus on conceptions of science teaching |
| Samuelowicz & Bain | 1992 | 13 academics in science and social sciences | Australia and Britain | British University was distance teaching one |
| Trigwell et al. | 1994 | 24 teachers of 1st year physics and chemistry | Australia | Concentrates on intention and approach |
| Trigwell & Prosser | 1996 | 58 chemistry and physics lecturers | Australia | Developed questionnaire to examine the relationship between intention and approach |

that of Pratt (1992) which focuses upon adult educators. This study was included, though, as at least some proportion of the sample were university academics and adult students are commonly found in higher education. The studies were located in diverse countries, but Australia was particularly strongly represented.

The reviewed work was limited to those studies which gathered data from university academics on their conceptions of teaching, so did not include speculative or theoretical treatises. The study by Fox (1983) was borderline in this respect as the article did not describe in any detail the way in which data were gathered and analysed. It seems as though the data gathering may have been somewhat impressionistic. However, as the categories were illustrated with vivid, easily understood metaphors and there turned out to be a good concurrence with other work, the article was used.

Other work used semi-structured interviews to gather information about university academics beliefs or conceptions of teaching. In the main, the questioning appears to have allowed the interviewee to talk about broadly related topics.

The interview transcripts were analysed by searching for categories with common themes, which were allowed to emerge from the data. About half the studies are described by their authors as using phenomenographic methods as devised by Marton (1981, 1988).

## COMPARISON OF CATEGORIES

Comparison of the labels and descriptions given for the categories indicates a high degree of commonality in the categories. Precisely the same wording or terminology may not be used, but it seems reasonable to interpret categories as similar if the descriptors appear to have the same or similar meanings. The groupings are further strengthened by comparing the category descriptors and sample quotations that are usually given in the papers. The finding that a number of largely independent studies has a high degree of consistency in identified categories considerably strengthens the credibility of the research.

Table 1.2 presents an attempt to show the commonality of the categories of conceptions of teaching identified by the individual studies. The organising framework for the table is based on the relationship between the teacher, students and the content. The conceptions identified in the various studies are arranged under a framework ranging from a teacher-centred/content-oriented pole to a student-centred/learning-oriented pole.

In Table 1.2 vertical relationships indicate perceived similarities between the categories for describing conceptions derived in the reviewed studies. There is obviously an element of subjectivity in judging the equivalence of described categories and compiling such a table. Direct equivalence is not necessarily implied as reducing the table elements to the author's category label inevitably results in the loss of the subtlety of the accompanying description. Some of the authors themselves, though, (e.g. Prosser, Trigwell & Taylor, 1994; Samuelowicz & Bain, 1992) have remarked upon the relationship of their categories to those of some subset of the other authors' work in the table.

The first two categories for Dall'Alba (1991) and Prosser et al. (1994) have two categories within the one column. By comparison with other categorisation schemes these were interpreted as subcategories of the same conception. The studies by Trigwell, Prosser and Taylor (1994) and Trigwell and Prosser (1996) examined intentions and strategies.

There is one identified conception in the study by Pratt (1992) which does not fit within the table because the focus is an ideal which overshadowed the elements of the teacher, the student and the content, chosen for the framework. Pratt discovered a variety of beliefs such as religious doctrines or political ideologies which underpinned this conception. In each case, though, the strength of conviction led to the ideal dominating any other element in the teaching process. Pratt's study was with adult educators and it seems unlikely that this conception would be common in universities. Basing teaching upon a single fervently held ideal would normally be seen as inconsistent with the goals of universities, founded on Western models, which stress critical thinking and encourage the plurality of viewpoints.

## CATEGORIES FOR CONCEPTIONS OF TEACHING

This section discusses the categories of conceptions of teaching shown in Table 1.2. For each of the categories identified in the meta-

TABLE 1.2    Comparison of categories for conceptions of teaching

| Author(s) | Date | Imparting information | Transmitting structured knowledge | Student-teacher interaction |
|---|---|---|---|---|
| Dall'Alba | 1991 | Presenting information<br><br>Transmitting information | Theory to practice<br><br>Developing concepts | |
| Dunkin<br><br>Dunkin & Precians | 1990<br>1991<br><br>1992 | | Structuring learning | Motivating learning |
| Fox | 1983 | Transfer | Shaping | |
| Gow & Kember<br>Kember & Gow | 1993<br>1994 | Knowledge transmission | | |
| Martin & Balla | 1991 | Presenting information | | Encouraging active learning |
| Martin & Ramsden | 1992 | Presenting content of process | Organising content and/ or procedures | |
| Pratt | 1992 | Delivering content | | |
| Prosser et al. | 1994 | Transmitting concepts<br><br>Transmitting teachers' knowledge | Helping students acquire concepts<br><br>Helping students acquire teachers' knowledge | |
| Samuelowicz & Bain | 1992 | Imparting information | Transmitting knowledge | |
| Trigwell et al.<br><br>Trigwell & Prosser | 1994<br><br>1996 | Information transmission/ teacher-focused* | Concept-acquisition/ teacher-focused* | Concept acquisition/ student-teacher interaction* |

* The intention is shown before the / and the strategy after.

| | Facilitating understanding | Conceptual change/intellectual development | |
|---|---|---|---|
| Developing capacity to be expert | Exploring ways of understanding | Bringing about conceptual change | |
| | Encouraging activity and independence in learning | | Establishing interpersonal relationships conducive to learning |
| Building | Travelling | | Growing |
| | Learning facilitation | | |
| | Relating teaching to learning | | |
| | Organising learning environment | | Facilitating understanding through engagement with content and process |
| Modelling ways of being | Cultivating the intellect | | Facilitating personal agency |
| | Helping students develop conceptions | Helping students change conceptions | |
| | Facilitating understanding | Changing student conceptions | Supporting student learning |
| | Conceptual development/ student-focused | Conceptual change/ student-focused | |

analysis, quotations from the original works are used to illuminate the category. Table 1.2 is ordered from information transmission on the left to intellectual development on the right. In the latter sections of the chapter, I discuss whether this ordering is consistent with a developmental continuum. To maintain consistency with my initial theme, the descriptions of categories starts with the intellectual development pole and, therefore, works from right to left across the table.

## CONCEPTUAL CHANGE/INTELLECTUAL DEVELOPMENT

The conception which seems closest to that of the teachers at my children's school is given the label 'conceptual change/intellectual development'. In the table these are shown as two columns at the student-centred/learning-oriented pole, as two distinct labels are used in the studies. It is noteworthy, though, that only the work of Samuelowicz and Bain (1992) has conceptions in both columns. This perhaps suggests that these two identified conceptions are alternative aspects or descriptions of one position. Changing student conceptions is not an easy process and perhaps needs the establishment of a sympathetic and supportive environment. In this chapter the two conceptions are, therefore, treated as different facets of the one conception.

The first facet envisages a holistic developmental process resulting from the establishment of inter-personal relationships between teacher and student. Good junior school teachers clearly conceptualise their roles in terms of the development of the children in their class. The structure of reports and the topic of parent-teacher discussions often centre on how a child has developed since the last meeting. An analogy to nurturing is made by Pratt (1992), and by Northedge (1976) in the quotation below.

> ... we view the ground as already covered with vegetation (concept systems), some of which is clearly worth retaining and cultivating.... In the garden plants will tend to grow quite readily regardless of intervention from the gardener, and it is his aim to encourage certain plants at the expense of others; finding ways of acting as a catalyst in bringing out the best he can from the available ground. The gardener does not work towards a precisely defined end, since the garden is continually changing as different plants come to their prime. He has broad plans as to how he wants the garden to develop (probably rather flexible ones, which change as possibilities within the garden reveal themselves), but

he does not attempt to specify the exact dimensions that each plant (or concept structure) is to achieve. (Northedge, 1976, p. 68)

The other aspect or related conception focuses upon changing student conceptions:

What I want to achieve with [these techniques] is confronting students with their preconceived ideas about the subject, which quite often conflict with what we are talking about – the official dogma as it were. So you've got to bring out that conflict and make the people aware that what they already know may not be what is the official line. (Trigwell et al., 1994, p. 81)

[Conceptual understanding is developed] by arguing about things, and trying to apply ideas, and being again confronted by differences between what you think and what actually happens ... to get people to make predictions about what's going to happen, maybe they might backtrack and revise their ideas about things ... what's going on in their heads ... What we're trying to achieve in learning physics, is for people to shift their view from the layperson's view, to what we would call a scientific/physicist's view ... view of the world. I think that's what I'm on about. (Prosser et al., 1994, p. 225)

FACILITATING UNDERSTANDING

The other conception consistent with student-centred/learning-oriented beliefs has a variety of labels but appears consistently in virtually all of the reviewed studies. The common elements are facilitating the development of understanding or conceptions of knowledge, so the label 'facilitating understanding' is used.

The role of the teacher is recognised by those holding this conception as that of helping the student to learn. They accept that they do have a responsibility towards students learning and that they can influence outcomes. The emphasis is on student learning outcomes rather than upon defining content. Teaching becomes a process of helping students towards desirable outcomes.

You've got to be able to make an environment where students really want to learn. If you do that, they are much more likely to understand why they learn. And then I think after that, the teacher should be a resource person, ... generally to guide the students, I don't see it as spoon-feeding. (Kember & Gow, 1994, p. 63)

The outcome of the teaching process is understanding. The student demonstrates this by applying the knowledge, rather than through regurgitation. 'They [students] have learned because they could apply it in some real situation and make sense of it' (Samuelowicz & Bain, 1992, p. 100). Students are recognised as individuals rather than as an audience to be lectured to. The teachers recognise that students may not interpret what they were saying in the intended way:

> I'm aware of how much I used to assume. I now try to take nothing for granted and to question my assumptions about what students know and how they see things. Also I don't expect my sessions to have the effect I intend. I'm looking for evidence of learning before I assume it. I try to be in a position where I expect the unexpected response. (Martin & Balla, 1991, p. 301)

## STUDENT-TEACHER INTERACTION

There is a conception which is seen as intermediate between the student-centred/learning-oriented and teacher-centred/content-oriented poles. It is characterised by a recognition that interaction between teacher and student is important. A quotation illustrates this position in the context of a science practical class:

> But I don't want the students to take everything I say at face value. I like them to think for themselves so I try to get them to interpret before I tell them, if possible. So if I do a demonstration, I won't tell them what the result will be... I often ask them to predict the result, having given them the principles. (Trigwell et al., 1994, p. 80)

The following quotation suggests that the lecturer has moved on to the previous conception. In reaching that conception, though, there must have been a realisation that it was necessary to interact with students in class. As well as illustrating the particular category, the quotation suggests that the categories can be seen as a developmental continuum, an idea which is further explored in the final sections of the chapter.

> Initially, I basically talked and they listened – that type of attitude. Now I am trying to get much more, you know, they talk and I listen. And I am there as a guide – to guide them, not to force something down their throats. (Kember & Gow, 1994, p. 63)

Three studies identify conceptions which see the student as needing to be shaped towards a particular role or form of expertise – the teacher thus has the role of model or expert. Again it is possible to view these categories as a further aspect of the one intermediate position. Dall'Alba (1991) calls this conception 'developing the capacity to be an expert' and illustrates this aspect with the quotation below:

> One of the barriers you would want to break down ... is the barrier which says all the time ... there are authors and there are critics... But never I am an author, I am a critic ... and as a reader, as a writer, I'm part of this ongoing process... And for this reason I proposed a course in which the writing of texts of all sorts ... is an important element ... they are involved week by week in being authors and critics themselves. (p. 295)

Pratt (1992) envisages this conception as a fusion of the teacher and the content – the teacher signifying the knowledge and content to be learnt. There is then a greater stress on learning activities such as experiments or problem solving classes as the student needs to learn how to perform like the master.

## TRANSMITTING STRUCTURED KNOWLEDGE

For the conceptions under the teacher-centred/content-oriented pole, the student is, at best, recognised as a passive receiver. For the transmitting structured knowledge conception, the lecturer does at least recognise that there is a receiver out there who does need to catch what is thrown. The ball, then, needs to be thrown carefully and accurately so that it can be caught.

> Teaching is transmission of concepts and skills in such a way that students can acquire them ... that sounds a very rudimentary sort of approach, but I think there is a body of knowledge and skills that students need to start off with. (Samuelowicz & Bain, 1992, p. 101)

The conception focuses upon transmitting knowledge but recognises that if the knowledge is to be caught it needs to be presented clearly. Fox (1983) describes the devotees as 'conscientious transferers' who

> spend a great deal of time preparing the material and making sure that it is accurate and up-to-date. Some of them also go to great lengths to develop and refine their method of transfer and they often devise

elaborate teaching aids to inject the essence of their subjects accurately into the heart of the container. (p. 152)

There may be a need for simplifying material so that it can be understood by the student. For this aspect of the presentation Fox uses a baby food manufacturing analogy: 'the teacher sees his job as one of processing very tough material into more easily digestible nutrient for rather simple minds' (p. 153).

Sound academic knowledge is the most important attribute of a good teacher, but there is also emphasis on the quality of the presentation which can be viewed as a stage performance.

> I have a set of lecture notes that's my safety belt and sometimes I stick very closely to those and other times if the circumstances are right when things click I leave my lecture notes well behind and wander off and march up and down and make jokes fly free so to speak. (Samuelowicz & Bain, 1992, p. 101)

The importance of arranging the material in a logical manner is recognised so that the student has more chance of receiving the information. One of the lecturers, used as a case study by Martin and Ramsden (1992), saw the importance of structuring the material which was being taught:

> You learn the theory that underpins the systems and that helps you to see what you're doing when you're working with the systems.... It's most helpful if it's properly structured. There should be some concepts which are fundamental and those have to be dealt with first.... If you can set up the structure of that content then it shouldn't be the problem I found it, for instance.... It's a structured body of knowledge that models the operation of computer programs. (p. 8)

Another lecturer envisages the process as developing a picture. 'If they could see the picture even just once, they would be helped.... They have to have an image of where they are going.... Once they can see the pathways' (Martin & Ramsden, 1992, p. 8).

## IMPARTING INFORMATION

The most teacher-centred conception views teaching as purely presenting information. The student is viewed as a passive recipient of a body of content, if indeed the student appears in the vision at all.

In its extreme form the student hardly enters the picture. At the most the student is a vessel into which knowledge is poured.

It is common to see teaching defined in this way and several of the papers have interview quotations which virtually paraphrase the conception title. 'Pass information onto students, that is the major goal' (Kember & Gow, 1994, p. 64), '[teaching] means that you're imparting information ... that they [students] are expected to get because they are enrolled in that course' (Samuelowicz & Bain, 1992, p. 101).

Of Fox's (1983) metaphors the broadcast variant of the transfer theory best illustrates this conception:

> ... views teaching as scattering seeds to the wind rather than transfer-ring them to specific containers. All that is required of a teacher is that he deliver himself of his nuggets of wisdom. Whether or not these are relevant or applicable in particular contexts or whether they make any sense to anybody but himself is not his concern. His responsibility is solely concerned with ensuring the purity of the seed. (p. 153)

The focus is upon the lecturer, and his or her knowledge, so a good teacher is considered to be one with sound academic knowl-edge:

> ... knowledgeable, they must be sound. They must convey their field very well. And they must be able to teach, that is, to convey what they have learned to the students. I mean they can't just go to the lecture and talk nonsense. (Kember & Gow, 1994, p. 64)

Those in this category describe their teaching as lecturing and focus upon the notes they prepare:

> I'll write my notes in such a way so that the students don't have to decide when to take notes. I'll tell them to. I'll dictate to them. I have handouts prepared. I have gaps in them that they fill in and I take that decision away from the students about when and how to take notes. (Trigwell et al., 1994, p. 80)

It is not just researchers, but students too, who have observed this conception. 'They try to stuff us with information. Employers have complained that we are like robots, lacking in independent thinking and disinterested in the things happening around us' (Gow & Kember, 1990, p. 320).

## TWO LEVEL CATEGORY SCHEME

The exercise of comparing the category schemes for describing conceptions of teaching in the various studies suggests that the outcomes can be synthesised into a common model. The teacher-centred/content-oriented and student-centred/learning-oriented framework does seem to provide a suitable basis for ordering the conceptions. These dimensions were those most commonly used in the studies to characterise and distinguish the categories, though other dimensions such as the 'conception of knowledge' were used in some studies as additional distinguishing characteristics.

Indeed the utility of these dimensions in analysing the categories suggests that, rather than listing conceptions implying a single level structure, it would be more revealing to portray them in two levels of categories. This description is akin to a first and second order factor structure. The higher level category would consist of two broad orientations, the first a teacher-centred/content-oriented orientation and the other a student-centred/learning-oriented orientation.

Figure 1.1 shows a two level categorisation model. The model posits two broad higher level orientations labelled teacher-centred/content-oriented and student-centred/learning-oriented. Subordinate to each orientation are two conceptions. A fifth intermediate conception, in which teacher-student interaction is first recognised as necessary, is included as a transitionary bridge between the two orientations and their subordinate conceptions.

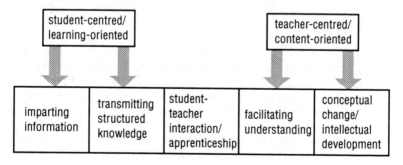

FIGURE 1.1    A two level model for categorising conceptions of teaching

Returning to my starting point, this analysis has shown that there are some university academics who hold similar beliefs about teaching to the junior school teachers at my children's school. These would be in the conceptual change/intellectual development category. Others are ranged across a spectrum towards the imparting information pole. Indeed it is reasonable to see the category schemes at the lower levels as a continuum. Prosser et al. (1994) also talk of a 'spectrum' with two ends, while Samuelowicz and Bain (1992) state that there is 'broad agreement that these conceptions can be arranged on a continuum' (p. 93). I will discuss later whether it is reasonable to see it as a developmental continuum.

## THE EFFECT ON STUDENT LEARNING

At this point it is appropriate to consider the significance and utility of these efforts to characterise beliefs about teaching. Is it just an academic exercise which has generated a healthy number of publications or do the findings have implications for our practice? I would argue that it is definitely the latter since there is evidence of links between the teaching beliefs and teaching strategies and, more significantly, with the learning approaches of students.

Trigwell et al. (1994) found a logical relationship between identified intentions of lecturers and the strategies they claimed to adopt. Those who intended to transmit information adopted teacher-focused strategies while others who believed in conceptual development or change adopted student-focused strategies.

Trigwell and Prosser (1996) developed, from this study, a questionnaire which contained scales corresponding to two intentions (information transfer and conceptual change) and three strategies. Factor analysis showed that the information transmission intention was related to teacher-focused strategies. The conceptual change intention went with more student-focused strategies involving student-teacher interaction.

Gow and Kember (1993) found a relationship between lecturers' conceptions of learning and measures for changes in students' approaches to learning between the beginning and end of degree programs. Departmental scores were obtained for two main orientations to teaching; knowledge transmission and learning facilitation. These were related to measures of students' approaches to learning from the Study Process Questionnaire (Biggs, 1987), which gives values for deep, surface and achieving approaches, and can be applied in a repeated measure design to show change in approach during a course. The results showed that orientations to teaching had significant correlations with changes in students' learning approaches. By the normal standards of educational research many of the observed correlations were quite appreciable. Departments more attuned to learning facilitation were less likely to promote a surface approach to learning. Departments with high mean scores for the knowledge transmission orientation tended to depress the use of a deep approach to learning.

Sheppard and Gilbert (1991) found that the development of student epistemology was influenced by the lecturer's theories of teaching and the students' perception of the learning environment and in turn the learning approaches they adopted. By students' epistemologies the authors referred to the students' belief about the structure of knowledge in their discipline. The research consisted of case studies of four departments. It found that meaningful learning outcomes were more likely to be associated with courses in the departments which explicitly considered alternative conceptions of knowledge.

Together these studies suggest a relationship from teaching conceptions, through approaches or strategies for teaching, to student learning approaches which will in turn influence student learning outcomes. The relationship may be envisaged as a variant of the Biggs 3P model of student learning (e.g. 1987).

Figure 1.2 shows a pictorial representation of the model. Conceptions of teaching are included in the Presage area. Teaching approaches and student learning approaches are in the Process section. Biggs (1987, p. 9) includes teaching method as a presage variable but that diagram was described as a general model of student learning. The focus of this discussion is more on teaching, so it seems reasonable to see the process element as including both teaching and learning processes. The Product part consists of student learning outcomes which are recognised as intimately related to learning approaches, but may not have high correlations with formal outcome measures such as GPA and examination results.

Other variables have been added to the model only if relevant to the discussion, which follows, on the significance of teaching

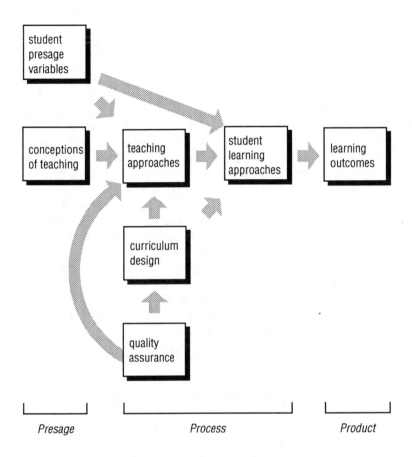

FIGURE 1.2    Conceptions of teaching, teaching approaches and learning outcomes related in a 3P model

conceptions for efforts to improve the quality of teaching and learning. The model, therefore relates to quality assurance systems and educational development activities. There are obviously other variables related to these factors, the most pertinent of which are shown in the portrayal of the model by Biggs.

## TEACHING APPROACHES

Before looking at the implications for educational development, it is necessary to clarify the relationship between teaching conceptions and approaches to teaching. At the information transmission end of the continuum, there is likely to be an almost exclusive reliance upon a unidirectional lecture approach. Even classes designated as tutorials are likely to end up largely as monologues. It is hard to see anyone holding such beliefs engaging in more interactive teaching methods such as dialogue or role play.

Those holding conceptions towards the opposite end of the framework will need to employ more interactive and student-centred teaching methods if they are to be consistent with their beliefs. There will not, though, always be an automatic relationship between underlying beliefs and observable teaching approaches at this end of the spectrum. Those holding student-centred conceptions of teaching may at times still have to employ approaches which appear inconsistent with that belief. They are likely to use methods such as lecturing and spend a proportion of their time communicating content and bodies of knowledge. This does not imply, though, that while they are doing this they have changed or switched off their underlying beliefs. The lecturing would be just one element in a wider effort to facilitate learning.

## EDUCATIONAL DEVELOPMENT IMPLICATIONS

The model in Figure 1.2 has considerable implications for both educational development and quality assurance schemes. The model, and the research on which it is based, suggest that underlying beliefs about teaching have a marked influence upon the teaching approaches adopted, which in turn affect student learning approaches and outcomes. However, both educational development activities and quality assurance mechanisms usually focus upon teaching approaches and take no account of the conceptions of teaching which underpin the approach.

The most common educational development activities (Moses, 1985) are workshops, consultancies and short courses which focus upon teaching methods and developing teaching skills. The relationship between beliefs and learning approaches suggests that it is those towards the information transmission end of the continuum who are most in need of educational development support. However, because of their beliefs it is this very group who are least likely to attend voluntary activities and most unlikely to put into effect any ideas on interactive or small group teaching. Any workshop is likely to have limited outcomes if the underlying beliefs of the participants are inconsistent with the conceptual framework of the initiative.

Quality assurance schemes also monitor teaching approaches since these can be reported, measured and examined. Peer review panels expect teaching approaches to be described and then discussed and perhaps observed. Student feedback questionnaires examine the manifest signs and outcomes of the teaching method. Recommendations for change inevitably concern the teaching method or the content. Quality assurance rarely, if ever, questions underlying beliefs about teaching which means that those assessed may fail to properly implement the recommendations because they are incompatible with their alternative conception of teaching.

In Figure 1.2, the model shows quality assurance influencing curriculum design and in turn teaching approaches. These are also affected by student presage variables. In view of the above discussion, the lack of an arrow from either quality assurance or curriculum design to conceptions of teaching should be seen as a significant and intentional absence.

## CHANGING BELIEFS

An alternative approach to educational development visualises the spectrum of beliefs on teaching as a developmental continuum. That it is a developmental continuum is not yet firmly established, but there is evidence, given in the remainder of this section, to suggest that lecturers can change their beliefs over time towards the student-centred/learning-oriented pole.

A logical position for improving teaching quality follows from the interpretation of beliefs about teaching as a developmental continuum. If beliefs about or conceptions of teaching can be changed there should be a corresponding influence upon teaching approaches and in turn an improvement in the quality of student learning. Educational development activities should, therefore, incorporate opportunities for participants to shift beliefs along the continuum towards the student-centred/learning-oriented pole.

However, advancing this as a logical position is easier than finding ways to put it into practice. Changing beliefs is never an easy process and is likely to be particularly difficult when academic conventions and long-held deep-seated beliefs are involved. Merely telling lecturers about the alternative conceptions and asking them to change theirs will inevitably prove futile. Any initiative which concentrated exclusively on teaching conceptions could be perceived as a crude attempt at mind-washing with inevitable negative consequences.

The few documented attempts to promote conceptual change with teachers at the tertiary level take a long term approach. The process of conceptual change is embedded naturally within another activity in which the participants confront their teaching beliefs and practices. Bowden (1988) describes a workshop which aims to expose disparities between espoused theory and theory in use, although, as Bowden points out, such workshops are only the start of a process because significant changes to teaching and learning require sustained effort over a lengthy period of time.

Martin and Ramsden (1992) report outcomes from a one year course for tertiary teaching which monitored changes in conceptions of teaching of the participants. The three presented case studies clearly show that the lecturers change their conceptions of teaching during the course. Again, though, it is obvious that change takes time, so Martin and Ramsden recommend that any such courses extend over a period of at least one year.

My own attempts to bring about changes in teaching orientation have followed an action research format (Kember & Gow, 1992; Kember & Kelly, 1993; Kember & McKay, 1996). Action research follows spirals or cycles of planning, acting, observing and reflecting, so there is an opportunity to work with academic staff over an extended period to allow time for conceptual change. The observation or evaluation phase of the action research cycle can be seen as a process for lecturers to confront the outcomes of their own teaching. The initial project cycles often reveal more fundamental problems at the course or department level. This can lead to the core participants trying to alter the teaching orientations of their colleagues.

It should be noted that each of these three approaches take place over an extended period and operate within the framework of either a short course or a project. Within these the participants observe or evaluate the impact of their teaching upon their students' learning. This in itself can cause the teachers to examine the intended or unintended outcomes of their own actions and beliefs. Reflection upon these actions, preferably as part of a small supportive group, can be a mechanism for changing beliefs.

## ACADEMICS *AND* TEACHERS?

The school teachers I highlighted at the beginning of this chapter clearly envisage teaching as a student-centred learning-oriented activity. They see it as their responsibility to facilitate the development of the children in their class. The development process encompasses the personal development of the children, their understanding of concepts and appreciation of values. Much of the work involves conceptual change and there are some enormous conceptual leaps to be made.

Many university academics, though, would be quite offended to be called a 'teacher'. Rather, they tend to refer to themselves in terms of their academic discipline or their professional affiliation – as physicists, historians, mechanical engineers or surveyors, for example. Their role is then simply that of conveying the knowledge and expertise of their discipline or profession.

However, the student does not receive due attention in this perspective. It is all very well to scatter the gems of wisdom to the winds, but what if they are not caught or fall on barren ground?

Educational developers and those concerned with quality assurance need to consider whether their schemes address the underlying beliefs about teaching held by academics. They need to get academics to think of themselves as teachers as well as specialists in their discipline area. Both the how and the what of teaching are important, though, so they should not argue that lecturers become teachers rather than discipline experts. The message is that an academic needs to be a discipline expert and a teacher.

## References

Biggs, J. (1987). *Student approaches to learning and studying*. Melbourne: Australian Council for Educational Research.

Bowden, J. (1988). Achieving change in teaching practices. In P. Ramsden (Ed.), *Improving learning*. London: Kogan Page.

Clark, M., & Peterson, P. (1986). Teachers' thought processes. In M. Wittrock (Ed.), *Handbook of research on teaching* (3rd ed., pp. 255–296). New York: Macmillan.

Conway, R., & Kember, D. (1993). Effecting changes in the teaching of practice management. *Optometric Education, 18*(4), 119–123.

Conway, R., Kember, D., Sivan, A., & Wu, M. (1993). Peer assessment of an individual's contribution to a group project. *Assessment and Evaluation in Higher Education, 18*(1), 45–56.

Dall'Alba, G. (1991). Foreshadowing conceptions of teaching. In B. Wright (Ed.), *Research and Development in Higher Education, Vol. 13, Teaching for Effective Learning* (pp. 293–297) Campbelltown, NSW: Higher Education Research and Development Society of Australasia (HERDSA).

Davies, H., Sivan, A., & Kember, D. (1994). Helping Hong Kong Business students to appreciate how they learn. *Higher Education, 27,* 367–378.

Dunkin, M.J. (1990). The induction of academic staff to a university: processes and products. *Higher Education, 20,* 47–66.

Dunkin, M.J. (1991). Orientations to teaching, induction experiences and background characteristics of university lecturers. *Australian Educational Researcher, 18*(1), 31–52.

Dunkin, M.J., & Precians, R.P. (1992). Award winning university teachers' concepts of teaching. *Higher Education, 24,* 483–502.

Fox, D. (1983). Personal theories of teaching. *Studies in Higher Education, 8*(2), 151–163.

Gow, L., & Kember, D. (1990). Does higher education promote independent learning? *Higher Education, 19,* 307–322.

Gow, L., & Kember, D. (1993). Conceptions of teaching and their relationship to student learning. *British Journal of Educational Psychology, 63,* 20–33.

Jones, A., & Kember, D. (1994). Approaches to learning and student acceptance of self–study packages. *Educational and Training Technology International, 31*(2), 93–97.

Kember, D., & Gow, L. (1992) Action research as a form of staff development in higher education. *Higher Education, 23*(3), 297–310.

Kember, D., & Gow, L. (1994). Orientations to teaching and their effect on the quality of student learning. *Journal of Higher Education, 65*(1), 58–74.

Kember, D., & Kelly, M. (1993). Improving teaching through action research. *N.S.W.: HERDSA Green Guide,* 14.

Kember, D., & McKay, J. (1996). Action research into the quality of student learning: A paradigm for faculty development. *Journal of Higher Education, 67*(5), 528–554.

Martin, E., & Balla, M. (1991). Conceptions of teaching and implications for learning. *Research and Development in Higher Education, 13*, Brisbane (pp. 298–304).

Martin, E., & Ramsden, P. (1992). *An expanding awareness: how lecturers change their understanding of teaching.* Paper presented at the 1992 HERDSA Conference, Gippsland.

Marton, F. (1981) Phenomenography: Describing conceptions of the world around us. *Instructional Science, 10*, 177–200.

Marton, F. (1988). Phenomenography: Exploring different conceptions of reality. In: D.M. Fetterman (Ed.), *Qualitative approaches to evaluation in education: the silent scientific revolution.* New York: Praeger.

Moses, I. (1985). Academic development units and the improvement of teaching. *Higher Education, 14*, 75–100.

Northedge, A. (1976). Examining our implicit analogies for learning processes. *Programmed Learning and Educational Technology, 13* (4), 67–78.

Pajares, M.F. (1992). Teachers' beliefs and educational research: Cleaning up a messy construct. *Review of Educational Research, 62*(3), 307–332.

Pratt, D.D. (1992). Conceptions of teaching. *Adult Education Quarterly, 42*(4), 203–220.

Prosser, M., Trigwell, K., & Taylor, P. (1994). A phenomenographic study of academics' conceptions of science learning and teaching. *Learning and Instruction, 4*, 217–231.

Samuelowicz, K., & Bain, J.D. (1992). Conceptions of teaching held by academic teachers. *Higher Education, 24*, 93–111.

Sheppard, C., & Gilbert, J. (1991). Course design, teaching method and student epistemology. *Higher Education, 22*, 229–249.

Sivan, A., & Kember, D. (1996). Structuring learning activities. *Innovations in Education and Training International, 33*(4), 203–212.

Sivan, A., Leung, R.W., Gow, L., & Kember, D. (1991). Towards more active forms of teaching and learning in hospitality studies. *The International Journal of Hospitality Management, 10*(4), 369–379

Trigwell, K., & Prosser, M. (1996). Congruence between intention and strategy in university science teachers' approaches to teaching. *Higher Education, 32*, 77–87.

Trigwell, K., Prosser, M., & Taylor, P. (1994). Qualitative differences in approaches to teaching first year university science. *Higher Education, 27*, 75–84.

# CHAPTER 2

# Approaches to Teaching Creative Writing

*Elaine Martin and*
*Paul Ramsden*

## INTRODUCTION

This chapter examines aspects of teaching the subject of *creative writing* in two first year university courses. The formal descriptions of these subjects, their aims and objectives, their content and teaching methods are documented and described in similar ways. We will see, however, that lecturers represent the field of creative writing in different ways, express different ideas of how students should be brought into a relationship with the subject and have different understandings of what it takes to teach and learn it.

## CREATIVE WRITING AS A UNIVERSITY SUBJECT

Creative writing used to be a subject that was taught in primary schools and in the earlier years of secondary school. Its purpose and merits as a topic of study have been debated (see, for example, Barnes, 1985). Its supporters have seen it as a means of encouraging young people with limited experience of literature to practise writing and to think about their own potential for effective and creative communication. On the other hand, because the ability to work with words and sounds and with subtleties of feeling and meaning may take priority over formal grammar and syntax, others have accused the subject of being responsible for a perceived decline in standards of written English.

The study of English at university level traditionally had little to do with developing literary ability in students. Although, for example, students might sometimes be required to write a sonnet, in order to understand better the structure of the poetic form, this detour into individual creativity was seen as a means to an end, rather than an end in itself. The purpose of a degree course in English was to study the literature of the English language.

Over the past 20 years there has been a steady increase in the number of university courses which have offered creative writing subjects to their students. Fifteen years ago, for example, none of Melbourne's three universities offered such a subject. Today, four of the city's six universities offer creative writing either as a whole subject or as a substantial topic within a subject. The rise in popularity of these courses has been linked to a change in emphasis in the English curriculum, from a study of the works of great men and women towards the deconstruction of texts and the questioning of once accepted merit and meaning. It has been asserted that it is not only the great writers who have something to say; all men and women might contribute to the continuing story of men and women in their world (Tracy & White, 1988).

Pressure to introduce such subjects has also come from students who have risen through a school system which taught and encouraged creative writing. Students and younger lecturers have often become powerful partners in a push to establish creative writing courses in otherwise traditional curricula (Martin, 1994). Moreover, creative writing has been interpreted as an extension of a more generalised ability to communicate and it has been suggested that an increase in subjects focused on writing, including those on creative writing, would be likely to improve the capacity of students to communicate effectively in writing (Moodie, 1986).

Students' competence in writing is an issue that has been studied extensively at university level (see, for example, Taylor, et al., 1988; Prosser & Webb, 1994). Most of this literature has focused on assignment and essay writing, however, and not on the development of creative writing. Stylistic and aesthetic considerations, and the desire to excite emotion as well as thought, which are central to creative writing, have not been emphasised. An interesting exception is 'Approaches to Learning and to Essay Writing' by Biggs (1988), in which the author explores the challenge of 'composing' and comments on the concerns of students of English and journalism courses about the 'feel' or 'cadence' of a particular word. Students may spend a good deal of time and effort attempting to find the right word or the right string of words. Biggs draws parallels with literary writing and emphasises the need to balance textual and semantic demands and get appropriate links between what is said and what is meant and how else it might be put. These comments are salient in the context of this chapter on the teaching of creative writing and we will return to them later.

## THEORETICAL BACKGROUND

The present study formed part of a larger Australian Research Council (ARC) project which examined the different ways in which lecturers approach their teaching (Martin & Balla, 1991; Patrick, 1992; Ramsden, Balla & Patrick, 1992). As Biggs (1996) has shown, teachers generally make decisions about how to teach in line with an explicit or implicit theory of teaching; our work sought to describe differences in how academics think about the subject they teach, how they represent to students the particular subject matter they are expected to learn, and how they actually bring their students into a relationship with this subject matter. How the teacher established this relation was seen as shaping the kind of learning which was expected; how the teacher framed the subject matter established what was to be learned. The theoretical ideas developed in the ARC Study are exemplified in the doctoral work of Patrick (1992). The central idea of Patrick's study of Year 12 physics and history teaching in Victorian high schools was that teachers construct an 'object of study' for their students and that teachers present their students with different objects of study which embody different conceptions of what is to be learned. In doing this, teachers can be seen as legitimate and necessary makers of curricula.

This model is consistent with the broad theoretical tradition of non-dualism in educational research, which asserts that meaning is created or constituted by the learner, in opposition to the dualist view that knowledge exists independently of the knower and can be learned and applied separately from its context. Much research into student learning and teaching, both in schools and in higher education, has been conducted from the latter tradition, which closely resembles what Marton has called a 'first order' perspective (Marton, 1986) in which the intention is to describe aspects of teaching from the perspective of an independent observer (Clark & Peterson, 1986). The work by Patrick and the present Study are based on a 'second order', non-dualist view of learning and teaching in which the focus is placed on the learner's experience of learning and the teacher's experience of teaching (Biggs, 1996; Prosser & Trigwell, 1996). One approach to educational research based on this second order perspective is phenomenography (Marton, 1986). Phenomenography attempts to map the range of ways in which people think about a given phenomenon – in this case, the learning and teaching of creative writing. The main outcome of the analysis is a set of precisely-constituted categories. What is being sought are the most distinctive characteristics of the range of experiences investigated, together with an understanding of how these distinctive character-istics relate one to the other. What is mapped is the essential variation in ways of understanding a phenomenon. The structure may be charted on two dimensions, one representing *what* is being focused on in attending to the phenomenon (the 'referential' as-pect) and the other representing *how* the focusing is done (the 'structural' aspect). Typically, the resulting variation represents more and less sophisticated ways of understanding a phenomenon and the outcome space suggests a hierarchy. What emerges are categories of description which, though originating from a contextualised understanding, are subsequently decontextualised and can there-fore be applied to contexts other than the original one.

In the analysis undertaken in this Study, we examine qualitative variation in the ways in which six lecturers approached the teach-ing of creative writing.

## CONDUCT OF THE STUDY

Two first year creative writing subjects in two English courses (in neighbouring universities) formed the source of the research data. Both subjects had very similar aims and methods. One subject was being studied by 100 students with five staff forming the teaching team. The other subject involved 40 students and two staff. Four teachers from the first subject and both the teachers from the sec-ond subject agreed to be interviewed and observed.

We carried out an initial one hour interview with each lecturer at which the Study was explained and curricula material gathered. Each lecturer was asked to talk about their understanding of what the subject was, what they wanted to achieve and how they would achieve it. Prior to each of three observations of teaching, we asked lecturers to talk about their aims for the session and the teaching methods to be adopted. Following the teaching sessions, there were debriefing interviews when the lecturers talked about the extent to which they had achieved their intentions. Open-ended questionnaires were administered to students after each session asking them for comments on the observed sessions and, after the final observation, for their experiences of the subject as a whole.

## CATEGORIES OF DESCRIPTION OF TEACHERS' APPROACHES TO TEACHING CREATIVE WRITING

The analysis identified four categories which describe the essential features of the variation in approaches to the teaching of creative writing.

### Category A
Teaching is approached by a focus on existing literature. Creative writing is taught by requiring students to read this literature. The assumption is that by reading good literature students will have models of what good writing looks like and consequently learn how to write themselves.

### Category B
Teaching is approached by a focus on developing the skills and the craft of writing. It is taught by requiring students to listen to writing and to write themselves. The assumption is that the sound of words is important because sound contributes to the meaning, by affecting the way the reader feels about the passage.

### Category C
Teaching is approached by a focus on developing the skills and craft of writing. It is taught by requiring students to listen to writing and to write themselves and also to think about how what they want to say is affected by what they write. The assumption is that the selection of particular words or phrases will change the 'message' and students can use this as a device to reflect on what they say.

### Category D

Teaching is approached by a focus on what it is students have to say. It is taught by requiring students to reflect intently on what it is they have to say and to work with words to explore ways of saying what they have to say.

The structural relationship between these categories is shown in Table 2.1. This shows the analysis in terms of referential and structural aspects of teaching creative writing.

TABLE 2.1   Relationship between categories of approaches to the teaching of creative writing

| How is the teaching carried out? | What is the focus of teaching? | | |
|---|---|---|---|
| | Established literature | Skills and craft | Having something to say |
| Requiring students to read | A (X) | | |
| Requiring students to write | | B (X X) | |
| Requiring students to reflect on what they have to say | | C (X X) | D (X) |

A, B, C, D = categories of teachers' approaches
(X) indicates the distribution of teachers in the sample against the categories

Category A is the only category which has as its primary focus the reading of established literature and which sees reading as a way of teaching creative writing. Category B acknowledges the importance of reading existing literature, but this is not the focus. The emphasis is on the development of the skills and the craft of writing and this is done by getting students to listen to literature and to write themselves. Students are encouraged to think about the sound of words and sentences and the effect this has on the feelings and thoughts of those who read the text.

Category C is referentially similar to Category B, in that the focus is on craft and skills, but the way in which this focus is established, through the teaching, is different. In this category, teachers encourage students to think about what the writer wants to say and then to consider how the use of certain words or literary devices might subtly change meaning. Category D differs from C, and all other categories, in that the focus of teaching creative writing is on encouraging students to come to know what it is they have to tell the world. The means of doing this, the development of appropriate skills to convey knowledge and emotion, is secondary to the message.

In common with most phenomenographic analyses, the resulting categories of description appear to form an inclusive hierarchy with the lower level categories (Category A, in particular) representing an unproblematic understanding of the teaching and learning of creative writing and the higher categories representing a more complex understanding of what creative writing is and how students might be brought into a relationship with it.

## CASE STUDIES

The phenomeonographic analysis provides a map of what our small sample of six teachers focused upon and an indication of the variation in that sample. It does not provide a detailed description of their intentions and the processes by which they realised them – with evidence, in other words, of how teachers 'aligned' their objectives, assessment and teaching strategies (Biggs, 1996). In the second part of this chapter we provide these more detailed descriptions using case studies of teachers who represent categories (A), (C) and (D) in the phenomenographic outcome space. We present these descriptions under three headings. The first two reflect the central questions of this Study: *What did knowledge of this subject consist of for this teacher? How were students taught the subject matter and how was it assumed that students would learn?* The final heading, *How do students respond?* is not intended to be a thorough analysis of learning outcomes, but to provide readers with an insight into how students commented on their experiences of the classes. These data were collected from the open-ended questionnaires administered after each of the three observation sessions.

## CATEGORY A – JOHN

*What did knowledge of this subject consist of for this teacher?*
John explained that in order to write English, you have to know English, consequently it was essential to be a good student of literature to do well in this subject. For John, the significance of the creative writing subject in the course was that it influenced students' understanding of the existing literature and their understanding of writers and poets and their life and times:

> You can't know how hard it is to write – a piece of romantic poetry, for example – until you've tried. You begin to get a whole new understanding of the people and the times when you do try. To get into that way of thinking and composing is to see an age and its writing in a very special way.

John did talk of writing, but it was not central to his focus on the subject. It was a means to an end rather than an end in itself:

> Writing is not just something which comes naturally to a few gifted people, it's something we can all be helped to engage in more effectively... Most of us won't be recognised for our writing, but through writing we can learn a lot ... a lot about life and society and people in different times operating under different assumptions and restraints. A lot can be learned about literature and about history, through writing.

*How were students taught the subject matter and how was it assumed they would learn?*
John understood literature as something that was read privately and analysed thoroughly and reflectively, rather than something which was read in class and commented upon spontaneously. The study of literature was a matter of knowing, rather than of feeling:

> Students need to work with these pieces beforehand and to think hard about them. They need to dig deeply and painstakingly. It's not a matter of just responding intuitively, it's a matter of analysing intelligently.

In class, John himself provided detailed biographical and historical information together with analysis, while students took notes and listened. The analysis was detailed and systematic. Students were invited to interrupt at any time and they did, but the comments were all analytical rather than emotional. Around 15 minutes of each class was set aside for comment on students' writing. The writing of one or two students had been circulated at the end of each class, to be read in advance and discussed by the group the following week. The class discussion of student work was analytic and critical, but not unkind:

> I see my task as providing encouragement but also direction for improvement. I temper my comments accordingly.

John believed that by learning about existing acclaimed literature, students would acquire the skills and knowledge to write themselves. The practice of writing they did in their own time, but feedback and guidance was provided for them in class as a group activity.

### How did students respond?

In their comments students emphasised the emphasis on the literary and analytical nature of the subject:

> This subject is very analytical. Sometimes I would like to say that I like a piece or hate a piece or how I feel about a piece.

They also commented that they would like more of an emphasis on writing rather than reading:

> We spend a lot of time reading and analysing when this is supposed to be about writing.

But most students were appreciative of John's expertise and commitment to literature and the opportunity to have feedback on their own writing and they responded positively:

> We get good feedback on our own writing and a very thorough understanding of the writing in other ages...

> He really knows the material .

> There are a lot of good writers in this class it is very beneficial to see what they write and to hear how it might be improved.

> It's good to have an opportunity to write and to have real critical feedback on that writing.

In summary, it can be said that John focused on literary analysis. He saw this as an essential tool for understanding writing style and a prerequisite for students to write themselves. His focus was always on knowing and understanding literature. There was no reference to the way writing made readers feel.

## CATEGORY C – JUNE

*What did knowledge of this subject consist of for this teacher?*
June described the subject as offering students the opportunity to develop both as writers and as students of literature. She said that in order to understand what literature is and what creative writing is, students needed to get a feel for the historical and geographical perspectives of where and how a genre emerged. They also had to know something of the technical and craft problems in reproducing that genre. So they needed to try to write, for example, a Shakespearian sonnet or a contemporary protest poem.

For June, the subject was about developing skills as a writer. To assist this, students studied existing literature but they also practised writing and had their own writing criticised as much as they criticised the work of established writers:

> Students should make an attempt to develop work either in imitation of forms and styles encountered in the course, or as parody of them, or in some way be influenced by them ... the aim is to produce crafted writing themselves.

*How were students taught the subject matter and how was it assumed they would learn?*
A class in this subject involved June herself reading aloud a series of two or three short pieces and analysing the pieces with the students. She always read pieces aloud, 'because the sound of words is so important'. Her analysis involved examining the way the piece was written, the syntax, the language, the imagery and how and why it worked or did not work:

> Writing means making us feel, as well as making us know, and the use of syntax as well as words is central to that. It's not just having a good vocab. It's much more [than] that; it's knowing [how] to work with language like a craftsman, knowing how to fashion a sentence, a paragraph, a page to make it do what you want it to do.

June emphasised that working with language and meaning was an iterative process:

> The thing is, you start to say something and then you realise that the language has taken it off in another direction and actually you might

rather like that and you follow where the language is leading you. It's part of the joy of creation. Students need to be encouraged to experiment and play with language in this way. This is the way they gain confidence and competence with the medium.

Each class had a theme, such as the use of dialogue. June read and discussed selected pieces for 15 minutes and for the remainder of the one hour class students wrote and discussed their own writing. They were given an exercise and perhaps 10 minutes to write to the exercise. They then read their pieces to each other in pairs and finally selected pieces to read to the whole group.

June did not lead the discussion or analysis, but she was clear about what she wanted students to get out of the exercise and she directed discussion accordingly. Always there was an emphasis on how writing made students feel, as well as what styles and authors it drew on, and how it might have been changed or developed. The writer's meaning was not central to the discussion; it was the mood or feelings evoked which were emphasised. The exercises were seen as preparation for the two more significant pieces of creative writing which students prepared as assessment tasks. There was a great buoyancy in the classes. June emphasised that a class should be enjoyable as well as instructive for her as well as for the students:

> I enjoy the subject. I enjoy reading the pieces I select. I genuinely am interested to hear the comments of students ... I'm lucky to work with these people, so many of them really want to write and enjoy writing ... I guess they're lucky to be here too.

### How did students respond?

Without exception June's students were enthusiastic about the topic. In particular, they emphasised how much they had learned about writing:

> At school we did a lot of creative writing, but here we actually learn how to do it.

> I have developed a lot as a writer through this subject.

There was also comment on June's enthusiasm:

> I never leave a class feeling low.

> I always go away wanting to read something or write something.

To sum up, June focused on helping students to develop skill and craftsmanship in writing. She emphasised the way words and syntax could be manipulated to influence emotion. She stressed the aesthetics of words and sentences, what they sounded like, what pictures and feelings they called up in the reader, and how they made the reader feel.

### CATEGORY D – SAM

*What did knowledge of this subject consist of for this teacher?*
For Sam, this subject was about helping students to know what they had to say, by getting them to grow in understanding of themselves. They did this through reading literature relevant to their own experience and then writing in a way which was 'powerfully honest'. Like June and John, she saw reading of literature as important, but she selected more recent and local literature as being most appropriate:

> There is much excellent writing, from everywhere and every time ... but this subject is about helping contemporary students find their own voice. The literature likely to help with that is more limited.

Sam argued that the perennial questions for young people were: Who am I? What do I have to say? and How can I make myself heard? She suggested that this subject helped students to address these critical questions.

### How were students taught the subject matter and how was it assumed they would learn?
Sam selected readings which she felt would make students reflect on some particularly salient aspect of their own experience. She invited students themselves to suggest pieces which they had found particularly evocative and she sometimes used pieces written by students in the previous year. She said she used these readings not as examples of skilled writing, but as examples of compelling messages. The task for the students (also the major assessment task) was to develop and craft their own message. The weekly classes aimed to assist this process.

Each week, out of class time, students were expected to read a selection of readings. Each week, in class time, they were asked to respond to one of the readings with one or two pieces of writing of their own. This could be a piece of writing to help them work through the way they thought about an issue or it could be a response which emphasised the way they felt about an issue. They were given 10 minutes to write and then they put the piece into one of two piles on the floor. One pile was for pieces emphasising thoughts and ideas; the other for writing which emphasised feelings and emotions. Students were called upon to pick pieces out of the two piles and to read them aloud. There was then comment and discussion both about the quality and craft of writing and about the issues and emotions explored.

Sam said that in working through the two piles she hoped to indicate that a balance was necessary between the salience of what is said and the beauty and aptness of how it was said:

> The intuitive way a writer feels, in a million subtle ways about a topic, should control the language and imagery and syntax. The skill is to temper honesty with impact, not to do something just for effect.

Sam took the pieces away, typed them up and circulated them to all students later.

### How did students respond?
Students were extremely positive:

> This subject has helped me think as well as write.

> It's given me a new insight into literature and writing and myself.

Perhaps the most telling evidence of Sam's success was that over the past five years, two of her students have been awarded literary prizes.

In summary, Sam's focus was on what students had to say and in finding ways to say that effectively and honestly. Her belief was that an essential first step in writing was to be sure of the message to be got across, then to consider the medium. Sam, like the other teachers, was aware of the importance of learning from existing literature, though she was selective in her choice of literature. She was also, like some of her colleagues, eager for students to develop writing skills and craft and for them to learn to invoke emotion through their craft. But she was the only one of the teachers who emphasised the pre-eminence of the message and considered that in balancing style with meaning, meaning must be dominant.

## DISCUSSION

The focus of this Study has been on the ways in which six lecturers differently interpret and represent a creative writing subject. A salient aspect is the clear connections between the ways in which teachers understand their subject, the ways in which they practise in the classroom, and the students' experiences. Similar connections have been documented in previous work (Ramsden, 1992; Biggs, 1993; Prosser & Trigwell, 1996) but it is the manufacture of differing content through the process of teaching that is the striking feature of the present results. As the case studies demonstrated, different representations of the subject matter mean that essentially different curricula are presented for students to learn. It is worth noting that, in all the case studies, students made complimentary comments on the quality of the teaching they experienced. In all cases the teachers could be described as devoted and competent. How they taught and what they taught varied significantly, however, and so did what the students learned.

This issue of teachers interpreting this creative writing subject differently can be seen in the context of two sets of comments made by Biggs (1988) and cited earlier in this paper. The first set relates to the topic of writing itself and emphasises the connections between literary writing and assignment writing and 'the need to get the right interaction between what is said and what is meant and how else it might be put' (p. 205). The second set relates to teachers having implicit or explicit theories of teaching and making decisions about how to teach in line with these theories of teaching (Biggs, 1996). Clearly, the interviews reveal different implicit theories or conceptions of teaching. These are associated with different teaching decisions and, apparently, different forms of understanding among students.

In the case of the topic of writing itself, it might be argued that the main difference between assignment writing and creative writing is in the balance between message and that aspect of writing craft called style. In assignment writing the focus is typically on the message, with little attention to style and aesthetics or attempts to evoke emotion. In creative writing the order of priorities is reversed. Biggs (1988) argues that in both assignment writing and literary writing an equilibrium needs to be struck between style and content. In the present study, however, we have found such a balance to be uncommon. The belief that in creative writing meaning can be sacrificed to the pursuit of style appears prevalent amongst university teachers of creative writing. Whether the corresponding belief that style can be forfeited to content is common among teachers who set assignments in other subject areas is an attractive speculation.

In the case of these teachers' conceptions of teaching, the variations in approaches to creative writing identified in this study bear interesting relations to the categories described in Biggs's SOLO taxonomy (Biggs & Collis, 1982). As Prosser and Trigwell (1996) have shown, university science teachers' conceptions of teaching and learning are to some extent consistent with the SOLO categories. The lecturers in Prosser and Tigwell's research who held conceptions of teaching as transmitting the syllabus, and conceptions of student learning as acquiring the information in that syllabus, seemed to understand the connections between teaching and learning in a unistructural way; they could not 'see the point' of explaining what they meant by learning. Teachers who could explain what they meant by teaching *and* learning, but explained them independently of each other, could be seen to be working at a multistructural level; while those who could explain how the two aspects of the educational process were related were operating at a relational level.

In the present case of teaching creative writing, Category A is the least developed conception. It might be described as unistructural, since the teacher's focus is only on the analysis of existing literature and the intent is to get students to know this literature. Category B is a multistructural response: students have to be familiar with existing literature and they have to be able to develop the craft of writing; they have to know about analysis and they have to be aware of the emotion evoked through language, but there is little emphasis on relating literary knowledge and skill to knowing and feeling. Category C seems to be a form of relational response: it relates an emphasis on literature and on craft to an emphasis on meaning and feeling. Category D resembles an extended abstract response. These teachers see the subject matter of creative writing as being more than a craft which competently combines message and medium, thought and feeling; it is conceptualised as a mechanism for personal interrogation, for finding an important message to send, and for identifying an honest way of sending that message.

## References

Barnes, D. (1985). *From communication to curriculum.* London: Penguin.

Biggs, J.B. (1988). Approaches to learning and to essay writing. In R.R. Schmeck (Ed.), *Learning strategies and learning styles.* New York: Plenum Press.

Biggs, J.B. (1993). From theory to practice: a cognitive systems approach. *Higher Education Research and Development, 12,* 73–85.

Biggs, J.B. (1996). Enhancing teaching through constructive alignment. *Higher Education, 32,* 347–364.

Biggs, J.B., & Collis, K.E. (1982). *Evaluating the quality of learning: The SOLO taxonomy.* New York: Academic Press.

Clark M., & Peterson. P. (1986). Teachers' thought processes. In M. Wittrock (Ed.), *Handbook of research on teaching* (3rd ed., pp. 225–296). New York: Macmillan.

Martin, E. (1994). Variations in awareness: How academics teach creative writing. *Occasional Paper 94.1,* Educational Quality Assurance Research and Development, Royal Melbourne Institute of Technology.

Martin, E., & Balla, M. (1991). Conceptions of teaching and implications for learning. *Research and Development in Higher Education, 13,* 298–304.

Marton, F. (1986). Phenomenography: A research approach to investigating different understandings of reality. *Journal of Thought, 21,* 28–49.

Moodie, G. (1986). *Standards and criteria in higher education.* Guildford: Society for Research into Higher Education and NFER Nelson.

Patrick, K. (1992). *Teachers and curriculum, at year 12: Constructing an object of study.* Paper presented at the AARE, Deakin University, Australia.

Prosser, M., & Trigwell, K.(1996). Relations between perceptions of the teaching environment and approaches to teaching. *British Journal of Educational Psychology, 67,* 25–35.

Prosser, M., & Webb, C. (1994). Relating the process of undergraduate essay writing to the finished product. *Studies in Higher Education, 19,* 125–138.

Ramsden, P. (1992). *Learning to teach in higher education.* London: Routledge.

Ramsden, P., Balla, M., & Patrick, K. (1992*). Teachers and curriculum in the first year courses.* Paper presented at the Australian Association for Research in Education (AARE), Deakin University, Australia.

Taylor, G., Ballard, B., Beasley, V., Bock, H., Clanchy, J., & Nightingale, P. (Eds.). (1988). *Literacy by degrees.* Milton Keynes: Society for Research into Higher Education and Open University Press.

Tracey, D., & White, P. (1988). *Fiction and the unconscious.* Milton Keynes: Open University Press.

# CHAPTER 3

# A Medley of Individual Differences

*J. H. F. Meyer*

## INTRODUCTION

You have to memorise some facts and important points ... because to understand certain things you have to connect different ideas and information, and by using facts you can develop your own ideas about something. I think memorisation is, in a way, giving you a core of information, and understanding allows you to connect different parts. (First year engineering student)

When I was at school I would just open a book at any time and I would memorise the whole book, without taking a break, and I would tomorrow write a test and get a very excellent mark, without having any worries at all. So now here at the 'varsity things have gone a different way, and every time I want to learn, any time, I find it so difficult to try and learn. (Second year science student)

I see learning as an ongoing process. It is a change in the way I see things, change of worldview, change in understanding. It involves experience and reflection ... I know that I often alter my opinion about something after I have been exposed to another perspective. (Third year education student)

This chapter deals with some aspects of the *individual differences* that characterise the manner in which students engage the content and the context of learning. The most important question that can be directed at the manifestation of such differences is that of *consequentiality* – the 'so what if' question. In order to inform educational theory and practice at the most basic level of application –

that of the individual learner – we presume that we can gather information, and thus form knowledge, about contextualised learning behaviour that can help us to predict or anticipate the consequences of inferred individual differences. Such knowledge is of profound strategic value to educational practice.

Learning in a relational and transformative sense is referred to here as 'virtuous'; it is a complex multivariate phenomenon in both process and outcome terms; it is shaped by a web of dynamically interwoven influences, many of which are closed to external observation. But there are many things that we can observe or infer about learning, either in terms of what students do or from what they tell us. The data gathering tools that we use to collect and shape this information are important, and they broadly favour either quantitative or qualitative research methodologies. In either case there is a fundamental requirement to address and interpret the presence of inter-individual *variation* in the data which is of theoretical or practical consequence.

Methodologically there may be different assumptions about the properties of the data gathered, as well as its latent (or unobserved) structure. But, again, this diversity is not in itself a cause for concern provided that full justice is done to the inter-individual variation present in the data. Hypothetically it really makes no difference whether a dimension of inter-individual variation in learning behaviour emerges as a 'category of description' in the outcome space of a phenomenographic analysis of interview transcripts, in the common joint space of an unfolding solution, or in the linear structure of a common-factor solution. But concerns do arise when we want to locate, and model, individual differences in such a hypothetical dimension of the data structure.

In general, concerns here are essentially those of complete individual-response location within data structures, and the 'fitting' of conceptual models to such structures for interpretive or inferential purposes. These are not trivial problems for educational researchers to overcome (Meyer, 1996).

## THE ANALYSIS OF INDIVIDUAL DIFFERENCE DATA

At a conceptual level, we can infer all sorts of consequences from the simple truths students tell us when we ask them equally simple questions about how they go about, and experience, learning.

We thus have access to valuable information, but data gathering tools, conceptual models, and analytical procedures (including statistical models) are required to help us shape that information if we are going to harness it for theoretical or practical purposes. The most widely used of these tools, models and procedures all bring with them their own particular assumptions and limitations. A brief exposure to some of these constraints forms the background to arguments that are developed further on in this chapter.

## PHENOMENOGRAPHY

Some of the most penetrating insights into the experience of learning have come from analyses (of interviews) that seek to interpret and preserve the internal horizons of learners themselves. From an individual-difference modelling perspective it is therefore paradoxical that the phenomenographic paradigm, which initially places so much conceptual emphasis on the experience of the individual (interviewee), subsequently *loses* the status of the individual response in terms of analytical method. This loss occurs in both the initial concentration of individual 'similarities of variation' into categories, and in any differences that may emerge between such categories. While it may remain theoretically possible to locate an individual partial response (experience) within a definitional category to which that response has contributed, it is usually impossible to locate the complete response within the overall structure of the outcome space.

There is an added tension within the phenomenographic paradigm itself in terms of 'logically' resolving the possible uniqueness of a single individual response in relation to categories of description that are either being 'discovered' or have been 'constructed'. Indeed, 'outlying' responses may simply be *discarded* as an arguably legitimate part of the analytic process. Phenomenography, quite simply, does not attempt to preserve individual differences across the dimensions of the outcome space. These, and other tensions, are only partially attributable to what Bowden and Walsh (1994) discuss as 'variations in method'.

It is also difficult to map some basic data description concepts onto phenomenographic 'categories of description'. Such a single category of individual responses, for example, can be ambiguously interpreted as either a measure of location, a measure of dispersion, or both. 'Reliability' in its various interpretations of internal consistency within, or reproducibility of, 'categories of description' is also a problematic concept in phenomenography. There are, in fact, some serious methodological and theoretical inconsistencies surrounding the concept of phenomenographic 'reliability' as Sandberg (1995) has begun to flesh out.

## MULTIVARIATE CORRELATION MODELS

There are many families of models of this form that are routinely used in educational research. These models have the attractive capacity to analyse complex multivariate data in terms of various experimental designs and test hypotheses concerning posited explanatory relationships in the data. Such models also bring with them the assumption of *linearity;* any inferences based on their application are therefore limited to a vision of the observables being constrained to interact in a particular manner.

Some linear models (such as common-factor models) have the capacity to reduce multivariate complexity to a parsimonious form that can provide powerful insights into the latent structure of the observables. This is an application that has been widely employed in studies of student learning. A common-factor model also has the theoretical capacity to represent individual differences, but a limitation is that it does so in an abstract sense that is not directly determinable from what has actually been observed. This limitation is discussed more fully further on.

Linear models in their more esoteric forms can provide powerful and testable insights into how many aspects of the world of the observables plausibly function. It is therefore appropriate, in the context of this chapter, to dwell for a moment on the nature of a linear model, and what such a model implies in student learning terms. The simplest linear model that can be fitted to two observables (variables $x$ and $y$, say) is reflected in the ubiquitous correlation coefficient. The calculation of a correlation coefficient carries with it an implicit test (or presumption) of hypothetical linear association between two variables.

If there is evidence for such an association that is perfect (as indicated by a correlation coefficient with an absolute value of one) then it means that the variation in $y$ is proportional (or inversely so) to the variation in $x$, and that the relationship between the two can be fixed in the form of an equation: $y = a+bx$ where $a$ is a constant (called the intercept), and *b* is the constant of proportionality (called the regression coefficient).

In the perfect case this equation would hold true for all the observations in question. So, if *y* is an outcome measure of, say, zero to full 'understanding' on some scale, and *x* is similarly a measure of learning 'process', then the conceptual question here is whether it makes sense to posit the existence of such a linear relationship as the basis for explaining *differences* between individual student outcomes. To imply, in essence, that individuals differ from one another in terms of fixed multipliers of the differences between observables seems an odd way to explain the free spirit of human learning behaviour. If such an explanation seems odd in the special (perfect) case, it is even more odd in the real world of observation, and measurement error, where the correlations are usually far from perfect, and the corresponding regression equations are based on optimal approximations.

## INDIVIDUAL-DIFFERENCE MODELS

In contrast, some quantitative analytical methods (such as multidimensional unfolding analysis) are based on non-linear individual-difference statistical models. These models emphasise the uniqueness of *all* observed individual responses and they seek to *preserve* such observed uniqueness, or at least reproduce it within known and acceptable limits of error. Data are not discarded because of a lack of inter-individual conformity.

Unfolding analysis, in particular, can be performed in the absence of linear assumptions. This is an important property for, in practice, the relationship between what students do and what they accomplish is usually non-linear across the full range of the outcome measure. As a descriptive technique the unfolding model has the potential to represent differences between how individuals engage learning in a more sensitive and natural way compared to other quantitative methods. A detailed technical, and non-technical, introduction to unfolding analysis (with numerous examples) is provided in Meyer and Muller (1990).

## INTENTION, MOTIVATION AND PROCESS

In thus introducing the world of explanatory observables, we need to note at the outset that observation tools (by virtue of the manner in which we use them), and conceptual and statistical models (by virtue of their assumptions), often expose contrasting aspects of observed or inferred phenomena. But even when this is the case, every tool and every model still has the potential capacity to provide an insight that might otherwise have remained hidden. This potential arises precisely because the tools that we choose to use to gather data, and the analytical methods that we employ, both impose limits on what can be observed and therefore interpreted. We come, then, to the questions of what *should* be observed, and why. For prospective scholars of student learning there is a need to begin somewhere; there is a need to establish and maintain a firm conceptual grip on the phenomenon that can serve as a solid foundation for the task at hand and for subsequent development. A good starting point is to seek some basic common sense explanations of human endeavour, and then examine how some contemporary models of student learning relate to them.

Psychologically, many of the most outstanding and praiseworthy feats of human endeavour are rooted in the driving forces represented by *intention* and *motivation*. (This insight applies equally well to the most deplorable acts of human endeavour; any criminal investigation seeks initially to establish an explanatory intention and a motivation.) The two central questions here thus concern the 'what' and the 'why' of human endeavour. The 'what' question (as in 'trying to do') concerns the intended accomplishment, while the 'why' question concerns the reason behind the intention. In terms of even the most everyday actions and accomplishments, people are motivated by a range of feelings (interest, enjoyment, anger, love, greed, pride, hunger, and so on) that traverse the entire spectrum of human experience.

Explanatory motivational forces apply equally well to learning endeavours. Contrasting forms of intention and motivation represent primary sources of explanatory variation in student learning; they begin to explain why some individuals differ in relation to one another.

A response to the 'what' question, in educational terms, can reflect any one of a variety of contrasting intentions, or even a multiple intention. The broadest intentional distinction in common use is between the internal transformation of information into knowledge (construction of personal meaning) and the accumulation and reproduction (literal or mechanical storage and recall) of information. Another family of strategic intentions is typically more focused on the measured outcomes of higher education; a classical example of tactical astuteness is the student who, unable to cope with several courses, 'buys more time' by deliberately aiming for a borderline failure in one of them so as to ensure a resit or supplementary examination.

A response to the 'what' question, in whatever form, is usually coupled with a congruent response to the 'why' question, and again there is a contrasting range of motivational forces (broadly distinguishable as either intrinsic or extrinsic to the person and, perhaps, even the task) that can be present, either singly or in combination. (For example, an interest in what is being learned, a fear of failure, a felt obligation to please others, a need to prove oneself, a competitive spirit, a materialistic desire, and so on.) The point here is that, at least at one level of consciousness amenable to external observation, an intention is more likely to be realised if it is supported by a *congruent* motivation.

Individual differences in learning behaviour thus begin to emerge even at this bivariate conceptual level, since two students can differ in both their stated intentions and motivations. Equally, two students with the same stated intention can differ in terms of the underlying motivation and vice versa. The corresponding or associated consequences (in terms of actions such as learning processes and resultant outcomes) may also therefore be different.

However, individual differences are also associated with manifestations of apparently *incongruent* combinations of intention and motivation; for example, there is a difference between an intention to seek understanding based on (congruent) intrinsic motivation and one based on (incongruent) fear of failure. Furthermore, in the latter incongruent case, the stated intention of 'understanding' may be based on an unsophisticated conception of what the term means, thereby creating a further difference.

To build a more sensitive model of student learning on a foundation of intention and motivation, there is a need to identify additional sources of explanatory variation. A common sense illustration again provides a useful starting point. To successfully climb a mountain or rob a bank requires more than just intention and motivation. The important methodological question of 'how' arises. There is a need to invoke some sort of process; a modus operandi, the choice of which can drastically affect the outcome of any intentional endeavour. In learning terms, a competitively motivated strategic intention to obtain high marks, for example, does not guarantee that high marks will be obtained. At the very least some form of organised cognitive process and/or learning method will need to be skilfully applied and carefully regulated.

The point here is that process is not simply a temporal consideration in purposeful learning activity; process is partially determined, or at least influenced, by the underlying intention and motivation. Again a common sense example: the same act of passion can be motivated by either love or hatred and, in either case, the method will most likely also vary accordingly. So too with learning. A declared intention to make sense of a difficult topic can equally well be motivated by personal interest, competitiveness, or fear of failure and, again, the employed method and/or process might vary accordingly.

In more general terms an extrinsically motivated intention to simply commit information to memory for subsequent recall in an examination is likely to invoke an appropriate (and congruent) process such as verbal recitation or repeated written forms of rehearsal. On the other hand, a contrasting intrinsically motivated intention to make sense of a difficult concept is likely to invoke a more elaborate and multifaceted relational process. A strategically motivated intention, in turn, might be realised by 'playing the system' and intelligent guesswork. In all cases effort is expended, but on different types of processes and with varying degrees of skill, regulation, and even contextual manipulation.

The 'big three' questions in student learning behaviour thus basically concern the 'what' (intention), the 'why' (motivation) and the 'how' (processes) of learning behaviour. These sources of variation essentially describe (and explain) contrasting forms of engagement with the content, as well as the context, of learning. There is thus a conceptual basis for a *first approximation* model of student learning of a form amenable to observation via suitable psychometric instrumentation or interview methodology. We can now examine how these basic sources of variation in student learning can be modelled, and further augmented in terms of more complex multivariate modelling.

## A FOUNDATION MODEL: THE WORK OF JOHN BIGGS

Before outlining the broad conceptual structure of the Biggs model, it needs to be observed that there is a lack of uniformity in the way various researchers use and interpret the meaning of some of the terms that are used to characterise models of student learning. Four such terms that are of particular interest here are 'strategy', 'approach', 'intention', and 'orientation'. When initially introducing these terms in a particular model-specific sense, their original intended interpretations within that model will be adhered to. Variation in the meaning of these terms across different models will be discussed where appropriate.

The general model of student learning proposed by Biggs (1978) consists of three stages: Presage, Process and Product (or the 3P model for short). The first stage deals with the personological attributes of the student, as well as situational or contextual factors. The second stage encompasses process factors, while the third reflects the outcomes of learning. It is in the formulation of this model, and in the design of its associated data gathering instrumentation (the Study Process Questionnaire (SPQ)) that Biggs has made a definitive contribution to research on student learning in higher education; he has provided both the model and the means for students to externalise the central (process) part of it. (The domain of the SPQ does not address the full multivariate complexity of the general 3P model.)

The model has, as its focus, what are termed 'process factors' which make up the 'learning process complex' that mediates between the presage factors and learning outcomes. The complex itself basically consists of three motives and three 'strategies'. For each of the three motives – subsequently named 'deep', 'surface' and 'achieving', there is a corresponding 'strategy'; the terms 'deep' and 'surface' follow the nomenclature of Marton and Säljö (1976). Biggs (1985, p. 202) furthermore considers motives to be prior to strategies; that is, strategies arise out of motivational states.

In thus acknowledging that motivation and strategy often coexist in a relatively stable relationship, the 'learning process complex' in the Biggs model further posits a more elegant structure of three higher order contrasting dimensions of variation (or 'approaches'). Conceptually each of these three dimensions is more robust than either of its corresponding (two) components in isolation. The SPQ itself has been employed in numerous quantitative studies of student learning that have been summarised, for example, by Kember and Gow (1990).

In a Biggsian sense, an 'approach' implies a motive and a form of process (the 'strategy'). But *strategies* as 'processes', as further explicated by Biggs (1985, p. 187), refer (for 'deep' and 'surface') to '...ways in which students engage the content of the task...', while for 'achieving' the emphasis is on how '...students organise the temporal and spatial contexts in which the task is carried out'. In the wording of some of the corresponding SPQ items, 'processes' are linked to *intention* as, for example, in the statement 'I try to work (intention) consistently throughout the term (process) and review regularly when the exams are close (process)'.

Variation in strategy does not therefore necessarily strictly imply a variation in cognitive processes related to learning tasks only; it can also encompass variation in intention and, indeed, *regulation,* as in 'I test myself on important points (self-regulatory process) until I understand them completely (intention)'. In terms of an observable (SPQ) model of student learning the developmental work of Biggs (1978, 1979, 1985) has had a profound effect on the manner in which researchers and students alike have thought, and continue to think, about individual variation in student learning.

There is a timeless attraction in the Biggs model for exploring individual differences in student learning. It represents a conceptually powerful foundation member of an evolving family of interrelated conceptual schemata, or 'mental models of learning', that help us to understand why, as Perry (1988) so succinctly put it, we have 'different worlds in the same classroom'.

## A MORE COMPLEX MODEL

A model of student learning proposed by Entwistle (1981) also places emphasis on process factors, but does so in a manner that is explicitly more complex than in the Biggs model. The Entwistle and Biggs models have many conceptual parallels. Both models share a common motivational base and, to some extent, also a common process base, across the 'deep', 'surface', and 'achieving' distinctions. But there is a different emphasis in the manner in which some of these common conceptual features are operationalised in the Entwistle model via its associated instrumentation, the Approaches to Studying Inventory (ASI).

There is, in particular, a degree of conceptual separation in the Entwistle model between intentions (which are referred to as 'approaches'), and processes. For example, the statement 'I usually set out to understand thoroughly the meaning of what I am required to learn' is interpreted as signifying an intention (to understand) rather than a process. Variation in 'deep' processes, in particular, is captured in terms of 'relating ideas' within and between subjects, and the critical 'use of evidence' in supporting argument and conclusion. Learning 'styles' and 'pathologies' (after the work of Pask, 1976) are also included as are other forms of learning engagement such as 'disorganised studying'.

The resultant four-dimensional model, as explicated in Entwistle and Ramsden (1983), is essentially reflected in terms of second-order structures called study 'orientations'. These second-order structures are the conceptually more complicated equivalents of the second-order 'approaches' in the Biggs model.

The essential point about the ASI model from an individual difference perspective is that, compared to the SPQ model, it admits additional sources of variation in student learning. To the extent that this conceptual multivariate complexity is also reflected in any associated empirical structures, it becomes possible to make finer distinctions in explaining any manifested inter-individual differences. The ASI model, in both a contracted and in an expanded form, has also been widely employed in studies of student learning, as reviewed by Richardson (1994).

## ADDITIONAL SOURCES OF VARIATION

The intentions, motivations and processes that have been discussed thus far do not occur in isolation. Their manifestation is influenced in varying degrees by, and within, the general environment of learning. Such influence also includes perceptions of self within the learning environment, gender, as well as the cultures and epistemologies of specific disciplines. As a further part of the quest for sources of explanatory variation and, therefore, manifestations of individual differences, these and other temporal influences also need to be considered.

## THE CONTEXT OF LEARNING

Everyday life experiences attest to the simple fact that our behaviour is often shaped by perceived circumstances or situational demands. An obvious illustration arises when a performance of competency, skill or ability is going to be critically scrutinised. It does not matter whether the performance is the presentation of an annual report to a shareholders' meeting, a guitar recital, driving a motorcar or caramelising onions. The preparation for the performance, and the act itself, will be shaped by perceptions of *what is required* to successfully pass the scrutiny in each particular context respectively.

Learning in a formal sense thus carries with it, as part of the grammar of the concept, a focus on both its content and its context. This contextual focus, in situational terms, is an important part of the presage component of the Biggs 3P model that has been further developed by a number of researchers. The work of Ramsden (1988) in particular, although not specifically linked to the Biggs model, has mapped out the issues involved in some detail. Correctly 'reading', and explicitly extracting, if necessary, the cues embedded in the context of learning (especially cues related to task demands) are an important part of what might be called 'skill in learning'. Such 'skill' represents yet another source of explanatory variation in student learning. In the case of written learning materials even simple textually embedded cues like learning objectives and revision exercises can constitute powerful differential regulatory mechanisms (Vermunt, 1996).

Sources of variation attributable to the context of learning thus represent a fundamental component of any model of student learning and they can be conceptualised in systemic relational terms (Meyer, 1988). More specifically, *perceptions* that students form about the context of learning are intimately associated at an individual process level with other sources of variation (Meyer & Muller, 1990). In fact the *same student* may manifest distinguishably different learning patterns and behaviours across different learning contexts as evidenced in the studies by Meyer and Watson (1991) and Eley (1992). There is thus inter- *and* intra-individual variation in contextualised learning that is potentially of consequence to learning outcomes.

## REGULATION AND LOCUS OF CONTROL

Vermunt and van Rijswyk (1988) have demonstrated that various forms of *regulatory mechanisms* (those mechanisms that clarify and direct learning activities) further help to explain inter-individual variation in learning. Indeed in the Biggsian sense it can be argued that structural level (of learning conception or self-knowledge) even regulates concomitant process and outcome. The work of Boulton-Lewis (1994), Meyer (1996) and Vermunt (1996), provides a synthetic basis for this argument.

Individuals also vary in the degree to which they perceive causal attribution for academic success (and failure) to be within, or beyond, their control in internal/external terms. Studies such as the one by van Overwalle (1989) have confirmed the importance of locus of control as a determinant of learning outcome in higher education. There is also evidence that, in both a dynamic and temporal sense, causal attribution provides valuable insights into unstable (and especially deteriorating) forms of learning behaviour (Meyer, 1996). These observations are consistent with the overall framework of the Biggs model in which locus of control explicitly forms a part of the presage factors. Biggs (1985) in fact also discusses in some detail the role of locus of control in relation to metalearning. 'Metalearning awareness' is thus also a potentially useful source of variation, stemming as it does from an initial self-awareness of motivation, but also embracing a range of other factors relating to students' awareness of their own learning processes.

## CONCEPTIONS OF LEARNING

Students' beliefs about learning, and their knowledge of their own learning, thus play an important role in shaping how they approach learning in general. Conceptually, the presage component of the Biggs 3P model accommodates associated sources of variation explicitly in terms of students' *prior knowledge*. The interest here lies in the observation that students differ considerably in terms of their conceptions of what 'learning' is (Säljö, 1979; Marton, Dall'Alba & Beaty, 1993). The distinction is broadly between *accumulative* and *transformative* conceptions; in simple terms, information is either collected in a quantitative sense for possible future use, or internally rearranged as part of the process of constructing knowledge, developing personal meaning and thereby changing as a person.

It has been verified empirically that, in terms of process linkages, such conceptual differences potentially represent a valuable source of inter-individual variation (Meyer, 1995b); contrasting conceptions of learning are associated with differing forms of learning behaviour. Students also differ in terms of what they *know* about their own learning in both a declarative and (SOLO) structural sense (Boulton-Lewis, 1994). The 'what', the 'why' and the 'how' of learning are thus also shaped and filtered by beliefs about, and conceptions of, what 'knowledge' and 'learning' are.

Beliefs about, and conceptions of, learning are not explicitly operationalised in the models referred to earlier. In order to explore individual differences in this domain it is therefore necessary to develop an instrument especially for this purpose. Meyer and Boulton-Lewis (1997) have reported progress in the development of such an instrument: the Reflections on Learning Inventory (RoLI).

## CULTURAL FACTORS

The earlier reference to 'virtuous' learning (in a transformative sense) also carries with it a degree of cultural presumption. It is important to realise that any belief as to what constitutes 'virtuous' learning behaviour must also be shaped by culturally embedded values and practices. In certain cultures in which there is a strong oral tradition, for example, the faithful reproduction of received wisdom is a virtuous act that may favour what Perry (1970) describes as a dualistic rather than a relativistic view of knowledge.

An exploratory quantitative study of conceptions of learning by Meyer (1995b), as well as phenomenographic studies on the theme of the 'Chinese Paradox' such as the one by Marton, Dall'Alba and Tse (1993), demonstrate the dangers of assuming a culture-free interpretation of basic learning processes associated with 'memorisation' in its many different forms. In short, in application modelling terms, there comes a point when the general purpose models of learning behaviour that have been espoused thus far may require cultural adjustment, specification, and extension, for the interpretation of any consequentiality of variation within them to remain valid beyond the contexts within which they were developed. An exploratory study by Kiley and Meyer (1996), for example, has produced some evidence to suggest that a construct as basic as a 'deep approach' does not behave very well psychometrically in an Indonesian context.

## DISCIPLINE SPECIFICITY

A limitation of what has been discussed thus far stems from the general purpose descriptions (and nature) of the primary sources of variation in student learning. In a discipline-specific sense none of these sources are uniquely located. For modelling purposes it thus needs to be recognised that, since learning is essentially content focused, there is an obvious need to address sources of explanatory variation that may be very specific to a particular discipline.

These sources may be either a function of the content itself (as in, for example, pure mathematics), or of the broader context within which the content is embedded and is perceived to be a part (for example the mathematical content of engineering or economics). Research in this area is still developmental, but clearly very promising as demonstrated, for example, in the studies by Marton, Carlsson and Halasz (1992) related to the reading of literary texts, by Ramsden, Whelan and Cooper (1989) to clinical diagnosis in medicine, and by Meyer and Dunne (1991) to clinical learning environments in nursing. In similar vein, and as a basis for building an inferential model, Meyer and Eley (1996) have begun to explore discipline-specific sources of motivational variation in the studying of pure mathematics. They have developed a specialised instrument for this purpose: the Experiences of Studying Mathematics Inventory (ESMI). Using this instrument they have provisionally identified at least three forms of motivational influences that relate to what they have termed 'beauty' (an appreciation for elegance and beauty in mathematical proof and argument), 'truth' (which refers to the absoluteness of mathematical knowledge), and 'enjoyment' (which refers to the intrinsic pleasure derived from indulging in mathematical pursuits).

There are thus a number of studies that have in common the identification of *specific* dimensions of variation that cannot, by definition, be included in any general purpose operational model of student learning. Stated differently, general purpose models of student learning and the individual differences that they potentially represent are, by definition, insensitive to discipline-specific (as well as gendered) constructs as a source of variation.

## GENDER RELATED DIFFERENCES

Despite a vast literature on gender issues in education, gender as a source of explanatory variation in learning behaviour is a relatively neglected issue in studies of student learning. While much attention has been given to gender related performance differentials in school and university subjects (like physics and mathematics) very little attention has focused on the possible differential processes involved.

The issue of gender related differences in learning behaviour does create some controversy. In contrast to the sources of variation that have been discussed thus far, a gender based construct may need to look at quite different aspects of a gendered engagement of learning. It may, for example, need to distinguish between sources of variation that are sensitive to biological influences (such as women's ways of 'knowing'), developmental influences (such as the academic socialisation of gender groups), and contextual influences (such as the gendered nature of some disciplines like engineering, or even the perspectives of a feminist epistemology).

From an individual-difference modelling perspective the question here is whether models of student learning, and the sources of variation from which they are constructed, are gender free. At the heart of this question lies the conjecture that men and women experience learning in ways that are not only qualitatively different, but that they do so in a distinctive manner that is of consequence to educational theory and practice. Ingleton (1995), for example, has argued that *emotion* is an important component of the learning experience, particularly for women students. The concern here is not to question whether manifested differences are a function of biological or developmental factors, but rather to explore whether such differences represent sustainable objects of intellectual inquiry.

A study by Meyer, Dunne and Richardson (1994) set out to explore the manifestation of gender based differences in learning behaviour using a nested hierarchy of models. The instrument used in this study was based on a modified and extended version of the ASI. At the base level of the hierarchy this instrument allowed for the exploration of a motive and intention/strategy model. This model, in conceptual terms, approximates the Biggs SPQ model.

Gender based differences emerged very clearly in a statistical evaluation of the base model; gendered responses indicated a statistically significant difference in covariance structure that was further explored using both principal component and factor analyses. Of particular interest was that the initial differences indicated within the base model were largely preserved within the more complex models of the hierarchy. There was thus an implicit confirmation of the explanatory power of the Biggs 'learning process complex' at a construct level.

Further accumulating evidence in support of gender related differences, although insufficient to sustain a substantive argument and conclusion, seems promising. There is consistent evidence to support the differential influence of some 'gendered' learning contexts on learning behaviour. But it is difficult to generalise, even in these narrow contexts, because of the compounding influences attributable to developmental and other factors.

There is also variation in the methodological focus of what a gender based 'difference' is. Some studies such as the meta-analysis by Severiens and Ten Dam (1994) focus on differences in *location* (mean scores), while other studies focus on differences in correlation or covariance *structure* (see Meyer, Dunne & Richardson, 1994; Meyer, 1995a). The argument here hinges on whether differences in mean scores (in relation, for example, to competitive forms of 'achievement' motivation) are necessarily of consequence in terms of significantly different relationships with other sources of explanatory variation. Differences in mean scores may simply reflect a gender biased response pattern and, statistically, such differences do not imply differences in correlation structure.

An exploratory study by Meyer (1995c) has produced evidence that the intersection of two sets of items, where each item set has been independently and empirically defined on a gender specific basis, can represent the basis of a statistically significant difference in terms of correlation structure. The implication of this finding is that some of the basic (item based) sources of variation used in model construction may be defined differently in terms of gendered responses – a possibility which favours, as a logical consequence, the construction of *gendered models* of student learning.

## CONCEPTUAL AND METHODOLOGICAL ISSUES

The explanatory sources of variation that have been discussed thus far present a number of conceptual and methodological modelling challenges to the educational researcher. Conceptually there is a need to admit sources of variation that are appropriate to the modelling task, and methodologically there is a need to fit appropriate models to observed data for inferential purposes. In both instances there is a range of assumptions and approximations that have to be made. The basic idea is that if a (conceptual) model fits observed data (perhaps via an intermediate empirical structure), and the data represents real individuals, then (in theory) the model can be used to make inferences about manifested individual differences.

## THE COMMON-FACTOR MODEL

A common analytical methodology, employed in many quantitative studies of student learning, relies on the aggregation of individual responses into group-level structures. This approach is reflected, in particular, in the large number of studies based on the adoption of a common-factor statistical model. The attraction of this model is that it is easy to apply, that it reduces the multivariate complexity of the observables, and that it can be used for hypothesis testing in a confirmatory sense. At face value the successful fitting of a common-factor model to observed data also produces empirical (and conceptually interpretable) *dimensions of variation* (the factor structures) within which all of the individuals contributing to the analysis will vary. It follows that each individual (response) can therefore be located, in some simultaneous sense, across all of the dimensions in question for inferential purposes.

Consider, for example, a three factor solution representing the popular dimensions of 'deep', 'surface' and 'strategic' variation respectively. There will be inter-individual variation within all three of these dimensions. In theory a particular individual (response) can thus be 'located' within such an empirical structure. Notionally this can be thought of in terms of the simultaneous 'scoring' of the individual response on each of the common factors.

Common-factor scores, however, are *not* determined from scores on the observables; they are *estimated* on the basis of assumptions required to specify the values within any particular factor-scoring method. There are, furthermore, several such scoring methods. In his book *The foundations of factor analysis* Mulaik (1972) states quite clearly that by 'estimation' is meant that it is mathematically impossible

> to determine uniquely or exactly the common-factor scores from scores on the observed variables even if one knows the population values for

the correlations among the observed variables and the correlations between the observed variables and the common factors. (p. 327)

In further discussing the properties of factor scores he goes on to caution against selecting variables for factor analysis without some conception of what common factors may be present. The danger, as he puts it, is that the common factors

> may be only poorly represented among the variables, and no linear combination of the observed variables will relate very strongly to the common factors. When that occurs, factor scores will be next to useless as intermediate measures of the common factors. (p. 328)

Conceptually, then, while it may be true that under certain circumstances common-factor scores may *approximate* individual responses in some comparative sense, they do so in a manner that is non-uniquely abstracted from the real world of what has actually been observed. Factor scores, although potentially useful for modelling purposes, are thus limited in their capacity to represent individual responses in terms of the observables, and especially so in an inferential sense.

## GROUP REPRESENTATION OF INDIVIDUALS

One of the most basic assumptions in the factor analytic approach is that a group adequately represents its constituent members; that is, that the variation in any manifestation of learning at an *aggregate* level of analysis adequately reflects variation in learning at an *individual* level. As discussed earlier, another important assumption that is implicit in the adoption of multivariate correlation forms of statistical modelling (which includes factor analysis) is that of *linear structure* as a source of explanatory variation.

Numerous difficulties thus arise when an attempt is made to model individual differences. These difficulties begin with the often invalid assumption of the group-level representation of either the individual, or of constituent individual-similarity subgroups. There is an inherent danger in analysing undifferentiated data as the studies by Biggs and Kirby (1984) and Entwistle, Meyer and Tait (1991) clearly indicate.

The most seemingly conceptually plausible undifferentiated structures can camouflage the existence of significant classification differences (such as gender, for example) as clearly demonstrated at the most basic level in the studies by Meyer (1995a, 1995b). These difficulties are further compounded by the simple fact that the phenomenon being modelled is, fundamentally, non-linear. The depressingly small (linear) correlation coefficients that are an unfortunate hallmark of so much published educational research frequently point to the absurdity of imposing a linear model on the data rather than any shortcomings in the observables. And even when there is an adequate assumption of group level representation, and even when a linear model does fit the observed data reasonably well in a given context, there is still the problem of representing the status of the individual within the empirical structure.

## INDIVIDUALS AS UNIQUE ENTITIES

A contrasting analytical approach (such as unfolding analysis) that seeks to preserve the uniqueness of the individual response is thus desirable. Alternatively an approach, such as the one adopted by Meyer (1996), is required in which individuals are aggregated into individual-similarity subgroups on the basis of categorical differences in the observed data prior to statistical modelling. Both of these approaches are naturally amenable to non-linear forms of statistical modelling.

The study by Meyer (1991), in particular, illustrates very clearly the complexity of inter-individual variation in contextualised learning behaviour based on the concept of 'study orchestration'. Volet and Chalmers (1992) have also used an unfolding model to investigate qualitative differences in discipline-specific goals. Their conclusions have supported the conceptualisation of such goals along a continuum in a manner that links progression along that continuum to altered perceptions of studying and different levels of academic achievement.

Unfolding analysis has demonstrated the complex nature of individual differences in the relationship between perceptions of the learning environment and approaches to studying (Meyer & Muller, 1990). It has also been used to investigate intra-individual variation in learning engagement, both across cognate disciplines (Meyer, Dunne & Sass, 1992) and within the same discipline (Meyer, Parsons & Dunne, 1990).

## ATYPICAL MANIFESTATIONS OF LEARNING BEHAVIOUR

The study by Biggs and Kirby (1984) provides a classic example of how the 'logical' dimensional structure of the Biggs motive and strategy 'learning process complex' can vary according to the attributes of differentiated responses; in this case in terms of four subgroups of scholars constituted in terms of median splits on 'reasoning' and 'memory' ability. Motive and strategy (principal component) structures of differing complexity were associated with each of these subgroups. Of particular interest is that the subgroup that was constituted as 'low reasoning' and 'low memory' manifested a collapsed and atypical (one component) structure. Biggs (1985) interpreted the apparent failure of this subgroup to distinguish between contrasting motives and strategies as an indication that the learning process complex was 'opaque and meaningless' for them.

Atypical factor structures have also been associated with subgroups of failing students in studies by Meyer and Dunne (1991) and Entwistle, Meyer and Tait (1991). Attention has thus been drawn to structures that fail, empirically, to verify conceptually posited discriminations between contrasting aspects of learning behaviour and perceptions of the learning environment. Meyer and Muller (1990) have explored in some detail the manifestation of atypical forms of *study orchestration* using unfolding analysis. They have confirmed that, at an individual level of response, there are students who are apparently unable to orchestrate motives, intentions, processes, and perceptions of their learning environment, in a conceptually coherent manner. Some such manifestations elude rational interpretation – the corresponding (preference) structures appear to be incoherent or conceptually disintegrated (Meyer, 1991).

## CATEGORISING INDIVIDUAL DIFFERENCES

Where there is an interest in individual differences (especially atypical differences) there is also an interest in isolating such differences for descriptive or modelling purposes. The preceding discussion has emphasised that student learning is fundamentally a complex multivariate phenomenon. It is of limited value to *conceptually* compress this multivariate complexity into neat decontextualised dimensions of variations of, for example, 'deep', 'surface' or 'strategic' forms of learning behaviour. To overcome the risks of reductionism there are a number of interrelated issues that need to be addressed.

To begin with, there is a need to overcome the latent subjectivity that is inherent in the conceptual interpretation of individual differences in observed data. Failure to do so introduces elements of nuance and ambiguity in interpretation that compromise the reliability of the conceptual categorisation. Furthermore, as the number of conceptually admissible categories increases, so does the need to define the basis of finer distinctions between them. In short, the challenge is to establish a set of conceptually defensible 'rules' that can be reliably applied (preferably via programmable logic) to an individual multivariate response set of observables.

## THE BIGGS CATEGORISATION PROCEDURE

A practical procedure has been proposed by Biggs (1985, 1988) for categorising an individual set of (six) inventory subscale scores derived within the SPQ model. This procedure essentially assigns one of three symbolic average values ('+', '0', or '-') to each score according to its relative magnitude. For each conceptually admissible combination of motivation and strategy (the 'approach') there is thus a corresponding *symbol pair* that can be used as a categorical basis for inter-individual comparison.

There are, however, problems in applying this categorisation procedure for modelling purposes. The most serious of these problems is the multi-way nature of the categorisation; three symbol pairs are required to categorise a single response within three posited 'approaches'. But each extension beyond the three preferred 'approaches' that might be required to accommodate a case of apparently individualistic, hybrid and/or atypical form of complexity, effectively introduces an *additional* symbol pair as part of the categorisation. If the preferred motive/strategy constraint is relaxed, then there are nine possible ways of pairing a motive with a strategy, and each such pair can assume one of nine possible states in terms of either 'highs', 'lows' or 'averages'. The categorisation procedure accordingly becomes conceptually intractable.

## THE MEYER CATEGORISATION PROCEDURE

An alternative 'interference' approach has been proposed by Meyer (1996), and was inspired by the challenge to categorise the individual preference structures which are the unit of analysis in an individual-difference (unfolding) statistical model. For examples of such preference structures see Meyer (1991). Conceptually the variables in this particular 'interference' application substantively reflect 14 of the 16 variables contained in the original ASI model (and these, in turn, also reflect the motive/strategy distinctions of the SPQ as a subset), plus an additional set of contextual perception variables.

The basis of the Meyer categorisation procedure can be visualised in terms of a simple example. Consider two preference sub-structures, one virtuous the other pathological:

| *Virtuous* | *Pathological* |
|---|---|
| deep approach | improvidence |
| relating ideas | globetrotting |
| use of evidence | fragmentation |

These two substructures, independently permuted, can be interlaced in a finite number of ways to form a single substructure. These single substructures, in turn, can be arranged in columns to form a conceptually discontinuous lattice. Each column in this lattice now represents a set of categorical *interference conditions* that can be searched for as an embedded feature of a more complex preference structure. If present these initial conditions can inform a partial ordinal categorisation of the preference structure as a whole. For example:

| | | | |
|---|---|---|---|
| deep approach | | deep approach | in |
| relating ideas | is | fragmentation | terms |
| use of evidence | better | relating ideas | of |
| improvidence | than | use of evidence | inferred |
| globetrotting | | globetrotting | outcomes |
| fragmentation | | improvidence | |

because, in the first substructure, the 'virtuous' components are 'preferred' above the 'pathological' components, while in the second substructure 'virtuous' approach and process are 'interfered with' by the pathology of fragmentation.

As operationalised, an observed preference structure is approximated, for each individual, by ranking the item-averaged response scores. There is, within all possible ranked structures that can theoretically occur, considerable conceptual redundancy (in terms of inferred consequentiality) that is used to advantage in the categorisation procedure.

There are four stages in the categorisation procedure. The first two stages, in an extension of the simple example above, distinguish independently between two finite sets of progressive 'interference' conditions under which the primary 'virtuous effect' (of deep intention and supporting processes) is conceptually compromised by pathological and non-pathological discontinuities respectively. Each of these 'interference' conditions is represented by a single numerical classification. The pathological discontinuities are represented by improvidence, globetrotting and fragmentation and the non-pathological discontinuities by memorisation, disorganised studying and workload. There is, furthermore, an assumption of conceptual equivalency between independent permutations within the virtuous, pathological and non-pathological substructures.

A secondary virtuous effect addresses the degree to which the overall preference structure exhibits a *contextualised* pattern of learning as well as other features such as the degree of tactical astuteness and learning style 'versatility' (after the work of Pask (1976) as operationalised in the ASI). These and other features are assigned numerical values in the third stage of the categorisation procedure. The fourth stage produces a single categorisation coefficient from the (two-way) primary interference conditions and the (virtuous one-way) secondary effect.

The 'interference' approach is, in fact, very versatile and it can be used in modelling applications to control the constitution of a wide range of individual-similarity groups using expanded or contracted forms of the categorisation coefficient. Some of these applications are reflected in the studies by Meyer and Sass (1993), Meyer and Scrivener (1995), and Meyer (1996).

## A GENERAL 'INTERFERENCE' MODEL

A general 'interference' model is defined here as a non-hierarchical model that contains at least two separately distinct, and conceptually contrasting, dimensions of variation. The dimensions may be either non-linear or linear structures, any one of which may typically be conceptualised in virtuous or non-virtuous terms that contrasts with one or more of the others. The neatest 'interference' arises at a conceptual level when individual observations violate the boundaries of contrasting variation.

While such conceptual violation can thus typically occur between the dimensions of the model, it can also be less neatly empirically reflected, for an atypical subgroup, in the internal composition of one or more of the dimensions themselves. Here the conceptual violation occurs as a characteristic property of the observed data. In either case a conceptual boundary can be violated in a number of ways that are amenable to categorisation. These phenomena are clearly illustrated in terms of non-linear structures in the study by Meyer and Muller (1990).

However, since group-level manifestations of student learning are partially approximated and easily conceptualised in terms of linear (correlation) structure, a common-factor model will be used here for illustrative purposes. Consider a simple 'interference' model (manifested as a factor structure), and based on undifferentiated data, in which there are two conceptually contrasting dimensions of variation; one of which is virtuous, the other not. Such dimensions of variation (the factors) are typically either independent of one another or negatively correlated, and it is assumed here that each represents a conceptually distinct entity.

Such a model of contrasting factors is assumed to represent individual differences in a coherent (albeit unobservable) sense. If the empirical model is conceptually interpretable, there is an expectation that individual variation, which occurs across both dimensions of variation *simultaneously*, will also occur in a manner that is conceptually coherent; that is, the conceptual distinction between the factors will not be compromised. In this case the conceptual model is presumed to 'fit' the data. This 'fit' carries with it the implicit assumption that the group-level variation (as evidenced in the factor structure) also adequately represents the variation of individuals within the group. However, since this basic assumption is seldom justified in practice, some individual responses can covary across contrasting dimensions of variation in a manner that violates the integrity of the conceptual model.

Thus, for some observations, the conceptual boundary between the two distinctively separate (and contrasting) factors is 'interfered' with, or violated, for reasons other than those attributable to measurement error. In other words, otherwise submerged atypical individual responses can violate the conceptual constraints of an empirical structure within which they are assumed to be accurately represented (by virtue of group membership). If separately analysed as a subgroup they can also produce empirical factor structures that violate conceptual boundaries as studies on failing students by Meyer and Dunne (1991) and Entwistle, Meyer and Tait (1991) have demonstrated. When such violations of conceptual boundaries within, or across, structures is observed to occur for reasons other than those attributable to measurement error, or too constrained a model, the atypical observations in question become a legitimate object of inquiry.

## THE DANGERS OF CONSTRAINED MODELS

It needs finally to be observed that contemporary models of student learning do not generally embrace an exhaustive set of first order response variables; they reflect, instead, varying degrees of conceptual and contextual *redundancy* (such as in the compression of intention and process). Sources of variation are either excluded on framework dependent grounds (they may, for example, originate outside the chosen model), or they are ignored by virtue of their interrelatedness with other included variables in the model. And, as we have seen, further interpretive constraints can also be imposed in the design of an instrument that goes with a particular model. A useful comparison of six contemporary instruments in use can be found in Tait and Entwistle (1996).

The problem remains that, from an individual-difference modelling perspective, inferences need to be as accurate as a given instrument, model and context of discovery will allow. In limiting the horizon of the observables because of practical constraints there is a risk that spurious inferences will be drawn on the basis of incomplete evidence. But, as has already been pointed out, any increase in the multivariate complexity of the observables also increases the problem of conceptually categorising observed individual responses within a chosen model.

Consider, for example, an otherwise clear manifestation of achievement motivation combined with deep-level learning strategy that is *also* associated (in the presence of suitable further observed variables) with the pathology of improvidence (an over-reliance on factual detail in the absence of a integrative framework), and generally disorganised study behaviour. In the strict motivation and strategy model the interpretation (and inferred consequence) is unambiguous, but in the more complex model it is not. If the more complex model also incorporates perceptions of the learning environment, then additional nuances have to be interpreted. Further distinctions would then need to be made, for example, between one individual with a perception of a heavy workload (and its related syndrome) and one without such a perception.

The point is that a complex operationalisation of learning behaviour introduces a range of additional variation that can actually *contradict* a more constrained interpretation based on fewer observables. In focusing on the interpretation of manifestations of individual differences in learning there is thus always a need to select, or construct, models and instruments that are appropriate to the task at hand. It is in the careful execution of these processes that the real art of modelling individual differences ultimately lies.

## References

Biggs, J.B. (1978). Individual and group differences in study processes. *British Journal of Educational Psychology, 48*, 266–279.

Biggs, J.B. (1979). Individual differences in study processes and the quality of learning outcomes. *Higher Education, 8*, 381–394.

Biggs, J.B. (1985). The role of metalearning in study processes. *British Journal of Educational Psychology, 55*, 185–212.

Biggs, J.B. (1988). Assessing student approaches to learning. *Australian Psychologist, 23*, 197–206.

Biggs, J.B., & Kirby, J.R. (1984). Differentiation of learning processes within ability groups. *Educational Psychology, 4*, 21–39.

Boulton–Lewis, G.M. (1994). Tertiary students' knowledge of their own learning and a SOLO taxonomy. *Higher Education, 28*, 387–402.

Bowden, J.A., & Walsh, E. (Eds.). (1994). *Phenomenographic research: variations in method.* Melbourne: Royal Melbourne Institute of Technology.

Eley, M.G. (1992). Differential adoption of study approaches within individual students. *Higher Education, 23*, 231–254.

Entwistle, N. (1981). *Styles of learning and teaching.* New York: John Wiley.

Entwistle, N.J., Meyer, J.H.F., & Tait, H. (1991). Student failure: Disintegrated perceptions of study strategies and perceptions of the learning environment. *Higher Education, 21,* 249–261.

Entwistle, N.J., & Ramsden, P. (1983). *Understanding student learning.* London: Croom Helm.

Ingleton, C. (1995). Gender and learning: Does emotion make a difference? *Higher Education, 30,* 323–335.

Kember, D., & Gow, L. (1990). Cultural specificity of approaches to study. *British Journal of Educational Psychology, 60,* 356–363.

Kiley, M., & Meyer, J.H.F. (1996). Indonesian postgraduate students' conceptions of learning. *Research and Development in Higher Education, 19,* 371–376. (Proceedings of the HERDSA '96 conference, University of Western Australia, Perth, July 8–12).

Marton, F., Carlsson, M.A., & Halasz, L. (1992). Differences in understanding and the use of reflective variation in reading. *British Journal of Educational Psychology, 62,* 1–16.

Marton, F., Dall'Alba G., & Beaty, E. (1993). Conceptions of learning. *International Journal of Educational Research, 19,* 277–300.

Marton, F., Dall'Alba G., & Tse, L.K. (1993). The paradox of the Chinese learner. *Occasional paper 93.1,* Educational Research and Development Unit, Royal Melbourne Institute of Technology.

Marton, F., & Säljö, R. (1976). On qualitative differences in learning – I: Outcome and process. *British Journal of Educational Psychology, 46,* 4–11.

Meyer, J.H.F. (1988). Student perceptions of learning context and approaches to studying. *South African Journal of Higher Education, 2,* 73–82.

Meyer, J.H.F. (1991). Study Orchestration: the manifestation, interpretation and consequences of contextualised approaches to studying. *Higher Education, 22,* 297–316.

Meyer, J.H.F. (1995a). Gender-group differences in the learning behaviour of entering first-year university students. *Higher Education, 29,* 201–215.

Meyer, J.H.F (1995b). A quantitative exploration of conceptions of learning. *Research and Development in Higher Education, 18,* 545–550. (Proceedings of the HERDSA '95 conference, July 48,Rockhampton, Australia, 18, 545–550).

Meyer, J.H.F. (1995c). *Gender-related differences in learning behaviour: an empirical exploration at an item and factorial level.* Symposium paper presented at the 6th European Conference on Learning and Instruction held at the Katholieke Universiteit Nijmegen, the Netherlands, August 26–31, 1995.

Meyer, J.H.F. (1996). Some aspects of the individual-difference modelling of causal attribution. *Higher Education, 31*, (special edition on student learning), 51–71.

Meyer, J.H.F., & Boulton-Lewis, G.M. (1997). *The association between university students' perceived influences on their learning and their knowledge, experience, and conceptions, of learning.* Paper presented at the 7th European Conference for Research on Learning and Instruction, Athens, August 26–30.

Meyer, J.H.F., & Dunne, T.T. (1991). The study approaches of nursing students: Effects of an extended clinical context. *Medical Education, 25*, 497–516.

Meyer, J.H.F., Dunne, T.T., & Richardson, J.T.E. (1994). A gender comparison of contextualised study behaviour in higher education. *Higher Education, 27*, 469–485.

Meyer, J.H.F., Dunne, T.T., & Sass, A.R. (1992). Impressions of disadvantage – I: School versus university study orchestration and implications for academic support, *Higher Education, 24*, 291–316.

Meyer, J.H.F., & Eley, M.G. (1996). The experiences of studying mathematics inventory (ESMI): An exploratory instrument for modelling purposes. *Research and Development in Higher Education, 19*, 190–194. (Proceedings of the HERDSA '96 conference, University of Western Australia, Perth, July 8–12).

Meyer, J.H.F., & Muller, M.W. (1990). Evaluating the quality of student learning – I: An unfolding analysis of the association between perceptions of learning context and approaches to studying at an individual level. *Studies in Higher Education, 15*, 131–154.

Meyer, J.H.F., Parsons, P., & Dunne, T.T. (1990). Individual study orchestrations and their association with learning outcome, *Higher Education, 20*, 67–89.

Meyer, J.H.F., & Sass, A.R. (1993). The impact of the first year on the learning behaviour of engineering students. *International Journal of Engineering Education, 9*, 209–217.

Meyer, J.H.F., & Scrivener, K. (1995). A framework for evaluating and improving student learning. In G. Gibbs (Ed.), *Improving student learning through assessment and evaluation.* Oxford: OCSD, Oxford Brookes University.

Meyer, J.H.F., & Watson, R.M. (1991). Evaluating the quality of student learning – II: Study orchestration and the curriculum. *Studies in Higher Education, 16*, 251–275.

Mulaik, S.A. (1972). *The foundations of factor analysis.* New York: McGraw-Hill.

Pask, G. (1976). Styles and strategies of learning. *British Journal of Educational Psychology, 46*, 128–148.

Perry, W.G. (1970). *Forms of intellectual and ethical development in the college years: A scheme.* New York: Holt, Rinehart and Winston.

Perry, W.G. (1988). Different worlds in the same classroom. In P. Ram-sden (Ed.), *Improving Learning.* London: Kogan Page.

Ramsden, P. (1988). Context and strategy: Situational influences on learning. In R.R. Schmeck (Ed.), *Learning strategies and learning styles.* New York: Plenum Press, 159–184.

Ramsden, P., Whelan, G., & Cooper, D. (1989). Some phenomena of medical students' diagnostic problem solving. *Medical Education, 23,* 108–117.

Richardson, J.T.E. (1994). Cultural specificity of approaches to studying in higher education: A literature survey. *Higher Education, 27,* 449–486.

Säljö, R (1979). *Learning in the learner's perspective – I: Some common-sense conceptions.* (Reports from the Department of Education, No.76). University of Gothenburg.

Sandberg, J. (1995). Are phenomenographic results reliable? *Nordisk Pedagogic (Journal of Nordic Educational Research), 15,* 156–164.

Severiens, S.E., & Ten Dam, G.T.M. (1994). Gender differences in learning styles: A narrative review and quantitative meta-analysis. *Higher Education, 27,* 487–501.

Tait, H., & Entwistle, N. (1996). Identifying students at risk through ineffective study strategies. *Higher Education, 31,* (special edition on student learning), 97–116.

van Overwalle, F. (1989). Success and failure of freshmen at university: A search for determinants. *Higher Education, 18,* 287–308.

Vermunt, J.D. (1996). Metacognitive, cognitive and affective aspects of learning styles and strategies: A phenomenographic analysis. *Higher Education, 31,* (special edition on student learning, 25–50).

Vermunt, J.D.H.M., & Van Rijswijk, F.A.W.M. (1988). Analysis and development of students' skill in self regulated learning. *Higher Education, 17,* 647–682.

Volet, S.E., & Chalmers, D. (1992). Investigation of qualitative differences in university students' learning goals, based on an unfolding model of stage analysis. *British Journal of Educational Psychology, 62,* 17–34.

## PART TWO

# CHAPTER 4

# Approaches to Learning and Forms of Understanding

*Noel Entwistle*

## INTRODUCTION

There is now a substantial literature which describes the various ways in which the learning environment, and particularly assessment procedures and teaching methods, affect the quality of student learning (see, for example, Biggs, 1989, 1994b; Entwistle, 1992, in press; Gibbs, 1992; Hounsell, 1997; Laurillard, 1993; Ramsden, 1992; Trigwell, Prosser & Taylor, 1994). This literature has considered ways of improving teaching and assessment which are likely to encourage the deep approach and so lead to conceptual understanding. There has, however, been much less consideration of the nature of the deep approach, or of understanding itself.

A deep approach depends on an intention to understand – to establish personal meaning. But, what does personal understanding involve, and how is it experienced by the students? This chapter starts with a brief retrospective of earlier research affecting current definitions of the deep approach, which also opened up the debate about how differing learning processes lead to qualitatively different outcomes. Next, more recent work on the distinction between memorising and understanding is considered, before relating these ideas to different forms of understanding and the ways these are described by students. Finally, the links between approaches to learning and forms of understanding are explored, in terms of the experience of 'knowledge objects'.

## PROCESSES OF STUDYING

In developing his Study Process Questionnaire (SPQ), Biggs (1976) drew his descriptions of contrasting learning processes from work on cognitive psychology. Factor analysis of this inventory suggested the existence of distinct study processes, which have subsequently been identified as 'deep' and 'surface' approaches to learning. The deep approach describes active involvement stemming from interest in the content which leads to an elaboration of the learning material in seeking personal understanding. In contrast, the surface approach suggests anxiety or extrinsic motivation driving routine memorisation intended to reproduce aspects of the subject matter.

The qualitative research of Marton and his colleagues in Gothenburg helped to clarify the meaning of this distinction, and introduced the term 'approach to learning' (Marton & Säljö, 1976, 1997; Marton & Booth, 1997). They carried out a naturalistic experiment which showed how differing outcomes of learning could be attributed to contrasting intentions – either to develop personal understanding, or simply to cope instrumentally with the immediate task requirements. Subsequent quantitative and qualitative research within the everyday university context has developed the meaning of these two categories even further, as indicated in Table 4.1 (Biggs, 1987, 1993; Tait & Entwistle, 1996; Marton, Hounsell & Entwistle, 1997).

Biggs (1979) and Ramsden (1979) added to these descriptions of students' approaches to studying by including an achieving or strategic approach to studying. This approach derived from an intention to obtain the highest possible grades, and relied on organised studying and an awareness of assessment demands. Their work also suggested that each of these three approaches was related to a distinctive form of motivation – intrinsic (deep), extrinsic and fear of failure (surface) and need for achievement (strategic). An earlier study had also identified contrasting types of student, described in terms of differences in both motivation and personality (Entwistle & Wilson, 1977). Students motivated by need for achievement showed a stable personality associated with self-confidence and ruthlessness. Intrinsic motivation was linked to syllabus-freedom and independent thinking, while fear of failure was related to anxiety and syllabus boundness. However, these descriptions suggest too static a picture of student learning, which is necessarily reactive to

TABLE 4.1   Defining features of approaches to learning

| Deep Approach | Transforming |
|---|---|
| **Intention** – to understand ideas for yourself | **by** |
| Relating ideas to previous knowledge and experience<br>Looking for patterns and underlying principles | |
| Checking evidence and relating it to conclusions<br>Examining logic and argument cautiously and critically | |
| Becoming actively interested in the course content | |
| **Surface Approach** | **Reproducing** |
| **Intention** – to cope with course requirements | **by** |
| Studying without reflecting on either purpose or strategy<br>Treating the course as unrelated bits of knowledge<br>Memorising facts and procedures routinely | |
| Finding difficulty in making sense of new ideas presented<br>Feeling undue pressure and worry about work | |

Source: Adapted from Entwistle, 1997.

the learning context. Students' approaches are affected by their prior educational and personal histories, which produce habitual patterns of studying. However, the content and context of the task evoke strategies which are specific to that particular situation. Both consistency, up to a point, and a certain variability have thus to be incorporated into descriptions of student learning (Entwistle, 1979).

We are concentrating here on approaches in relation to understanding, and so the focus is on the deep approach with the defining features shown in Table 4.1. These features have been derived mainly from the studies mentioned above, but to some extent also from work on learning styles and strategies and developmental personality characteristics, as we shall see.

Pask (1976, 1988) asked students to learn the defining features of imaginary animals. He found that, in tackling this task, they used distinctively different strategies – holist and serialist – which seemed to reflect more consistent, underlying learning styles – comprehension learning and operation learning. The conditions used in Marton's original experiment allowed students to decide for themselves whether or not they would seek to understand the meaning of the article for themselves. In Pask's studies, students were

TABLE 4.2    Defining features of distinctive learning strategies

| | |
|---|---|
| **Serialist strategy** | Prefers step-by-step, tightly structured learning |
| | Focuses on the topic in isolation |
| | Concentrates on details and evidence |
| | Adopts a cautious logical stance, noting objections |
| leading to **Improvidence** | Fails to seek analogies or to use own experience |
| | Fails to make connections with related ideas |
| **Holist strategy** | Prefers personal organisation and a broad view |
| | Tries to build up own overview of topic |
| | Thrives on illustration, analogy, and anecdote |
| | Actively seeks connections between ideas |
| leading to **Globetrotting** | Fails to give sufficient attention to details |
| | Tends to generalise and reach conclusions too readily |

Source: Adapted from Pask, 1976.

required to reach a form of conceptual understanding, but they still went about it in quite different ways.

The main distinction was in the student's preference for learning in a particular way. A holist strategy and comprehension learning starts from a broad view of the task and constructs a personal, and often idiosyncratic, organising framework to support understanding. In contrast, a serialist strategy and operation learning relies on step-by-step learning concentrating on details and examining the logic of the argument cautiously. Over-reliance on one or other of these strategies leads to a characteristic pathology in learning – either globetrotting (holist) or improvidence (serialist). The defining features of these two strategies and their pathologies are shown in Table 4.2.

In Table 4.1, two pairs of learning processes were shown within the deep approach – looking for patterns and relating ideas on the one hand, and cautious use of evidence and logic on the other. These can now be identified as comprehension learning and operation learning. Bringing these two learning processes together was seen by Pask as essential to thorough understanding in what he called a versatile strategy. He also found that some students relied on rote learning, a process which he distinguished from operation learning and which represents a surface approach.

Using a quite different methodology – a longitudinal interview study – Heath (1964) explored the way opposing characteristics became integrated over time into a more mature personality, dubbed 'the Reasonable Adventurer', through combining two ways of thinking – the critical and the curious. In considering a problem, Heath suggested that the Reasonable Adventurer

> ... appears to experience an alternation of involvement and detachment. The phase of involvement is an intensive and exciting period characterised by curiosity, a narrowing of attention towards some point of interest ... This period of involvement is then followed by a period of detachment, an extensive phase, accompanied by a reduction of tension and a broadening range of perception ... reflect(ing) on the meaning of what was discovered during the involved stage. Meaning presumes the existence of a web of thought, a pattern of ideas to which the 'new' element can be related ... – the critical attitude ... We see, therefore, in (the Reasonable Adventurer) a combination of two mental attitudes: the curious and the critical. They do not occur simultaneously, but in alternation. (pp. 30–31)

One way of thinking feeds on the other, and understanding develops out of this interplay. It might even be seen as the alternation between left and right hemispheres of the brain, with their relative specialisations of function (Cohen, 1983; Sperry, 1983). The idea of alternation can also be found in Pask's thinking. The preference shown for one or other of the main learning strategies means that students will generally use that preferred strategy first, using the other strategy only later, and to the extent that it is essential to the task. In everyday studying, time constraints mean that it is often impossible to spend long enough on a task to complete the cycles necessary to build up full understanding. We should therefore anticipate outcomes of learning in which the characteristics of one or other learning style are found in conjunction with incomplete understanding.

## APPROACHES TO LEARNING AND LEVELS OF UNDERSTANDING

In the original work on approaches to learning, Svensson (1977, 1997) was particularly concerned about the nature of the outcome of learning. Instead of 'deep' and 'surface' which focused on intention and process, he preferred to use the terms 'holist' and 'atomist', which also indicated the way knowledge had been structured. Referring to the original experiment, he said:

> Within that investigation, the difference between a holistic and an atomistic approach was found to be the most crucial difference between interactions with complex learning materials. The difference is one between merely delimiting and ordering parts of the material interacted with, compared to integrating parts by use of some organising principle... To be skilled in learning, ... means to be deep, holistic and complete in approach and understanding... The most important aspect of this is the open exploration and use of the possibilities inherent in the material, allied to a consideration of relevant previous knowledge. It is this kind of exploration of relevant knowledge and of relevant principles of organisation that represents skill in learning in the deepest sense. (Svensson, 1997, pp. 64, 68)

Svensson found few students who had adopted an organising principle different from the one presented to them in the text. The main difference was between using, and not using, the one provided by the author. But this conclusion was based on the understanding shown by first year students who had been asked to read a single article. In Pask's (1988) work, students were required to develop their own structures of understanding, and his distinction between holist and serialist strategies can be seen, in part, as implying the use of different organising principles. The holist tends to transform the information provided into a personal framework of interpretation, often going well beyond the information given, even in unjustifiable ways as an holistic strategy spills over into globetrotting. The serialist, in contrast, seems much more likely to accept and use any clear structure already existing in the information provided. The contrast in Pask's work is not between understanding and reproducing, but between preferences and habits in the use of different kinds of interpretative frameworks in seeking understanding.

While Svensson included both process and outcome in his description of approach, Marton and Säljö (1976) described the approach to learning as preceding, and being responsible for, the outcome. Thus, an intention to understand leads to the processes required to understand, and those processes culminate in a particular level of understanding. In the original experiment, Marton and Säljö (1976) had found an empirical association between approach and outcome. The nature of this relationship was investigated more fully in a quantitative study carried out subsequently by Entwistle, Hanley and Ratcliffe (1979) in Lancaster. Students were asked to read an article and answer questions which related both to what they had learned and how they had learnt it. Their responses were coded to indicate outcome (in terms of level of understanding, integration, and knowledge of main points) and approach to learning (based on the characteristics of deep and surface approaches).

Principal components analyses were used to explore the interrelationships between approach and outcome. Of the three main factors, the first brought together the three components of a deep level of understanding with the approach characteristics of 'looking for meaning' and 'use of experience'. The second factor loaded highly on knowledge of the essential points, and picked up the other main component of the deep approach included in this study – 'relating facts to conclusion'. The final factor had high loadings on the surface characteristics of 'looking for information' and 'memorisation', combined with negative loadings on all but one of the indicators of deep approach and outcome. Whereas Marton (1976) had suggested that a deep approach would necessarily show all its defining features, these analyses indicated that some students concentrated more on facts and details in developing a deep understanding, whereas others were more concerned with personal meaning. This distinction paralleled Pask's description of holist and serialist strategies, but also showed links with rather different kinds of outcome.

Fransson (1977) had found differences in the learning outcomes of students which he attributed to both the amount of effort and the involvement shown during the learning process. Bringing these aspects together with the findings from Lancaster suggested the links between approach and outcome indicated in Table 4.3.

These differences in outcome can also be seen in relation to the SOLO taxonomy developed by Biggs and Collis (1982). This taxonomy describes how information is used in answering assessment questions. At the lowest levels – prestructural and unistructural – students drew on limited and often inaccurate information, equivalent to a surface passive outcome. The next level was multistructural, in which answers contained several unrelated but pertinent points (surface active). The relational level showed an integration of the main points presented by the teacher (deep passive), while the

TABLE 4.3    Approaches to learning and levels of understanding

| Approach to learning | Level of understanding |
|---|---|
| Deep active | Explains the author's conclusion and examines how it was justified |
| Deep passive | Summarises the main argument accurately, but without considering evidence |
| Surface active | Describes the main points made without integrating them into an argument |
| Surface passive | Mentions a few isolated points or examples |

Source: Adapted from Fransson, 1977, p. 250, and Entwistle, 1988, p. 85.

extended abstract category showed a much deeper grasp of the material derived from previous knowledge and independent thinking (deep active).

Differences in the outcomes of learning can, however, also be described in terms of the cycles of comprehension and operation learning required to reach a full understanding. In most of the Gothenburg studies, the outcomes of learning were produced within a naturalistic experiment, unaffected either by time constraints or by assessment pressures. In everyday studying, time constraints and competing pressures often prevent students from completing the processes which lead to full understanding, even when the intention is deep. Whether the reason for incomplete learning is a lack of effort, as Fransson suggests, or lack of time, the effect will be the same, and Pask's work suggests that stylistic distinctions will be found in the outcomes. The two factors covering a deep approach found in the Lancaster study, described previously, provide tentative evidence that this type of difference does occur and suggest a more elaborate description of the links between approach, process, and outcome shown in Table 4.4 (Entwistle, Hanley & Hounsell, 1979; Entwistle, 1988).

The original version of this Table implied that operation learning was rooted in an intention to reproduce, whereas it is now clear that this style of thinking makes an essential contribution to understanding, particularly in the sciences (Entwistle & Ramsden, 1983). When operation learning is carried out either casually, or without effective use of comprehension learning, however, it may well become indistinguishable from a surface approach. More generally,

TABLE 4.4 Approaches, processes and outcomes of learning

| Intention | Approach/Style | Process | | Outcome |
|---|---|---|---|---|
| | | Stage I | Stage II | |
| Understanding | Deep Approach/ Versatile | All four processes below used in alternation to develop a full understanding | | Deep level of understanding |
| Partial understanding | Comprehension learning | Building overall description of content area | Reorganising and relating ideas to prior knowledge | Incomplete understanding through globetrotting |
| | Operation learning | Detailed attention to evidence and to its provenance | Relating evidence to conclusions, critically | Incomplete understanding through improvidence |
| Reproducing | Surface Approach | Memorisation | Overlearning by routine repetition | Surface level of understanding |
| Achieving | Strategic, well-organised studying | Any combination of the six above processes considered to be necessary in carrying out the perceived task requirements successfully | | High grades with or without understanding |

Source: Adapted from Entwistle, Hanley & Hounsell, 1979, p. 376.

reliance on either comprehension or operation learning alone will lead to an incomplete form of understanding which exhibits the characteristic pathology of either globetrotting or improvidence.

## MEMORISING AND UNDERSTANDING WITHIN CONCEPTIONS OF LEARNING

In earlier work, the often quite consistent differences in the ways in which students tackle their academic work were attributed to personality and motivational traits. But these could equally well be seen as emanating from pre-existing conceptions of learning. Students enter higher education with beliefs about learning derived from their previous experiences of education and also from their own feelings about the nature of learning. Säljö (1979) introduced the idea of a hierarchy of such conceptions, which again could be reduced to an underlying dichotomy between memorisation and reproducing, and understanding through personal transformation of the material.

More recent research has suggested, however, that the distinction between memorising and understanding may not be clear- cut – at least in some countries. Biggs (1991) drew attention to the paradox of the Asian learner who concentrates on memorising study materials and yet typically does well, even in assessments designed to tap understanding. In addition, using the SPQ, he showed that students in Hong Kong had higher scores than Australian students on the deep approach. The apparent paradox could then be explained as a failure of Western educationists to recognise important cultural differences in the ways students learn in 'Confucian-heritage cultures' (Biggs, 1994a). Biggs made the crucial distinction between memorising in a routine manner (which is a surface approach) and memorising intended to ensure accurate recall of material already understood, which he described as 'deep memorising'. Because the intention is still to understand, repetition as a process of reinforcing understanding is not a surface approach, it is simply a strategy to ensure thorough understanding.

The processes of developing thorough understanding have been explored further using phenomenographic analyses of the conceptions of learning held by students in different countries (Marton & Booth, 1997). They bring out clearly the emphasis on understanding which Asian students describe as 'memorising'.

> In the process of memorising, the text being memorised is repeated several times which may be outwardly suggestive of rote learning. However ... (teachers) explained that, when a text is being memorised, it can be repeated in a way which deepens the understanding... (This) process of repetition contributes to understanding, which is different from the mechanical memorisation which characterises rote learning. (p. 35)

Two forms of memorising thus need to be considered – routine rote learning and meaningful repetition intended to reinforce and extend understanding. The distinction also contrasts committing to memory what the teacher has presented with understanding for oneself, where the initiative comes from the student. Furthermore, students were found to be describing learning in three consecutive phases – acquiring, knowing, and making use of what was known.

TABLE 4.5 The outcome space of learning

| Ways of experiencing learning | Temporal facet | | |
|---|---|---|---|
| | acquiring | knowing | making use of |
| committing to memory (teacher's words) | memorising (teacher's words) | remembering (teacher's words) | reproducing (teacher's words) |
| committing to memory (teacher's meaning) | memorising (teacher's meaning) | remembering (teacher's meaning) | reproducing (teacher's meaning) |
| understanding (meaning for oneself) | gaining understanding (for oneself) | having understanding (for oneself) | being able to do something differently, or different |
| understanding (the phenomenon) | gaining understanding (of the phenomenon) | having understanding (of the phenomenon) | relating |

Source: Adapted from Marton & Booth, 1997.

These conceptions of learning could then be summarised within the two-dimensional framework (outcome space) of depth and temporal sequence shown in Table 4.5.

Although these separate forms of memorising are being discussed currently in terms of cultural variants in conceptions of learning, Biggs (1994a) recognised that deep memorising also was found in Western education, particularly in preparing for examinations. Recent small-scale interview studies at the University of Edinburgh have also highlighted contrasts in the way memorising and understanding are used in preparing for examinations.

## UNDERSTANDING DEVELOPED IN PREPARING FOR FINALS

The interviews in Edinburgh began with a series of questions about revision strategies, but students were then asked about their experiences of seeking and reaching understanding, and how that understanding was represented in their revision notes and in writing their examination answers. Details of the research methods can be found elsewhere (Entwistle, N. & Entwistle, 1991).

In taking notes in lectures and from books, students were involved in the first phase of learning described by Marton and Booth, namely acquiring meaning. While this process is active, it does not involve repetition, at least in the final year. Because they have acquired extensive prior knowledge and understanding, most students assimilate the material quite readily by what has been called meaningful reception learning (Ausubel, Novak & Hanesian, 1978). Over time that initial grasp of the material fades. As a result, the first step in revising for finals typically involved students in reading through all their notes, deciding which topics were most important, seeking to understand those topics for themselves, making condensed, summary revision notes, and then 'learning' those notes. One of the students explained this last process as follows.

> I would ask myself if I remembered each bit (of the revision note), and if I could explain it, then that went off the list ... I had headings. But under the headings I would have the important points which showed the understanding ... It was basically names, experiments and important examples, which triggered off the understanding by reading it through. The understanding was still there, ... I could grasp it whenever I wanted, but by reading it through it seemed to underline the understanding. (Entwistle, N. & Entwistle, 1991, p. 218)

Students learned in this last phase by rehearsing explanations, either out loud or in writing, through a process which involved revisiting the material to deepen the understanding – rather like 'deep memorisation'. The 'triggering' which was reported seemed to go in both directions, with the understanding bringing to mind relevant details, and the names and facts suggesting the meaning that lay behind them. However, some of the information was much less easy to remember, and then rote memorisation came into play.

> You can learn some things and they can automatically pop up when you need them, and other things are slightly less easy to learn, or slightly less easy to remember. So, by repeating them to myself before I went into the exam, it gave me that short time to actually get at them. It's almost as though there was no connections for those things, so I almost needed an extra connection with the conscious brain. (Entwistle, N. & Entwistle, 1991, p. 218)

While the logical sequence of acquiring, knowing, and using, described by Marton and Booth, is also seen in preparing for examinations, there seems to be another phase which involves preparing one's understanding for specific assessment demands. From our interviews, the revision strategies indicated a first phase of checking whether the material was sufficiently understood for the anticipated examination requirements. If it was not, then the notes would be re-read, and alternative explanations might be sought in books. If understanding was felt to be adequate, then the next step was to rehearse it until there was confidence in being able to remember and explain it fully. At this stage, details were pulled in to fill out the explanation, but there was less concern about precision in the details, rather a feeling that they were potentially available to back up the description or argument – a feeling we shall return to later. Finally, students concentrated on thoroughly remembering a set of important facts by concentration and repetition. In the students' experience, most of these facts would be lost shortly after the examination, whereas the structure of the revision notes would be recalled fairly easily for some time afterwards.

## THE EXPERIENCE OF UNDERSTANDING IN PREPARING FOR FINALS

Besides looking at understanding indirectly as part of the revision process, students were also asked directly about their experiences of understanding. There was a good deal of agreement in what 'understanding' was like, with students describing understanding as a feeling of coherence, connectedness, and provisional wholeness – 'provisional' because it could be extended in the future (Entwistle, A. & Entwistle, 1992). A composite quote conveys the essence of students' experiences which echoes Svensson's (1997) description of holistic outcomes of learning.

> Understanding? To me that's the interconnection of lots of disparate things – the way it all hangs together, the feeling that you understand how the whole thing is connected up – you can make sense of it internally. You're making lots of connections which then make sense and it's logical... It is as though one's mind has finally 'locked in' to the pattern. Concepts seem to fit together in a meaningful way, when before the connections did not seem clear or appropriate or complete... If you really understand something, why it works, and what the idea is behind it, you can't not understand it afterwards – you can't 'de-understand' it! And you know you understand (when you can) construct an argument from scratch ... by yourself – can explain it so that you feel satisfied with the explanation. (Entwistle A. & Entwistle, 1992, p. 148)

### CONTRASTING FORMS OF UNDERSTANDING

While most students described attempts to 'understand' their notes, a careful analysis of the transcripts of the interviews suggested that 'understanding' was seen in importantly different ways. Students had sought and developed quite different forms of understanding. The way these were first described (Entwistle, N. & Entwistle, 1991) derived directly from students' revision strategies and the varying degrees of sophistication implied by their descriptions of understanding. The set of categories shown in the top half of Table 4.6 can now also be viewed in terms of differing conceptions of learning described by Marton and Booth (see Table 4.5). They form a hierarchy starting with essentially no attempt to develop understanding beyond 'committing to memory the teacher's words' (A). The second category suggests an understanding which remains close to the lecturer's own presentations (B) – committing the teacher's meaning to memory. The deeper levels of understanding (D and E), in contrast, involve substantial re-organisation of the learning material into what becomes an essentially personal framework of meaning (understanding the meaning for oneself).

The hierarchy can also be interpreted as a gradual diminution in the influence of the examination on the forms of understanding being sought by the student. In the fourth category (D), the student is developing personal understanding, but with a wary eye on the requirements of assessment. The final category (E) can be seen as

TABLE 4.6    Contrasting forms of understanding in revising for finals

---

**Forms of understanding in relation to approaches to studying and revising**

A. Absorbing facts, details, and procedures, without consideration of structure
B. Accepting and using the logical structures provided in the lecture notes
C. Developing own summary structures from notes solely to answer exam questions
D. Developing structures to represent own understanding and to control exam answers
E. Developing structures relating own understanding to the nature of the discipline

**Forms of understanding seen in terms of cognitive processes and structure**

Breadth of understanding
Depth or level of understanding
Structure used to organise the material being learned
  a. little or no structure being imposed on the facts learned
  b. relying exclusively on the lecturer's structures
  c. producing prepared answers to previous years' questions
  d. adapting own understanding to expected question types
  e. relying on an individual conception of the topic

---

Source: From Entwistle, N. & Entwistle, A., 1991, and Entwistle, N., 1995b.

an ideal form of academic understanding, deriving from a sophisticated conception of the discipline itself – 'understanding the phenomenon' – but it does involve a lack of strategic awareness in taking examinations.

To illustrate these differences, a student who was essentially recapitulating the lecturer's understanding (category B) said:

> The main thing that I really relied on during revision was going through all the past papers and finding all the questions on the topics I'd chosen to revise. Then I went through my lecture notes and made summaries of those topics. I did short essay plans and drew them as mind-maps, so I could remember them in the exam. Then, sometimes I was lucky, when the question seemed to say, in effect, "Rewrite your mind map in prose". But at other times, I had to adapt them as I went on and, by and large, those were worse answers than I would have written had the question been more favourable. (Entwistle, N. & Entwistle, 1991, p. 220)

Students who had sought their own understanding, but with an eye fixed on the examination (D), described their strategy for presenting their understanding 'gift-wrapped' for the examiner.

> The more I have done exams, the more I'd liken them to a performance, like being on a stage. Having not so much to present the fact that you know a vast amount, but having to perform well with what you do know. Sort of, playing to the gallery. In the exam, I was very conscious of being outside what I was writing. (Entwistle, N. & Entwistle, 1991, p. 220)

In contrast, students who had concentrated more on understanding the discipline itself (E) saw the examination as an unwelcome restriction on thorough explanation of their understanding.

> Well, in revising I had tried to understand things thoroughly, but in the exams there were cases where I knew too much. I had to go through all the stages of working through the topic and showing that I had understood it. I couldn't gloss over the surface. And once I started writing, it all just 'welled up'. I felt that I couldn't interrupt the argument halfway, as it was developing, because it ties together as a whole. It's very difficult to pick something like that apart, when you understand the theory like that. Half an understanding doesn't make sense! (Entwistle, N. & Entwistle, 1991, pp. 220–221)

This difference in forms of understanding was very evident even as the interviews were being conducted and was reflected in the first description of the five distinguishable categories. Later reflection on the nature of these differences, in terms of the processes and structure involved, led to the identification of three components within these forms of understanding – breadth, depth, and structure, as shown in the bottom half of Table 4.6.

## BREADTH, DEPTH, AND STRUCTURE IN UNDERSTANDING

While seeking understanding, most of the students were bringing together substantial amounts of information and ideas, but they differed markedly in the breadth or volume of material which they were attempting to integrate. Some students were just trying to make sense of their lecture notes supported by minimal outside reading, while others were tackling the much more daunting task of interconnecting ideas drawn from wide reading and continuing personal reflection. Marton and Booth (in press) have recently ascribed variations in the depth of learning to 'agency' – the extent to which the student relies on the teacher or initiates learning independently. The distinction between reproducing the teacher's meaning and developing one's own understanding (seen in Table 4.5) can also be seen within the depth dimension here, although in this analysis there were also differences in the amount of time and effort students put into seeking their own understanding. Finally, students varied in the extent to which they simply accepted the structure offered within the lectures as their way of coming to grips with the material, or sought to develop their own ways of looking at the subject within more idiosyncratic frameworks (Entwistle, A. & Entwistle, N., 1992).

These contrasts in structure parallel those described earlier from Svensson's (1996) work. Accepting and using the structure provided was seen as part of the deep, holistic approach in Svensson's study of first year students. Among final year students, however, this strategy becomes a surface device to avoid hard independent thinking, or provides a way of playing safe by reproducing what the examiner is most likely to accept.

## KNOWLEDGE OBJECTS

The questions asked about revision strategies also brought to light the widespread use of mnemonics and a reliance on visualising the structure of the notes, sometimes in the form of mind maps. Descriptions of these revision notes often stressed visualisation, and the way the image helped to trigger memory.

My revision notes were just little charts that linked everything up together with a diagram in the centre and sort of spokes coming out... I
used them for sorting an argument out in my head – sorting out where
everything was pigeon holed ... and also to remember specific names.
It's a mind map. It has branches coming out of the centre – they are the
label of an argument – and then, on the branches coming out from
each main branch, there would be subsidiary arguments, entailments
of the argument – which is right and which is wrong, according to
experiment, ... with the facts pinned at the end. What that fact triggers,
is the whole branch going backwards.

I can see that virtually as a picture, and I can review it, and bring in
more facts about each part... Looking at a particular part of the
diagram sort of triggers off other thoughts. I find schematics, in flow
diagrams and the like, very useful because a schematic acts a bit like a
syllabus; it tells you what you should know, without actually telling
you what it is. I think the facts are stored separately, ... and the
schematic is like an index, I suppose. (Entwistle, N. & Entwistle, A.,
1991, p. 219)

This extract intrigued Ference Marton and led to a joint re-analysis of aspects of the transcripts which contained references to
similar experiences of understanding (Entwistle & Marton, 1994).
One extensive introspection on the nature of this experience became the focus of the re-analysis. It 'seeded' the crystallisation of a
new concept – knowledge object. The student was talking about
differences between using an understanding in an examination and
explaining that understanding in a more relaxed context.

Take this graph [shows diagram], you may recall it in many ways. You
may remember it from having drawn it, from having thought about it;
but to actually reproduce it on paper, you may not have to go through
the visual process of remembering what it looked like on the page...
You may say you've got a visual memory of it, if you have to search for
it. But otherwise it just appears, and therefore it's just a memory which
may or may not be expressed visually... I don't perceive it in any particular way, I just know it. I don't actually hear it, see it, write it; it's
just present. And I know it's present without actually identifying it.

(In exams), I just clear my mind and something comes... You know
it's visual in some ways, but it's also just there without necessarily being visual... (It's not as if) you remember a page, and the page is locked
in your memory. What I'm saying is that the ideas are locked in your
memory and they display as a page when you're thinking about it, but
not necessarily when you're putting it down... You can sort of by-pass

the conscious perception of your memory: it may not be a visual memory, but (sometimes) it may have to be perceived as a visual memory... I think, in a stress situation like an examination, you don't actually (have to) reach for it, it comes out automatically. That may show that it's not actually a visual memory, as such, but a visual expression of 'central memory'. (Entwistle & Marton, 1994, pp. 172–173; Entwistle, 1995b, p. 49)

The subsequent analysis of the whole set of interviews suggested that this experience was not uncommon, although the majority of students found difficulty in articulating their experience. Piecing together the range of incomplete descriptions, it seemed that students were experiencing their understandings as having some internal form and structure – almost as entities in their own right which came to control their thinking paths (Entwistle & Marton, 1994; Entwistle, 1995b). In introducing the concept, it was explained that

the term was chosen to draw attention to the tight integration of knowledge achieved through intensive study, to the quasi-sensory nature of the 'perceptions' involved, and to the awareness of substantial amounts of related knowledge not immediately at the focus of attention. The term 'object' is, of course, used only as a metaphor for the multidimensional and ever evolving awareness which represents the full experience of understanding. (Entwistle & Marton, 1994, p. 166)

Table 4.7 summarises the defining features of a knowledge object.

TABLE 4.7   Defining features of 'knowledge objects'

| |
|---|
| Awareness of a tightly integrated body of knowledge |
| Visualisation and 'quasi-sensory' experiences |
| Awareness of unfocused aspects of knowledge |
| Use in controlling explanations |

All of the students who described 'quasi-sensory' experiences had carried out intensive revision in which they had successively summarised their notes into frameworks of some kind. By the end of their revision they had become confident about their understanding and were aware of a tightly integrated body of knowledge to which they felt they had ready access. Their experience involved impressions of a tight structure of which they were aware in a visual, but not wholly visual, manner – a 'quasi-sensory' experience. Often the summary notes were accessed visually, but the students were also aware of unfocused aspects of their knowledge. As they focused on the key points in their summary, these would 'pull up' additional information and specific details which they had memorised separately.

The final feature of the knowledge object is of particular interest. Knowledge objects seem to have an important function for the students in providing flexible control of an examination answer as it develops (Entwistle, 1995b). Students use the structure of their knowledge objects to provide a generic framework for a topic, but some of them also actively shape that structure to suit the specific demands of the question. This 'shaping' of a knowledge object can be illustrated through the following extract.

> I had tried to structure my revision so that I could understand what was going on... So, although I had this structure when I went into the exam, I still wanted it to be flexible, so that I could approach the question (itself)... At the time, as I was writing, I was just using anything that came into my mind (and fitted in). I had learned a good deal of detail, and yet I could use (only) a small percentage of it... (As I wrote), it was almost as though I could see it all fitting into an overall picture. I think you're almost developing what you know, and are playing it in a slightly different way. (Entwistle, 1995b, p. 50)

One student seemed to have experienced the knowledge object as monitoring the adequacy of the answer as it emerged on the page. The knowledge object provided a logical structure but, as a particular answer was written, it seemed to take on a life of its own as it controlled the answer.

> Following that logic through, *it* pulls in pictures and facts as it needs them... Each time I describe (a particular topic), it's likely to be different... Well, you start with evolution, say ... and suddenly you know where you're going next. Then, you might have a choice ... to go in that direction or that direction ... and follow it through various options *it's* offering... Hopefully, you'll make the right choice, and so this goes to this, goes to this – and you've explained it to the level you've got to. Then, *it* says "Okay, you can go on to talk about further criticisms in the time you've got left". (Entwistle, 1995b, p. 50, emphasis added)

Students also talked about how their perceptions of the examination requirements influenced their answers. Their explanations seemed to be controlled not only by the organisational structures or knowledge objects developed during revision, but also by the form and wording of the particular question set, the tight time constraints, and the audience – the examiners who would be reading the script.

> In an exam, you have to have background knowledge of the subject, and an ability to interpret the information in your own way... You don't sit down and think "How much can I remember about this particular subject?", you try and explain your ideas, using examples which come to mind... You can't use all the information for a particular line of argument, and you don't need to; you only need to use what you think is going to convince the examiner. (Entwistle, N. & Entwistle, A., 1991, p. 221)

## BRINGING AN UNDERSTANDING TO MIND

In the interviews, students were asked how well they could remember one of the essays they had written. Most of the students struggled to bring it to mind, but used the logical structure as a prop. And again visualisation was often part of that process.

> Sometimes I can visualise parts of it. I can think about, perhaps, where certain things were, but I don't have the kind of memory where I can think back to a certain page and remember everything that was written down there... It must be that, in my mind, I'm just going back to the same structure that I had to begin with... (When I think back now) the general points are there, and the actual details ... all come flooding back, as it were. The general arguments that I included tend to be remembered... I would probably remember certain points, and then they may lead off to other points, and then they might start bringing things out. I wouldn't remember detailed things like quotes and data; I would have to actually sit down and learn those, but I think I would remember the general arguments. (Entwistle, 1995b, p. 52)

There was, in the interviews, a good deal of evidence that knowledge objects retained their integrity for a week or more, but did they last any longer than that? Serendipitous anecdotal evidence of the continued presence of a knowledge object came from one of the students who had been interviewed previously. She had been involved, subsequently, in discussions about the existence of knowledge objects, and had agreed to review study advice for first year students. In reflecting on her own experiences of preparing for examinations, she suddenly saw herself as she had been five years previously – in a library looking over her revision notes. That scene was, however, soon replaced by two other images in quick succession, images which initially seemed unrelated and surprising. The first image was that of a bird flying over a landscape of hills; the second portrayed a bird in a cage. These unexpected images provoked reflection which soon produced a connecting link, and a recognisable knowledge object.

There was absolutely no (memory) search..; (the image) just appeared... (Then) I sort of questioned it: what was the caged bird? It wasn't active, as in searching for something, it was just – I stalked it, if you like, and said "What's that?". Then it, sort of, told me that these things ... were the different avenues that could possibly explain... (the apparently) 'magical' navigation of birds. It was basically by stopping there and pausing, these other things were sort of pulled in. So it was like stopping a reel in a film that could have gone past, and actively halting it; and then by stopping it, these other things appeared... almost as a set of sub-headings...

At that stage, I ... defocused on the caged bird – in effect I let the film run – and switched again to a picture of a bird in flight. But (then) this was more like a bird's eye view picture, of dark hills, ... so I was in fact being the bird, looking at the hills. And this knowledge – of the fact that you could use hills (for navigation) – then brought back the structure of the essay as a whole. I'd got these experiments on the one hand (the bird in the cage), and this local (navigation) knowledge on the other, and putting those together created a whole... And so this whole thing can be produced from two pictures; but it wasn't produced by the first picture that I saw.

(Again, I) thought back to the picture of the bird in a cage... (and) tried to go a stage further and see if there were any details that I could get to. I had general details...(but at first) I couldn't go any further with that. So, I went back to the bird in the cage to see if I could probe... When I actually stopped and looked at... the picture of the bird in the cage, ... a door seemed to open and the information came out... (Eventually I felt) "There's potentially specific knowledge, but I can't get at it". You get to a point where you know there is knowledge that you have come across in the past, but you can't find the way into it. (Extract from the transcript)

The initial memory of revising did not bring to mind the structure of the revision notes, but rather it was the associated vivid images which contained the essence of that structure. The knowledge object must have continued to exist in some form, but could only be brought to mind through these images. When questioned directly about other topics, no equivalent structures could be remembered.

The subtitle of the original article describing knowledge objects was 'understandings constituted through intensive academic study' (Entwistle & Marton, 1994). This phrase acknowledged that the knowledge objects had been found only under specific, and atypical, circumstances. Subsequent interviews showed that knowledge objects were formed in the process of researching and writing course work essays (Entwistle, 1995b), and recently another piece of anecdotal evidence has suggested other circumstances in which a knowledge object has been experienced. Again, the evidence comes from someone who was already familiar with the concept – David Perkins from Harvard (personal communication). And again vivid visual imagery was involved. He had been persuaded to give a presentation on facilitating group discussions. This was an area in which he had considerable practical experience; he had also talked about aspects of it before, but had never previously given a formal presentation, treating the topic as a whole.

The activity of bringing together what were initially rather loosely related ideas and experiences seemed to involve the creation of a knowledge object. He was conscious that such experiences were perhaps a step towards a knowledge object, and suggested the term 'knowledge ensemble' to indicate the less structured associations developed experientially. Previously, separate experiences had been explained as required. Preparing for the presentation, however, seemed to provide access to the whole topic in a more organised and complete way. Perkins himself described what had been produced as 'a highly coherent, easily surveyable representation', and he suggested that a knowledge object 'may be important in communicating coherently and effectively about a strong competence, even if it isn't necessary for exercising that competence'.

The framework which Perkins (1994) chose for his developing knowledge object involved an elaborate and sustained metaphor which would almost inevitably evoke strong visualisation. A group discussion had been imagined as 'an exploration of the space of possible ideas', and that led to a metaphor of space exploration.

The leader of the discussion was seen as being the mission controller, responsible for guiding the group through the opportunities and perils of the exploration. The mission controller has to be well prepared prior to launch, as the early stages are critical to success. Discussions tend to follow one or other of several recognisable sequences or orbits, and maintaining the orbit depends on keeping moving at a good speed and avoiding being knocked off course by distractions (meteor showers) or getting involved in disputes (star wars). Travel further afield depends on good navigation through limitless space (focusing the discussion). Finally, the mission controller is responsible for a safe landing, which happens in discussions through consolidation, summarising, and deciding future actions.

This rich metaphor, as it evolved, became an ideal knowledge object. It had a logical structure, a flow (time sequence), and it evoked the strong visual imagery needed to make it memorable.

## DISCUSSION

This chapter has considered approaches to learning in relation to forms of understanding. The earlier work on the relationship between approach and outcome concentrated on showing links between the deep and surface dichotomy and the levels of understanding reached. In the usual descriptions of these approaches, each of them has a single distinctive process of learning – seeking understanding or memorising – while levels are restricted to aspects of the content. These analyses were necessary starting points, but do not fully represent what is found in student learning: the process is much more intricate and complex than that.

The recent work provoked by the paradox of the Asian learner has developed the distinctions between conceptions of learning further, by identifying learning processes which involve committing understandings to memory through rehearsal and elaboration. It has also introduced the two dimensions of depth and temporal sequence. The research by Pask and Heath drew attention to stylistic differences in how people build up meaning for themselves, and the ways in which understanding develops through the alternation between 'the critical and the curious'.

When we consider how understanding is demonstrated through explanations, we come back to Svensson's idea about the importance of articulated wholeness through the use of appropriate integrating principles. Indeed, this idea can be seen as central to the phenomenographic perspective on learning subsequently formulated by Marton.

> In our view, learning proceeds, as a rule, from an undifferentiated and poorly integrated understanding of the whole to an increased differentiation and integration of the whole and its parts. Thus, learning does not proceed as much from parts to wholes, as from wholes to parts, and from wholes to wholes. (Marton & Booth, 1997)

This emphasis on the evolution of understanding through progressively more elaborated, differentiated, and yet tightly integrated wholes resonates with the message being developed in this chapter. The conceptualisation evolved through looking at the contrasting forms of understanding which students describe. These understandings are qualitatively different, due partly to the approach to learning adopted, partly to the degree of effort and engagement of the learner, and finally to the attempts made to build an idiosyncratic framework within which to integrate new information with previous understandings.

The analyses of students' revision strategies showed that the sequence proposed by Marton – acquiring, knowing, and using – while logically inevitable in general terms, needed further elaboration when describing learning within an everyday study context. Students typically were found to work through several revision stages in which different types of learning were used. In lectures, students took in (or down) information, but they were often aware of actively relating that knowledge to what they already knew, and so understanding it – at least in a provisional way. Ausubel saw this form of learning as meaningful reception learning. In starting revision, students typically read through their complete set of notes to 'refresh' and elaborate their initial understanding. Making revision notes began the process of simplifying and restructuring that understanding. Some students were content to leave the structure as the lecturer or book had presented it, but others went much further in building a more complete and personally satisfying framework which integrated a wider range of information and ideas. Whichever way that was done, most students produced a set of revision notes which they then 'learned' using a process similar to what Biggs has described as 'deep memorising'. By rehearsing and checking their understanding, and keeping in mind the summarising structure in the revision notes, they built up a tightly integrated form of understanding which could become, in the words of Perkins, 'a highly coherent, easily surveyable representation' – a knowledge object.

This quasi-sensory entity is constituted through an intensive effort intended to extract personal meaning. Although Perkins sees it, in cognitive psychological terms, as a 'mental representation' that label fails to capture its essence. Certainly, representations of students' understandings are involved in the process of revision, in the form of structured or patterned notes which are organised with shapes and bold lettering to aid subsequent recall. However, a knowledge object is much more than a mental image of a diagram. It can pull into awareness currently unfocused knowledge, almost in the way that hypertext in computing uses certain emphasised words to indicate the existence of additional information. In examinations, mnemonic diagrams are used to provide more reliable access to a knowledge object, which then pulls related material into focus as an answer is constructed.

From students' descriptions, understanding can be seen, not as a fixed representation of some 'target' understanding (Entwistle & Smith, 1997) which exists 'out there', but rather as a feeling of confidence that an understanding can be reconstructed at will from sets of inter-linked ideas and information.

> A schematic acts a bit like a syllabus; it tells you what you should know, without actually telling you what it is. I think the facts are stored separately. I can see that virtually as a picture, and I can review it, and bring in more facts about each part... Looking at a particular part of the diagram sort of triggers off other thoughts. The general points are there, and the actual details all come flooding back, as it were... I clear my mind and something comes. It may not actually be a visual memory, as such, but a visual expression of 'central memory'... (As I wrote), it was almost as though I could see it all fitting into an overall picture... Following that logic through, it pulls in pictures and facts as it needs them and suddenly you know where you're going next... I think you're almost developing what you know, and are playing it in a slightly different way. (Composite from previous quotes)

The idea of 'understanding' seems to refer partly to knowledge which has been confidently stored, and partly to a memory of how that knowledge has been successfully organised in the past. Representations in memory offer mnemonics which help in recalling the structure and key elements within the knowledge object. But it is the combination of knowledge and well established thinking pathways which allows explanations to be constructed to suit a specific question, a particular audience, and a perceived context.

Although knowledge objects were found initially after lengthy, and intensive, revision for finals, a subsequent study found knowledge objects associated with preparing for course work essays, at least when students had engaged personally with a topic and researched it actively. These knowledge objects were being recalled after an interval of several weeks, but the recall of the 'bird in the cage' showed that a knowledge object could be brought back to mind even after five years. Strong visual imagery within the subconscious had presumably triggered that recall, while a vivid metaphor had deliberately been created by Perkins in converting his loose 'knowledge ensemble' into a tightly structured knowledge object. The imagery produced by his metaphor of a space mission grew ever more elaborate as the various previous experiences of facilitating discussions were added in. We can imagine this metaphor creating the 'nodes' of the basic structure, which also implies a clear logical sequence for an explanation. The nodes are initially used to pull in other related aspects, and subsequently act as triggers to recall the relevant details as required.

The latter part of this description goes beyond Perkins's own memory of the experience. It relies, instead, on personal experiences of lecturing, where preparation of familiar topics feels like 'polishing up' a knowledge object. The explanations within the lecture then come from the generic structure of the knowledge object which pulls in relevant examples and details as required. The structure provided by the knowledge object is sufficiently flexible to modify explanations on the basis of feedback from the audience, or in response to questions. Attempts to answer testing questions may necessitate some restructuring of the knowledge object for future use.

Academic thinking often contains the essence of the experience of Perkins. It has its origins in a set of observations or ideas, all of which seem relevant to the topic, but which are only loosely structured. An emerging framework is then used to bring the components into logical and sequential relationships. This way of thinking is also found in scientific research, where knowledge objects can produce a sense of completeness well before detailed evidence and arguments support the intuition (Entwistle & Marton, 1994). The idea of knowledge objects also helps to explain the process, not just of writing essays, but also of constructing academic articles and preparing lectures.

Being able to explain, at least tentatively, the way understandings are developed, elaborated, rehearsed, and converted into explanations should help us to advise students on that most elusive aspect of essay writing – the organising framework – and also help lecturers and authors to build more effective organising principles into their planning of lectures, supporting materials, and writing.

## References

Ausubel, D.P., Novak, J.S., & Hanesian, H. (1978). *Educational psychology: A cognitive view.* New York: Holt, Rinehart & Winston.

Biggs, J.B. (1976). Dimensions of study behaviour: Another look at a.t.i. *British Journal of Educational Psychology, 46,* 68–80.

Biggs, J.B. (1979). Individual differences in study processes and the quality of learning outcomes. *Higher Education, 8,* 381–394.

Biggs, J.B. (1987). *Student approaches to learning and studying.* Melbourne: Australian Council for Educational Research.

Biggs, J.B. (1989). Approaches to the enhancement of tertiary teaching. *Higher Education Research & Development, 8,* 7–25.

Biggs, J.B. (1991). Approaches to learning in secondary and tertiary students in Hong Kong: Some comparative studies. *Educational Research Journal, 6,* 27–39.

Biggs, J.B. (1993). What do inventories of students' learning processes really measure? A theoretical review and clarification. *British Journal of Educational Psychology, 63,* 3–19.

Biggs, J.B. (1994a). Asian learners through Western eyes: An astigmatic paradox. *Australian & New Zealand Journal of Vocational Educational Research, 2*(2), 40–63.

Biggs, J.B. (1994b). Student learning theory and research. Where do we currently stand? In G. Gibbs (Ed.), *Improving student learning: Theory and practice*. Oxford: The Oxford Centre for Staff Development, Oxford Brookes University.

Biggs, J.B., & Collis, K.E. (1982). *Evaluating the quality of learning: The SOLO taxonomy*. New York: Academic Press.

Cohen, G. (1983). *The psychology of cognition*. London: Academic Press.

Entwistle, A.C., & Entwistle, N.J. (1992). Experiences of understanding in revising for degree examinations. *Learning & Instruction, 2*, 1–22.

Entwistle, N.J. (1979). Stages, levels, styles or strategies: Dilemmas in the description of thinking. *Educational Review, 31*, 123–132.

Entwistle. N.J. (1988). *Styles of learning and teaching*. London: David Fulton.

Entwistle, N.J. (1992). *The impact of teaching on learning outcomes in higher education*. Sheffield: Universities' and Colleges' Staff Development Unit.

Entwistle, N.J. (1995b). Frameworks for understanding as experienced in essay writing and in preparing for examinations. *Educational Psychologist, 30*, 47–54.

Entwistle. N.J. (1997). Contrasting perspectives on learning. In F. Marton, D.J. Hounsell & N.J. Entwistle (Eds.), *The experience of learning* (2nd ed.). Edinburgh: Scottish Academic Press.

Entwistle, N.J. (in press). Improving teaching through research on student learning. In J.J.F. Forest (Ed.), *University teaching: International perspectives*. New York: Garland.

Entwistle, N.J., & Entwistle, A. C. (1991). Contrasting forms of understanding for degree examinations: The student experience and its implications. *Higher Education, 22*, 205–227.

Entwistle, N.J., Hanley, M., & Hounsell, D.J. (1979). Identifying distinctive approaches to studying. *Higher Education, 8*, 365–380.

Entwistle, N.J., Hanley, M., & Ratcliffe, G. (1979). Approaches to learning and levels of understanding. *British Educational Research Journal, 5*, 99–114.

Entwistle, N.J., & Marton, F. (1994). Knowledge objects: Understandings constituted through intensive academic study. *British Journal of Educational Psychology, 64*, 161–178.

Entwistle, N.J., & Ramsden, P. (1983). *Understanding student learning*. London: Croom Helm.

Entwistle, N.J., & Smith, C. (1997). *Personal understanding and target understanding: A question of match*. Manuscript submitted for publication.

Entwistle, N.J., & Wilson, J.D. (1977). *Degrees of excellence: The academic achievement game*. London: Hodder & Stoughton.

Fransson, A. (1977). On qualitative differences in learning – IV: Effects of motivation and test anxiety on process and outcome. *British Journal of Educational Psychology*, 47, 244–257.

Gibbs, G. (1992). *Improving the quality of student learning*. Bristol: Technical & Educational Services.

Heath, R. (1964). *The reasonable adventurer*. Pittsburgh: University of Pittsburg Press.

Hounsell, D.J. (1997). Understanding teaching and teaching for understanding. In F. Marton, D.J. Hounsell, & N.J. Entwistle (Eds.), *The experience of learning* ( 2nd ed.). Edinburgh: Scottish Academic Press.

Laurillard, D. (1993). *Rethinking university teaching: A framework for the effective use of educational technology*. London: Routledge.

Marton, F. (1976). What does it take to learn? Some implications of an alternative view of learning. In N.J. Entwistle (Ed.), *Strategies for research and development in higher education*. Amsterdam: Swets & Zeitlinger.

Marton, F., & Booth, S. (1997). *Learning and awareness*. Mahwah, N.J.: Lawrence Erlbaum.

Marton, F., Hounsell, D.J., & Entwistle, N.J. (Eds.). (1997). *The experience of learning* (2nd ed.). Edinburgh: Scottish Academic Press.

Marton, F., & Säljö, R. (1977). On qualitative differences in learning – I: Outcome and process. *British Journal of Educational Psychology*, 46, 4–11.

Marton, F., & Säljö, R. (1996). Approaches to learning. In F. Marton, D. J. Hounsell, & N.J. Entwistle (Eds.), *The experience of learning* (2nd ed.). Edinburgh: Scottish Academic Press.

Pask, G. (1976). Styles and strategies of learning. *British Journal of Educational Psychology*, 46, 128–148.

Pask, G. (1988). Learning strategies, teaching strategies and conceptual or learning style. In R. R. Schmeck (Ed.), *Learning strategies and learning styles*. New York: Plenum Press.

Perkins, D. (1994). *Missions in possibility space*. (Internal paper). Boston, Mass.: Harvard University Graduate School of Education.

Ramsden, P. (1979). Student learning and perceptions of the academic environment. *Higher Education, 8*, 411–427.

Ramsden, P. (1992). *Learning to teach in higher education*. London: Kogan Page.

Säljö, R. (1979). *Learning in the learner's perspective – I: Some common-sense conceptions*. (Report 76). Gothenburg: University of Gothenburg, Department of Education.

Sperry, R. (1983). *Science and moral priority*. Oxford: Blackwell.

Svensson, L. (1977). On qualitative differences in learning – III: Study skill and learning. *British Journal of Educational Psychology*, 47, 233–243.

Svensson, L. (1997). Skill in learning and organising knowledge. In F. Marton, D.J. Hounsell, & N.J. Entwistle (Eds.), *The experience of learning* (2nd ed.). Edinburgh: Scottish Academic Press.

Tait, H., & Entwistle, N.J. (1996). Identifying students at risk through ineffective study strategies. *Higher Education, 31*, 97–116.

Trigwell, K., Prosser, M., & Taylor, P. (1994). Qualitative differences in approach to teaching first year science. *Higher Education, 27*, 74–84.

# CHAPTER 5

# Effects of Collaborative Learning on the Quality of Assignments

*Catherine Tang*

## CONCEPTIONS OF LEARNING

Academic learning involves complex cognitive activities engaged by students in a personal interaction with the learning tasks embedded in a particular learning context. Due to different personal characteristics, experiences and intentions, learning may have different meaning to different students, and hence there may be different answers to the same question of 'What does it mean to say we have learned something?'. The different ways in which students understand learning constitute the different conceptions of learning held, and also give perspectives on the learning process.

Extensive research has been conducted on the different conceptions of learning held by students (Marton, Dall'Alba & Beaty, 1993; Säljö, 1979). In summary, there are two basic conceptions of learning existing in educational thinking: quantitative and qualitative (Biggs, 1996a; Cole, 1990; Tang, 1991; Tang & Biggs, 1996).

### QUANTITATIVE AND QUALITATIVE CONCEPTIONS OF LEARNING

In the quantitative conception, learning is concerned with the acquisition of a large quantity of discrete units of declarative and procedural knowledge to be memorised for the purpose of reproduction or utilisation at a later time. Teaching from a quantitative perspective implies a transmission model, according to which discrete units of knowledge are transmitted from the teacher to the students.

In the qualitative conception, learning is concerned with an insight into the subject, and new ways of thinking about the world. Learners actively construct meaning of the content to be learned, resulting in a change of their conceptions about the external world. Teaching from a qualitative perspective implies a constructivist model, which is concerned with facilitating students in actively developing and constructing meaning and their own personal understandings of what is being learned (Steffe & Gale, 1995).

## CONCEPTIONS OF LEARNING AND IMPLICATIONS FOR ASSESSMENT

These different conceptions of learning not only drive the curriculum, how students learn, and how teachers teach, they also have a great impact on assessment. To assess outcomes of learning within a quantitative framework requires confirming that so many discrete binary knowledge units have been acquired. These units are assumed to be either correct or incorrect, and all are of equal importance. The extent of learning or competence in a subject is indicated by an aggregated score of all the correct units. Most objective test questions such as true/false and other forms of multiple choice questions are common quantitative assessment methods. Essay type questions, particularly those which are set and marked to preset answers, and where one point is awarded to each correct piece of knowledge, are also assessing learning in discrete quantities rather than in terms of the cohesive or structural qualities of learning.

Assessment methods designed to assess learning outcomes within a qualitative framework are concerned with the overall quality and integrity of learning. This may involve evaluating the understandings as constructed by the students, the learning processes used, and changes in their conceptions about the subject learned. Assessment by project, portfolio, and some appropriately set and graded essay questions are some of the ways of providing students with the opportunity to demonstrate the extent and quality of their learning in fulfillment of the objectives.

## DIFFERENT MODELS OF ASSESSMENT

Satterly (1981) defines educational assessment as a term which includes all processes and products describing the nature and extent of students' learning, its degree of correspondence with the aims/objectives of teaching, and its relationship with the environment which is designed to facilitate learning. Educational assessments are perceived to serve several functions such as selecting students, maintaining standards, motivating students, and providing feedback to students and teachers (Rowntree, 1987). These different functions of assessment are based on two different underlying models, the measurement model and the standards model, upon which assessments are designed (Biggs, 1995).

In the measurement model of assessment, test performance is assumed to reflect a stable ability of the individual which can be converted into a single quantifiable dimension, which in turn can be used in norm-referenced assessments. This model of assessment is usually summative in nature, and is used when students are to be compared with each other, as in the selection of students.

In the standards model, assessment is criterion-referenced, and performances are assessed in relation to set criteria and standards as defined in the objectives of the learning tasks. The focus of assessment is whether or not the learning outcome reflects the criteria for learning as stated in the objectives, rather than comparing individuals with each other. This model of assessment provides information that may be formative or summative.

Different modes of assessment more readily address different cognitive levels of processing. For instance, true/false and multiple choice items most easily confirm recognition of taught content, short answer its recall, while more open-ended formats allow the assessment of such higher order thinking as synthesising, integrating and application beyond the immediate learning context. Depending on the particular learning context, the course objectives and thus the expected quality of the learning outcomes, assessment may involve different models to serve different, or a combination of different, purposes.

## A CASE STUDY OF ASSESSMENT IN A PROFESSIONAL COURSE OF PHYSIOTHERAPY

The provision of physiotherapy education in Hong Kong involves a three year Bachelor degree program. The aim of this program is for students to develop the knowledge, skills and attitudes in the professional practice of physiotherapy, including the competence to analyse and evaluate the practice in the context of the local health care system (Physiotherapy Section, 1991). During the course, the students have to learn both basic pre-clinical science subjects and specialised professional therapeutic procedures. Not only do students need to be competent in the theoretical knowledge, they have, more importantly, to be able to integrate theory with practice and to be able to apply pre-clinical knowledge to clinical practice. Although this course objective is expected to be achieved in all subjects, it is most explicitly espoused and realised in the subject of 'Integrated Professional Studies' (IPS). The objectives of IPS are that the students should be able to synthesise the theoretical knowledge and professional skills learned in the individual subjects into a holistic perspective for the treatment and management of patients in the clinical setting. This integration would allow the students to propose, analyse and modify rehabilitation programs related to specific patient problems within the context of the health care environment. IPS therefore constitutes a very important component in preparing students for their clinical practice.

To achieve the objectives of IPS, students should develop high level cognitive activities involving critical thinking, relating, integrating, synthesising and applying knowledge. Such goals require a deep approach to learning (Biggs, 1987; Marton & Säljö 1976). The course objectives of the physiotherapy program are thus embedded in a qualitative conception of learning. Hence the assessment of the course in general, and of IPS in particular, should be designed so that these high level cognitive activities are addressed rather than the quantity of the learning outcomes.

## ASSESSMENT BY ESSAY TEST AND ASSIGNMENT

The assessment of IPS has traditionally been by using essay tests. Many teaching staff believe that a wide coverage of the pre-clinical theoretical knowledge is important in developing basic professional standards, and that the traditional essay test is the appropriate method to assess the coverage of the content. However, the teaching staff are at the same time ambivalent about the effectiveness of essay tests in assessing the quality of the learning outcomes, as the following comments illustrate.

> I think it is important that our students should learn all the basic ingredients and to ensure a basic professional standard and patient safety at the pre-clinical stage.

A test is just an assessment of the performance on paper but not necessarily whether or not the students can apply the knowledge. The general concept is that a test may be of low level of learning.

Written test can directly reflect if the students understand, or whether or not they are clear about the concepts... they have to answer the questions in their own words and cannot rote learn, so we can tell from their answers if they have understood or not.

Even the students share the same concern that essay tests, because of their wide coverage, are more likely to encourage rote learning.

The test syllabus is usually very long and it is impossible for me to try and understand everything. I really find that I have to rote learn just for the test, but then I will soon forget the things that I have studied.

So it appears that at least some teachers feel there is mis-alignment between the desired learning outcomes and the assessment method. Although content coverage may be perceived to be necessary in providing the students with a broad knowledge base for which essay questions will be the appropriate assessment method, essay tests are not likely to assess the kind or quality of learning outcomes stated as desirable in the course objectives.

In order to assess the espoused high level quality of learning outcomes required for competent professional practice, the assignment mode of assessment was later introduced as an alternative method on the assumption that assignments draw on higher cognitive levels that require students to adopt a deep learning approach. The assignment in the present context of physiotherapy education is an extended-response essay. The students are usually given a few topic areas to choose from according to their own interest. The students are required to submit an original assignment within a certain time limit. In preparing for the assignment, the students have total freedom in managing the time and resources for their work. The assessment of the assignments is mostly content-related: adequacy of coverage, relevance to the topic, and the overall presentation. The score of the assignment is awarded according to the assessment criteria for written work as indicated in the course document (Physiotherapy Section, 1991).

The majority of the teaching staff believe that assessment by assignment encourages more independent learning and a more active student role. Although the scope of coverage of assignments is narrow compared with tests, assignments are perceived to demand and to assess the sort of high level cognitive activities required of a competent physiotherapist, as illustrated by the following comments from members of the teaching staff.

> Of course the scope is much wider in a test, whereas for the assignment, it is more in depth in just a certain area.

> The assignment is looking more for how the students tackle the knowledge, how they relate it to other subjects, and how they handle the situation. For the assignment, the emphasis is not so much on the quantity but rather on the quality of the information, how the students arrange that information and how they establish their argument.

Again many students who have the experience of doing assignments also agree that assignments can encourage better and more independent learning, and that they can have a better understanding of the subject as one student explained.

> When we do the assignment, we can discuss with our classmates to clarify and talk about some of the concepts that we do not understand. It is very helpful for our understanding of the topic. I really understand more after doing the assignment and I also learn to be independent in my learning.

Another objective of assessing students by assignment is to assess their ability to integrate ideas at various levels, and to demonstrate a well discussed, argued and holistically structured representation of their understanding of the assignment topic. This quality of learning outcome is particularly important for the profession of physiotherapy. In clinical practice, therapists gather information from various sources. This information is usually presented as isolated facts. To be able to arrive at a holistic diagnosis of the patient's condition for the determination of a treatment protocol, it is important that therapists should not only be able to understand the meaning and implications of those facts but, more importantly, be able to also perform effective clinical reasoning through relating and integrating the various information to arrive at an accurate clinical diagnosis of the patient's condition. It is expected that one of the ways to facilitate and assess the development of this competence is via the assignment.

Therefore, there was a difference in opinion as to which was a more appropriate method of assessing student learning in this physiotherapy program: essay questions or assignment. Nevertheless, if the assessment is to be in line with the espoused course objectives, it should address high level cognitive processes. It then follows that the assessment should be based on the standards model, and qualitatively conceived, and this in turn implicates the assignment rather than the essay questions. To ascertain if the assignment, as a relatively new method of assessment, was able to fulfill the above purpose appropriate to the program, an indepth study was conducted to explore the effects of assessment by assignments on the actual learning strategies involved, and on the learning outcomes (Tang, 1991).

## THE STUDY

Thirty-nine student physiotherapists were randomly selected from a total of 156 first year students. Nearly all these students were 'A' level (grade 13) graduates, but many of them did not have any previous experience of doing assignments. These students were interviewed immediately after submission of assignments for the IPS assessment. During the interviews, the students were asked to report and elaborate on how they prepared for the assignment.

### ASSESSMENT OF THE ASSIGNMENTS

In this study, the assignments were assessed in two ways. The first (S1) was based on the prescribed criteria, involving adequacy of coverage, relevance to the question requirements, development of the discussion and argument, and the quality of the presentation. The second (S2) was intended to assess the structural quality and complexity of the assignment, and the presentation of a holistic view of the topic, since well structured and integrated thinking is important in the development of a holistic physiotherapy program for the management of patients, as discussed earlier. This second component of the assessment (S2) was based on the Structure of the Observed Learning Outcome (SOLO) Taxonomy (Biggs & Collis, 1982).

## THE SOLO TAXONOMY

Biggs and Collis argue that student learning takes place in stages of ascending structural complexity, with a consistent sequence across tasks. In the SOLO taxonomy, five levels are identified:

*Prestructural* – the task is engaged but the learning involved is irrelevant.

*Unistructural* – learning is relevant, but the learner only focuses on one aspect of the work.

*Multistructural* – the learner focuses on a number of relevant parts, but does not integrate them together.

*Relational* – the learner integrates the different parts with each other to arrive at a coherent whole structure and meaning.

*Extended abstract* – the learner generalises and extends the whole to take on new and more abstract features.

The qualitative interpretation of the structural complexity of the assignments was assessed according to the SOLO taxonomy. This provided an indication of the level of the structural complexity of the assignment content, and hence a qualitative assessment of the learning outcomes. The S2 scores consisted of a five point scale. Due to the nature of the assignment, it was anticipated that all the students would present more than one relevant idea, but also that they would not be generalising beyond the professional context. Hence the extreme SOLO levels, prestructural, unistructural and extended abstract, would not be appropriate in the assessment; therefore they were not included in the rating scale, and in fact were not found. The S2 scores for the assignments thus consisted only of the multistructural and relational levels: one multistructural and four relational. The scoring was as follows:

S2.1 – The student presented multiple isolated ideas without integration. This was the multistructural type of response, and thus scored one point.

S2.2 – If a student was able to integrate and relate the ideas into main ideas and principles, then the assignment would be graded at a relational level and a score of two to five points would be awarded depending on the complexity of the main ideas and principles that the student was able to construe. For students who were able to integrate points into main ideas within a paragraph (intra-paragraph ideas), two points would be awarded.

S2.3/S2.4 – If the student further integrated between paragraphs to arrive at main sectional ideas (inter-paragraph ideas), three or four points would be awarded.

S2.5 – The maximum score of five points would be awarded to students who could present a well structured and succinctly discussed overall theme for the assignment.

Hence a high S2 score (S2.3 or above) would be associated with a deep approach in the preparation of the assignment.

## RESULTS AND DISCUSSION

### STUDENTS' PERCEPTIONS OF THE REQUIREMENTS OF THE ASSIGNMENT

The interview data showed that although they lacked previous experience in doing assignments, some of the students were able to perceive that the assignment required of them a high cognitive level of processing as illustrated by this comment from one student.

> Assignment helps improve the theoretical knowledge e.g. to relate the treatment program to fracture union and consolidation stage. There is a need to reason the process, you need to go through the thinking process... You have to identify the case and the reasons in an assignment and so you understand better.

The interview results also revealed that a majority of the students, 34 (87%), reported the experience of spontaneous collaboration in preparing for their assignments (collaborating students), while the other five students (13%) did the assignments totally on their own (self-studying students). It appears that this spontaneous collaborative learning was developed as a coping strategy for the assessment (Tang, 1993, 1996).

Being assessed by assignment is a new experience for most students in first year. Lacking previous experience and knowledge of what was required of them in writing assignments, many students spontaneously formed small groups seeking assistance from each other in preparing for the assignments. They perceived that reading and comprehension of an extensive knowledge base from the reference materials were integral stages in the preparation of an assignment, as some of them reported in the interviews.

> The information given in class about each case cannot be too indepth. When doing the assignment, you need to go in more depth about the case you are doing before you can write about it, so you need to get more information concerning the case.

Just books and notes are not enough for assignments, they are not detailed enough as they just talk about that particular fracture, so if you want to know and understand more in order to write the assignment, you need to read more widely.

Both depth and breadth of the knowledge base are necessary for a deep study approach (Marton, 1988). However, to be able to process the information at a deep level involving understanding and to effectively express themselves in the assignments, students need a reasonable command of English (these students are taught and assessed in English which is a second language for them). The following comments demonstrate this concern.

English has to be good. As there is not much direct information, so we have to think and put things together, and so English has to be good.

English is very important. As there is a word limit, you need good English to be able to express all the points with fewer words.

## COLLABORATIVE LEARNING IN THE PREPARATION FOR ASSIGNMENT

The assignment itself was perceived by students to require high level cognitive processing. To enable them to understand clearly the reference materials, the students mutually supported each other through collaboration and discussion to promote understanding of the information. During the interviews, these students reported several collaborative group activities including sharing the reading of the reference materials, and helping each other to understand the assignment questions and the reference materials through group discussion.

During discussion, the students tried to identify the requirements of the question, select relevant information, clarify concepts, argue and share opinions, and different strategies were used in the processing of the information. After discussion, the students wrote their individual assignments based on their own understanding and interpretation of the ideas developed in the discussion, and they also developed their own structure of the assignment.

The five self-studying students did not form study groups, doing preparation for the assignment entirely on their own. These self-studying students felt that they did not want to be influenced by others when doing their assignments. They also preferred to do the assignment at their own pace without having to be tied down by

TABLE 5.1  Study strategies used by students in
preparing assignment

| Strategies | Collaborating students (%) | Self-studying students (%) |
|---|---|---|
| Organise information | 32 | 80 |
| Analyse question requirements | 24 | 20 |
| Copy from reference materials | 18 | 40 |
| Focus on basic concepts | 9 | 20 |
| Compare information | 18 | 0 |
| Supplement each others missing points | 18 | 0 |
| Relate information | 15 | 0 |
| Criticise each others ideas | 12 | 0 |
| Share and exchange ideas | 12 | 0 |
| Analyse information | 6 | 0 |
| Apply | 6 | 0 |
| Argue | 3 | 0 |

discussion schedules. The process of preparing for the assignment as reported by these self-studying students also involved literature search, reading the reference materials, and they also reported using some preparation strategies in the processing of the information. Table 5.1 shows the percentage of students in each group using the different strategies in preparing for the assignment.

The interview data showed that both groups of students went through similar stages in preparing the assignment, and these include searching for information, reading the reference materials and eventually writing up the assignment. The only difference was the way in which the information was processed. The collaborating students did that in small group discussions, while the self-studying students did so entirely on their own. From the reported data, some strategies were used by both groups of students while others were only used by the collaborating students. However, since these strategies were reported by the whole group, it does not necessarily follow that each student within the group used all the strategies reported.

The collaborating students collectively reported various preparation strategies during group discussion: analysing, applying, arguing with and criticising each other, sharing and comparing ideas.

These students also reported that these group learning strategies stimulated them to think at a deeper level individually. Hence, students who collaborated in the preparation of the assignment tended to engage in high level cognitive strategies, and were thus more likely to adopt a deep learning approach. This appeared to help them both to understand the question better, and to process the content of the assignment more deeply, as illustrated by the following comments.

> Understanding will be better with discussion. [Without discussion] you always tend to see things from your own point of view and your mind is pre-occupied... Discussion can help you realise missing points, and will also increase your interest when your ideas are accepted by others and when you accept others ideas.

> Group discussion is good. Everyone has a different level of understanding. During discussion, we can see how much the others have understood, and so it helps you understand some of the things that you did not understand before.

The self-studying students, preparing the assignment on their own, tended to copy from the reference materials, and to focus on the organisation of the information. They also tried to interpret the question requirement and focus on the basic concepts, but there was not much evidence of any strategies being used for a deeper processing of the information. Preparing on their own deprived this group of students of the opportunity of sharing and discussing ideas with their peers. The lack of social interaction and collaboration seemed likely to result in a higher tendency to adopt a more surface approach in the actual processing of the information, as indicated by the common response of just copying from the references.

The above findings suggest strongly that collaborative learning has positive effects on the learning process. Students who worked together were able to develop specific group learning strategies which helped them prepare the assignment. Many of these strategies such as arguing and criticising each other, sharing and supplementing each other's ideas, were specific to a group learning situation when the students interacted and learned in a social environment. These collaborative group strategies were not just of a high cognitive level, they were more closely aligned to the cognitive activities specified in the course objectives.

TABLE 5.2   Results of the assessment of the assignments

| Group | Mean scores | |
|-------|-------------|-------|
|       | S1          | S2    |
| Collaborating students (n=34) | 65.1 (SD=10.2) | 3.0 (SD=1.2) |
| Self-studying students (n=5)  | 57.8 (SD=9.9)  | 1.8 (SD=0.8) |

## THE RESULTS OF THE ASSESSMENT OF THE ASSIGNMENTS

As described in an earlier section, the assignments were assessed in two areas. The S1 score was the assessment of the adequacy and relevance of the content and the quality of presentation. The S2 score was the assessment of the structural quality of the assignment, the integration and the presentation of a holistic view of the understanding of the topic. The results of the assessment of the assignments are shown in Table 5.2.

The assignment assessment scores were compared between the self-studying and collaborating groups. The results showed no significant difference in the S1 scores (mean scores of 57.8 and 65.1 respectively), but the trend (non-significant) was that the students who collaborated did better than those who wrote the assignments on their own. As for the S2 scores, there was a significant difference ($P<0.05$) between the two groups of students.

The average S1 score of the collaborating group was 65.1. According to the assessment criteria for written work as indicated in the course documents, this score was equivalent to a credit level, indicating that the written work was a piece of 'Good work showing evidence of clear understanding of the concepts involved; analytical and evaluative reasoning; relevant content; comprehensive and logical presentation' (Physiotherapy Section, 1991, p. 34). An average of 57.8 (self-studying group) was equivalent to a mid-pass level, indicating that the assignment was a piece of 'satisfactory work showing understanding of the main concepts involved; evidence of analysis and evaluation of the topic; relevant content; comprehensive presentation.' (Physiotherapy Section, 1991, p. 34). Hence the collaborating students showed better content-related performance than the self-studying students.

Comparing the S2 scores of the two groups, it was found that the collaborating students again did better with an average S2 of 3.0 indicating a clear relational level, such that these students on the whole were able to achieve a complex structure of the assignment by integrating ideas across paragraphs. The self-studying students, on the other hand, scored an average of 1.8, indicating that they were more confined to a limited integration of ideas and a less holistic presentation of their views of the topic. The collaborating students clearly demonstrated a better performance in structuring their assignments. This significant difference indicated that students who collaborated in spontaneous group discussion in preparation for the assignments achieved qualitatively better learning outcomes. As shown in Table 5.1, it is clear that the cognitive activities engaged by these students are much more closely aligned to the objectives in the Physiotherapy Section document than those used by the self-studying group.

## IMPLICATIONS FOR PRACTICE

### COLLABORATIVE/CO-OPERATIVE LEARNING

Co-operative learning has been extensively studied and found to have positive effects on student learning when compared with individualistic and competitive learning situations (Bennett, 1991; Johnson & Johnson, 1991; Nichols & Miller, 1994; Slavin, 1987, 1991; Topping, 1992; Webb, 1985). Opportunity to study interactively with peers has been shown to have social and cognitive benefits (Cohen, 1994; Slavin, 1990). Students learning and helping each other in groups tend to become motivated to learn (Slavin, 1984) and more readily facilitated to develop reasoning and problem solving skills (Damon, 1984; Hooper, Temiyakarn & Williams, 1993; Meloth & Deering, 1992; Qin, Johnson & Johnson, 1995; Webb, 1989). During group learning, students pool their resources as to content, while participating and interacting in group discussion can help them develop multiple perspectives and so become more metacognitive in their learning process (Webb, 1985; Webb, 1990). It has been demonstrated that students who collaborate in drafting and revising computer-written tasks with their peers are able to improve the quality of the text, both in context and language (Zammuner, 1995).

Co-operative learning provides a non-threatening learning context for interaction between students. During co-operative learning, students are exposed to other perspectives and alternatives, they share and exchange ideas, criticise and provide feedback. Peer feedback can help students increase their awareness of their learning aims, and of the strategies to employ to achieve those aims. Collaboration provides a 'scaffolding' for mutual support and enables students to learn from each other. The function is a teaching function, although the major interaction is student-student, rather than teacher-student, as teaching is normally understood.

Co-operative learning, as reported in literature so far, is, however, teacher-structured in the sense that the teacher organises the different situations of group learning. Within the context of the study reported, the student-student interaction was student-structured. To capture this difference, the term Spontaneous Collaborative Learning (SCOLL) has been used, which is entirely student-centred, being a spontaneous effort from the students (Tang, 1993, 1996). The term 'co-operative' learning thus refers to what has been reported in the literature, by researchers such as Slavin and the Johnsons for example, but here the term 'collaborative' learning is used to underline the fact that students initiate their teaching-learning process.

Since collaborative learning has been demonstrated to facilitate the development of high level cognitive strategies and the adoption of a deep learning approach, it should be more extensively utilised by incorporating it in the formal teaching context, but retaining as much student-control as possible. To maximise the effects of collaborative learning, students may need to be provided with training in strategies to collaborate and to give elaborated explanation (Greenwood, Carta & Kamps, 1990; McAllister, 1995), and to focus thoughts and activities on text content (Meloth & Deering, 1994). Teachers should provide the context and tools for collaborative learning by structuring the learning and problem solving tasks to facilitate and encourage students to collaborate in learning. The strategy of asking the students to seek 'learning partners' (Saberton, 1985) is likely to be very useful in this context. Teachers should also provide students with appropriate preparation for an active and constructive participation, and at the same time be receptive to constructive criticism during group discussions. To be effective in collaborative learning, students need to have at their disposal the appropriate collaborative learning skills such as interpersonal communication skills, group management and interaction skills, and cognitive learning skills of appropriate level (Johnson & Johnson, 1991; Johnson, Johnson & Houlbec, 1990). It has been demonstrated that students who receive appropriate training in learning in groups operate more effectively in collaborative learning (Gillies & Ashman, 1996). They are more group conscious and more mutually supportive in helping each other, and obtain better achievement than those students who do not receive similar training.

## THE CONDITION FOR SPONTANEOUS COLLABORATIVE LEARNING

The spontaneous collaborative learning situation reported here has been developed as a coping strategy by students in response to a particular teaching and learning context. In the context of writing assignments, collaborative learning was adopted by a group of students as a strategy to help them cope with a new learning experience and the heavy demand of learning in a second language. Many of these first year students do not have any previous experience of doing assignments. When faced with the assessment task, although many students were able to identify the assignment requirements, they lacked the procedural knowledge in the actual preparation. So in order to help them complete the task, the students felt the need for collaboration and mutual support. As there was no infra-structure providing such support, the students spontaneously provided their own by forming groups and collaborating in preparing for the assignment.

Another aspect of the contextual perspective of collaborative learning is the language requirement. The majority of the students are Chinese with Chinese as their mother tongue. However, the formal language of instruction and assessment of the physiotherapy program is English. The students perceived that the language requirement in writing the assignment would be a potential difficulty, especially for the comprehension of the reference materials, and in actually writing their assignments. In order to help them deal with the language issue, many of the students saw the benefit of pooling resources in sharing the reading of the reference materials, and also to share and discuss the content in small groups. During group discussion, the students found that communicating in Chinese facilitated their understanding of the content and also stimulated their thinking.

## COLLABORATIVE LEARNING AND CONSTRUCTIVE ALIGNMENT

Learning has been considered as an active process in which students actively construct their own knowledge and understanding, while teaching is to provide the context in which learning can take place in order to achieve desirable learning outcomes. This constructivist theory forms an important basis for decision making at all stages of the teaching process: designing the curriculum objectives, deciding the teaching methods to use, and selecting appropriate assessment methods. Effective teaching in a constructivist framework requires that the relevant and appropriate high cognitive level activities that students should display are addressed both by the teaching methods and by the assessment tasks (which in any case become the curriculum to the students). This is 'constructively aligned' teaching (Biggs, 1996b).

This model of teaching is particularly appropriate in professional courses, where both teaching and assessment should be criterion-referenced; students are expected to demonstrate certain qualities of learning which are considered important for the professional practice, and the teaching is supposed to help them do so. In the present case, the assignment is considered to be an appropriate method of assessment, in alignment with the course objectives. To provide a criterion-referenced assessment in relation to the objectives, apart from assessing content-related competencies, it is more important to assess the overall structural quality and coherence of the assignment. In the present study, the SOLO taxonomy seemed to provide a more useful measurement of these qualities than the content-related measure prescribed in the course document.

According to constructive alignment and systems theory generally, the course objectives, the teaching context, and the assessment tasks should all address the same student learning-related cognitive activities (Biggs, 1995, 1996b). Biggs (1996b) suggests that alignment can be facilitated by looking at the learning-related verbs that each component in the system addresses. Here the curriculum verbs referred to integrating, synthesising, applying etc. Initially, the assessment task was essay questions, and the verbs elicited there did not align with what was expected (Tang, 1991). Accordingly, the assignment was adopted, and the students did perceive that this task required the sort of verbs needed to fulfill the task satisfactorily (see Table 5.1).

To be aligned with the assessment, the teaching context should have provided support for students in developing the necessary procedural knowledge to deal with the assignment. The university staff assumed this had been done in the schools, but it had not. When faced with a novel learning task, not only did the students lack the appropriate experience in writing assignments, the procedural knowledge for doing so was not provided by the teaching context. Apart from giving out the assignment questions, and probably some informal clarification of the questions, the students were entirely on their own, and they solved the problem on their own. Hence, the teaching component failed to align with the assessment, and there was a gap to be filled. The students themselves filled this gap by developing collaborative learning as a coping strategy.

Ideally, as part of the normal teaching, it may now be seen that the objectives of assessment by assignment should be clearly defined, along with the assessment criteria used, and the procedural knowledge necessary in preparing for the assignment. All this is part of the system, extending from objectives through to teaching and assessment. Generalising from this, it might be said that teaching, to be successful, needs to make sure that what the objectives specify, and what the assessment tasks demand, is provided for in the activities required of students. Although there was a gap in the teaching, it was fortunate that in this case the students were able, in most cases, to bridge the gap themselves. However, it is a good question to ask if it is better to allow students the freedom to solve the teaching-learning problems themselves, or to provide the structure for them. Whatever the answer, it is one that teachers should at least be aware of.

### SUMMARY AND CONCLUSIONS

Quality learning takes place in a context within which all the different components, the curriculum objectives and the teaching and assessment methods, are in equilibrium and constructively aligned. To align assessment with the course objectives, not only do the assessment tasks have to be appropriate and criterion-referenced so that they confirm the desirable qualities of learning, they also have to be appropriately assessed. In the case of physiotherapy education, the assignment was considered an appropriate assessment task as its demand on the level of cognitive processing was in alignment with the course objectives. In assessing the assignments, content-related assessment focusing on the adequacy and relevance of the content was not able to adequately address the activities and qualities of the specified learning outcomes. The SOLO taxonomy had, in this case, provided a useful tool for assessing the structural quality of the assignment. Using the various SOLO levels, it was possible to assess the extent of integration and the presentation of a coherent and holistic understanding of the assignment content.

In the present case, teaching was mis-aligned with the goals of the course and with the assessment. A gap existed as teaching failed to provide the students with the necessary procedural knowledge to cope with the assessment. To bridge the gap, students provided their own scaffolding by collaborating and mutually supporting each other in their learning. Investigation into the process of preparing the assignment has provided further evidence of the positive effects of collaborative learning on the quality of the learning outcomes. Not only did the collaborating students use higher level cognitive strategies in the preparation of the assignment through group discussion, they also achieved better learning outcomes especially in the structural quality of the assignment as assessed by the SOLO levels. It is likely that social interaction and collaboration provides a facilitative context for the development of better structural quality of academic written task such as assignments. This is one finding that is of value.

When the activities specified in both the objectives and in the assessment are not addressed by the teaching itself, the students are faced with a problem. How this is solved depends on many factors, based on the resourcefulness of the students themselves. However, it is interesting that in a collectivistic society, such as Hong Kong, the solution was spontaneous collaboration amongst the students. In Western universities, spontaneous collaboration has been observed (Goodnow, 1991), but nowhere to the extent of involving over 80 per cent of the class; possibly Western students choose a more individualistic or independent way of solving the problem.

To maximise the effects of collaborative learning, teaching should provide support and create a context to facilitate group learning.

This support may include appropriately structuring the teaching context so that group discussion is encouraged, and also by providing training in appropriate collaborative learning skills, yet retaining as much student-control as possible. Collaborative learning, with appropriate support and facilitation from teaching, provides the bridge in establishing equilibrium and alignment of the teaching and learning processes. This learning experience also facilitates the development of more desirable learning outcomes in general, and better quality assignment in particular.

## References

Bennett, N. (1991). Cooperative learning in classrooms: Process and outcomes. *Journal of Child Psychology and Psychiatry, 32,* 581–594.

Biggs, J.B. (1987). *Student approaches to learning and studying.* Melbourne: Australian Council for Educational Research.

Biggs, J.B. (1995). Assessing for learning: Some dimensions underlying new approaches to educational assessment. *Alberta Journal of Educational Research, 41,* 1–8.

Biggs, J.B. (Ed.). (1996a). *Testing: to educate or to select? Education in Hong Kong at the crossroads.* Hong Kong: Hong Kong Educational Publishing Company.

Biggs, J.B. (1996b). Enhancing teaching through constructive alignment. *Higher Education, 32*(3), 347–364.

Biggs, J.B., & Collis, K.F. (1982*). Evaluating the quality of learning: The SOLO taxonomy.* New York: Academic Press.

Cohen, E. (1994). Restructuring the classroom: Conditions for productive small groups. *Review of Educational Research, 19,* 237–248.

Cole, N.S. (1990). Conceptions of educational achievement. *Educational Researcher, 19*(3), 2–7.

Damon, W. (1984). Peer education: The untapped potential. *Journal of Applied Developmental Psychology, 5,* 331–343.

Gillies, R.M., & Ashman, D.F. (1996). Teaching collaborative skills to primary school children in classroom-based workshops. *Learning and Instruction, 6*(3), 187–200.

Goodnow, J.J. (1991). Cognitive values and educational practice. In J.B. Biggs (Ed.), *Teaching for learning: The view from cognitive psychology.* Melbourne: Australian Council for Educational Research.

Greenwood, C.R., Carta, J.J., & Kamps, D. (1990). The teacher-mediated versus peer-mediated instruction: A review of educational advantages and disadvantages. In H.C. Foot, M.J. Morgan, & R.J. Shute (Eds.), *Children helping children*. Chichester: Wiley.

Hooper, S., Temiyakarn, C., & Williams, H.D. (1993). The effects of cooperative learning and learner control on high- and average-ability students. *Educational Technology Research and Development, 41*(2), 5–18.

Johnson, D.W., & Johnson, R.T. (1991). Cooperative learning and achievement. In S. Sharan (Ed.), *Cooperative learning: Theory and research*. New York: Praeger.

Johnson, D.W., Johnson, R.T., & Houlbec. E.J. (1990). *Circles of learning: Cooperation in the classroom*. Edina, MN: Interaction.

Marton, F. (1988). Describing and improving learning. In R.R. Schmeck (Ed.), *Learning strategies and learning styles*. New York: Plenum.

Marton, F., & Säljö, R. (1976). On qualitative differences in learning – I: Outcome and process. *British Journal of Educational Psychology, 46*, 4–11.

Marton, F., Dall'Alba, G., & Beaty, E. (1993). Conceptions of learning. *International Journal of Educational Research, 19*, 277–300.

McAllister, W. (1995). Are pupils equipped for group work without training or instruction? *British Educational Research Journal, 21*(3), 395–404.

Meloth, M., & Deering, P. (1992). Effects of two cooperative conditions on peer-group discussions, reading comprehension, and metacognition. *Contemporary Educational Psychology, 17*(2), 175–193.

Meloth, M.S., & Deering, P.D. (1994). Task talk and task awareness under different cooperative learning conditions. *American Educational Research Journal, 31*(1), 138–165.

Nichols, J.D., & Miller, R.B. (1994). Cooperative learning and student motivation. *Contemporary Educational Psychology, 19*, 167–178.

Physiotherapy Section (1991). *Definitive document of the Bachelor of Science in Physiotherapy*. Hong Kong: Physiotherapy Section, Department of Rehabilitation Sciences, Hong Kong Polytechnic.

Qin, Z., Johnson, D.W., & Johnson, R.T. (1995). Cooperative versus competitive efforts and problem solving. *Review of Educational Research, 65*(2), 129–143.

Rowntree, D. (1987). *Assessing students: How shall we know them?* London: Kogan Page.

Saberton, S. (1985). Learning partnerships. *HERDSA News, 7*(1), 3–5.

Säljö, R. (1979). *Learning in the learner's perspective -I: Some commonsense conceptions* (Report 76). Gothenburg: University of Gothenburg, Department of Education.

Satterly, D. (1981). *Assessment in schools.* Oxford: Basil Blackwell.

Slavin, R.E. (1984). Students motivating students to excel: Cooperative incentives, cooperative tasks, and student achievement. *The Elementary School Journal, 85*(1), 53–63.

Slavin, R.E. (1987). *Cooperative learning: Student teams.* Washington D.C.: National Educational Association.

Slavin, R. (1990). *Cooperative learning: Theory research and practice.* Englewood Cliffs, N.J.: Prentice Hall.

Slavin, R. (1991). Synthesis of research in cooperative learning. *Educational Leadership, 48*(5), 71–82.

Steffe, L., & Gale, J. (Ed.). (1995). *Constructivism in education.* Hillsdale, NJ: Erlbaum.

Tang, K.C.C. (1991). *Effects of different assessment procedures on tertiary students' approaches to studying.* Unpublished doctoral dissertation, University of Hong Kong.

Tang, K.C.C. (1993). Spontaneous collaborative learning: a new dimension in student learning experience? *Higher Education Research and Development, 12*(2), 115–130.

Tang, C. (1996). Collaborative learning: the latent dimension in Chinese students' learning. In D.A. Watkins, & J. Biggs (Eds.), *The Chinese learner: Cultural, psychological and contextual influences* (pp. 183–204). Hong Kong/Melbourne: Comparative Education Research Centre/Australian Council for Educational Research.

Tang, C., & Biggs, J. (1996). How Hong Kong students cope with assessment? In D.A. Watkins, & J. Biggs (Eds.), *The Chinese learner: Cultural, psychological and contextual influences* (pp. 159–182). Hong Kong/Melbourne: Comparative Education Research Centre/Australian Council for Educational Research.

Topping, K. (1992). Cooperative learning and peer tutoring: An overview. *The Psychologist, 5*(4), 151–157.

Webb, N. (1985). Student interaction and learning in small groups: A research summary. In R.E. Slavin, S., Sharan, S. Kagan, R.H. Lazarowitz, C. Webb, & R. Schmeck (Eds.), *Learning to cooperate, cooperate to learn* (pp. 147–172). N.Y.: Plenum.

Webb, N. (1989). Peer interacting and learning in small groups. *International Journal of Educational Research, 13*, 21–40.

Webb, R. (1990). Working collaboratively on topic tasks. *Cambridge Journal of Education, 20*(1), 37–52.

Zammuner, V.L. (1995). Individual and cooperative computer-writing and revising: Who gets the best results? *Learning and Instruction, 5*(2), 101–124.

# CHAPTER 6

# Assessing Approaches to Learning:
# A Cross-Cultural Perspective

*David Watkins*

## INTRODUCTION

One of the main achievements of Professor Biggs has been to develop measuring instruments to assess approaches to learning based on a clear theoretical rationale grounded in the reality of how students actually go about the learning tasks set in their classrooms and lecture halls (see Biggs, 1987, 1993). However, the basis for this theory is research carried out into how Australian, British, North American, and Swedish students learn (Biggs 1987; Entwistle & Ramsden, 1983; Marton & Säljö, 1976). Moreover, the careful process of item construction and test validation which Biggs utilised to develop the school-level Learning Process Questionnaire (LPQ) and its tertiary equivalent the Study Process Questionnaire (SPQ) were also conducted with Australian (and earlier Canadian) students as subjects. But is this work relevant to non-Western culture?

Today, most developing countries around the world see education as a route to economic progress (Altbach & Selvaratnam, 1989). Surveys such as those in the well known International Education Achievement (IEA) series have told us much about what is being learnt in different countries around the world (though not without controversy as to the validity of the conclusions at times). The focus of these surveys is nearly always on the outcomes of learning (and often from a very quantitative perspective at that). Much less information is known about why international differences in such outcomes are achieved except in relatively macro-terms such as the percentage of gross national product spent on education, class sizes, teacher training, etc. To achieve such insights requires intensive research into the range of factors which influence how students learn and the outcomes they achieve as envisaged in the 3P model of learning.

Intensive research has been carried out in Western countries using both quantitative and qualitative methods and much more is known now about the teaching/learning complex and how high quality learning outcomes can be achieved (see, for instance, Marton, Housell, & Entwistle, 1984; Ramsden, 1988, 1992; Schmeck, 1988). A common cry from even developing countries such as India and the Philippines which have been relatively successful in their educational progress in quantitative terms is that the quality is lacking (Gonzales, 1989). So there is an urgent need for research to be conducted in non-Western countries to investigate whether Western findings can be generalised to also apply to them. It may well prove necessary to conduct subsequent research to find out the factors affecting quality of learning in particular non-Western countries.

While qualitative research utilising either phenomenographic or ethnographic perspectives would certainly be valuable to achieve full understanding it is also a very long, expensive process requiring a highly trained indigenous research team capable of conducting indepth interviews and/or detailed field observations. On the other hand, if a questionnaire were available which could accurately assess how students learn rapidly at little cost and requiring few if any local specialists then speedy progress may be possible. However, researchers from Third World countries have long warned about the 'imposition' of Western social science theories and measuring instruments on subjects from non-Western cultures (Enriquez, 1987). The purpose of this chapter is to assess the appropriateness of using the SPQ in non-Western cultures.

## THE STUDY PROCESS QUESTIONNAIRE

The SPQ, like the LPQ, was developed to reflect the findings of both qualitative and quantitative research into how students study. Both research paradigms have confirmed the two most basic approaches that students tend to utilise which were first identified in qualitative research by Marton and Säljö (1976). Students who are learning because of extrinsic motivational factors or fear of failure tend to adopt superficial strategies which are syllabus bound and ignore the deeper meaning and implications of what is being learnt. Those students who are interested in what they are studying are likely to adopt strategies which help their understanding of the material such as attempting to interrelate ideas to their previous knowledge and personal experience and to read widely. These contrasting ways of studying are known as the *surface* and the *deep* approach, respectively. Only the latter can lead to high quality learning outcomes. While students tend to be relatively consistent in terms of which of these approaches they adopt, they also modify their approach depending on their perceptions of course requirements and other factors (see Biggs, 1987; Entwistle & Ramsden, 1983).

To these two approaches Biggs (1987) and Entwistle & Ramsden (1983) added an *achieving* approach where the student's motivation is to obtain the highest possible grades and so strategies are adopted which he or she believes will maximise those grades. These typically include cue seeking strategies which depend on the learning context and traditional study skills such as being well organised, speed reading, and effective note taking. While the deep and surface approaches to a particular learning task are basically mutually exclusive (one cannot really both ignore and focus on the meaning of what is being learnt), the achieving approach can be combined with either of these approaches depending on which the student feels will result in learning outcomes that are best rewarded by the assessment system. Thus, if the student considers that understanding will be best rewarded, deep and achieving approaches may well be adopted. If, however, the student considers that detailed reproduction will be best rewarded then a combination of surface and achieving approaches is likely. Of course, weaker students may not be capable of using a deep approach successfully and so may not be able to benefit from the flexible nature of the achieving approach.

The SPQ is an instrument with 42 items equally divided among the above three approaches to learning into six motive and strategy scales (see Table 6.1). Each item is to be answered on a five point scale from '1 = never true' to '5 = always true' (the reader is referred to Biggs, 1987, for details of the construction of the SPQ). The SPQ scales have been translated using the usual translation/back-translation method (Hui & Triandis, 1985) into languages such as Chinese, Indonesian, Malaysian, Swedish and Arabic.

TABLE 6.1    Descriptions of scales of Study Process Questionnaire (SPQ)

| SPQ Scale | Description |
| --- | --- |
| *Surface Approach* | |
| Surface Motivation (SM) | Motivation is utilitarian: main aim is to gain qualifications at minimum allowable standard |
| Surface Strategy (SS) | Strategy is to reproduce bare essentials often using rote learning |
| *Deep Approach* | |
| Deep Motivation (DM) | Motivation is interest in subject and its related areas |
| Deep Strategy (DS) | Strategy is to understand what is to be learnt through interrelating ideas and reading widely |
| *Achieving Approach* | |
| Achievement Motivation (AM) | Motivation is to obtain highest possible grades |
| Achievement Strategy (AS) | Strategy is highly organised and designed to achieve high marks by being a 'model' student, e.g. being punctual, doing readings, etc. |

Source: Adapted from Biggs, 1987.

## CROSS-CULTURAL EQUIVALENCE

Cross-cultural methodologists have pointed out that the central notion that needs to be understood regarding the validity of measuring instruments in different cultures is that of 'equivalent usage'. Moreover, there is a hierarchy of usage, each level of which requires the demonstration of a corresponding hierarchy of assumptions (Hui & Triandis, 1985). The lowest level involves conceptual equivalence and the highest, metric (or scalar) equivalence. In this section it is first asked whether the constructs of conceptions of and approaches to learning at the heart of the Student Approaches to Learning position, which is the theoretical basis for the SPQ (Biggs, 1987; 1993), are relevant to non-Western cultures. If so, is the SPQ reliable and valid for use in such cultures? Finally, are we justified in directly comparing the SPQ scores of students in different cultures (metric equivalence)?

### Conceptual equivalence

The notions of conceptual equivalence and 'etic' and 'emic' approaches to research (Berry, 1989) are closely associated. The former approach seeks to compare cultures on what are thought to be universal categories. By way of contrast, the latter approach uses only concepts that emerge from within a particular culture and is associated with the traditions of Anthropology but also, more recently, with those of Indigenous Psychology (Kim & Berry, 1993). Triandis (1972) has pointed to the dangers of 'pseudoetic' research which involves the imposition of the concepts of one culture upon another as if they were universal without any prior research into the veracity of this assumption.

To assess the conceptual equivalence of the constructs underlying the SPQ requires qualitative analysis. To my knowledge such studies in non-Western cultures have been conducted to date with Chinese/Hong Kong, Nepalese, and Nigerian students.

There are several studies which support the proposition that the concepts underlying the SPQ are relevant to Nigerian students. An ethnographic study based on 120 hours of observations in Lagos primary schools claimed that Nigerian pupils are trained to believe that getting the right answer by any means, even cheating, is the essence of learning (Omokhodion, 1989). Neither the teachers nor the pupils considered the processes of understanding the problem and of obtaining the solution were of any importance. Thus it was concluded that a superficial, surface approach to learning was being encouraged. Further evidence comes from a study where 250 Nigerian university students responded to the question 'What strategies do you use to study?' (Ehindero, 1990). Content analysis indicated three main themes in the students' responses: diligence, building up understanding, and memorising content material without understanding. These themes seem to correspond to the notions of achieving, deep, and surface approaches to learning, respectively.

More recent evidence comes from a study by Watkins and Akande (1994) who content-analysed the answers of 150 typical Nigerian 14- to 16-year-old secondary school pupils to the question 'What do you mean by learning?'. Using a phenomenographic-type approach the analysis looked for not only the uniqueness of particular subject's responses but also for similarities across subjects. Eventually four categories emerged: *learning as an increase in knowledge, learning as memorising and reproducing, learning and applying,* and *learning as understanding.* The first three categories were congruent with the three quantitative conceptions of learning identified by Marton, Dall'Alba, & Beaty (1993) with United Kingdom Open University students. The fourth conception was also similar to the lowest order qualitative conception reported in the Marton et al. (1993) study where the focus is now on the meaning of what is being learnt. However, there was no evidence in this Nigerian study of the higher order qualitative conceptions involving insight and changing as a person, as found in the Open University research. So considering the findings of these Nigerian studies together, it appears that the approaches to learning and quantitative and qualitative conceptions of learning identified in Western studies and forming the theoretical basis for the SPQ are relevant to Nigerian students, but the present studies question whether higher level qualitative conceptions are reached by Nigerian students. However, this can only be determined by further indepth phenomenographic studies with more mature and select Nigerian university students and graduates such as utilised in the Open University studies.

There have been a number of recent qualitative investigations of the learning approaches and conceptions of Chinese learners in Hong Kong and China (Kember, 1996; Kember & Gow, 1991; Watkins & Biggs, 1996). These studies have partially supported the conceptual validity of the constructs underlying the SPQ for Chinese students, as deep and surface approaches to learning were clearly identifiable in their descriptions of how they went about tackling actual learning tasks. However, it is also clear that memorisation and understanding are more closely interwoven in the experience of learning of many more Chinese than Western students where these concepts are often seen virtually as opposites. Indeed, Kember (1996) has proposed that a new approach to learning may be needed for Chinese students involving an intention to both memorise and understand. With Chinese students the main difference is between rote memorisation and memorising with understanding (Watkins & Biggs, 1996). Also, these qualitative studies make clear that the interpretation of the word 'understanding' as in questions such as 'Do you try to understand what you are learning?' should vary according to whether the subject takes the word to mean knowing the dictionary meaning of the words you are learning (a common response with Hong

Kong students who are learning in a virtual 'foreign language', English); getting full marks on the examination; or grasping the meaning of the body of knowledge that is being learnt. Moreover, research has also queried the appropriateness of Western motivational constructs assessed by the SPQ for Chinese students (Salili, 1996; Watkins & Biggs, 1996). Whereas Western theories tend to regard intrinsic and extrinsic motivation as distinct and virtually mutually exclusive, Chinese students (and educators) are much more likely to combine both sources of motivation. In addition, while achievement motivation is perceived in the Western literature as an individual, ego-boosting motivation, Chinese students are more likely to report desiring high grades for the sake of their family.

Research with Nepalese students has more seriously questioned the cross-cultural validity of the constructs underlying the SPQ. Comparisons of LPQ and SPQ scale scores of Nepalese school and university students indicate that they possess deeper approaches to learning than comparable students from Australia, Hong Kong, and the Philippines (Watkins & Regmi, 1990; Watkins, Regmi, & Astilla, 1991). However, several subsequent qualitative studies have questioned the validity of such comparisons. In particular, a content analysis of the open-ended responses of 333 Master degree students (Watkins & Regmi, 1992) indicated that the view of learning as rote-memorisation and/or reproduction frequently reported by Western students was virtually absent in the Nepalese responses. Moreover, some of the hierarchy of learning identified by Marton et al. (1993) seemed to emerge at lower levels in the Nepalese sample. Further support for these findings came from indepth interviews carried out in Nepal with 45 Master degree students (Watkins & Regmi, 1995). Analysis also showed that few of the Nepalese students had anything but very superficial insight into their learning processes, typically used superficial learning strategies, and achieved a low quality of learning outcomes. The above results cast doubt on the conceptual validity of the SPQ for Nepalese students.

### Reliability

Like any measuring instrument, the scales of the SPQ need to be assessed for reliability in any culture where this questionnaire is to be used. Table 6.2 shows the internal consistency reliability estimates alpha for the SPQ scales for 14 independent samples of 6500 university students from 10 countries. The alpha's ranged as follows: SM .37 to .67 (median .55); SS .25 to .66 (median .55); DM .44 to .70 (median .64); DS .47 to .76 (median .69); AM .48 to .77 (median .68); and AS .56 to .77 (median .72). All but 13 of the 84 alpha coefficients exceeded .50; a magnitude, considered to be acceptable for a research instrument used for group comparisons but well below the level required for important academic decisions about an individual student (Nunnally, 1978). Not surprisingly, the reliability estimates were slightly higher for Australian students for whom it was developed and particularly low for the Nepalese for whom the concepts may not have been as relevant (see above) and whose level of English competence is relatively low. Also the internal consistencies of the two surface approach scales were generally lower than the other scales. Again this was not unexpected as these scales are less conceptually pure than the others as there are several motives (extrinsic or fear of failure) and strategies (from doing little to rote learning everything) which may be involved (see Biggs, 1993).

### *Within-construct validity*
As explicated in the classic writing of Cronbach & Meehl (1955), to demonstrate the construct validity of an instrument two aspects of the nomological network surrounding the construct being measured need to be investigated. Firstly, the within-construct validity of the SPQ will be examined by comparing the results of internal factor analysis of the SPQ scales for different cultures with each other and the theoretical model expected. Moreover, correlations between scales of inventories supposed to be tapping the same constructs as the SPQ should be statistically significant. Secondly, between-construct aspects will be assessed by testing hypotheses about the relations between the SPQ scales and other variables (see below).

### *Factor analysis*
Table 6.3 reports the factor loadings of the SPQ scales based on two factor solutions (which typically explained 65 per cent of the variance) obtained after principals axis factor analysis followed by rotation to oblique simple structure using the Oblimin procedure for samples of university students from eight countries. In all eight samples the results are clear-cut with distinct surface and deep approach factors. The achieving scales as explained earlier were not expected to load consistently on one or other of the

TABLE 6.2  Internal consistency reliability coefficients alpha of SPQ scales for students from 10 countries

| Country | Australia (n=823) | Brunei (n=524) | Hong Kong (1)[b] (n=2338) | Hong Kong (2) (n=162) | Hong Kong (3) (n=192) | Indonesia[a] (n=90) | Kenya (n=75) | Nepal (1) (n=342) | Nepal (2) (n=120) | Philippines (n=123) | South Africa (Black) (n=184) | South Africa (White) (n=179) | Sweden[a] (n=179) | United Arab Emirates[a] (n=246) |
|---|---|---|---|---|---|---|---|---|---|---|---|---|---|---|
| **Questionnaire Scales** | | | | | | | | | | | | | | |
| Surface Motivation | .61 | .58 | .53 | .56 | .56 | .37 | .67 | .40 | .63 | .51 | .54 | .54 | .41 | .49 |
| Surface Strategy | .66 | .48 | .65 | .61 | .55 | .30 | .43 | .25 | .43 | .51 | .60 | .60 | .57 | .54 |
| Deep Motivation | .65 | .58 | .60 | .62 | .67 | .67 | .64 | .44 | .49 | .57 | .65 | .65 | .70 | .56 |
| Deep Strategy | .75 | .73 | .75 | .68 | .76 | .70 | .57 | .47 | .57 | .60 | .62 | .62 | .75 | .68 |
| Achieving Motivation | .72 | .64 | .74 | .77 | .71 | .68 | .53 | .48 | .65 | .57 | .73 | .73 | .70 | .64 |
| Achieving Strategy | .77 | .76 | .69 | .74 | .77 | .74 | .63 | .56 | .69 | .57 | .77 | .77 | .63 | .71 |

[a] Translated versions of the SPQ were used  [b] A bi-lingual version of the SPQ was used

Source: see Note 1.

TABLE 6.3  Factor loadings from two factor oblique solution of responses to the SPQ for university student samples from eight countries

| Country of Subjects | Brunei | | Hong Kong | | Indonesia | | Nepal | | Nigeria | | South Africa | | Sweden | | United Arab Emirates | |
|---|---|---|---|---|---|---|---|---|---|---|---|---|---|---|---|---|
| | Factor I | Factor II | Factor I | Factor II | Factor I | Factor II | Factor I | Factor II | Factor I | Factor II | Factor I | Factor II | Factor I | Factor II | Factor I | Factor II |
| **Questionnaire Scales** | | | | | | | | | | | | | | | | |
| Surface Motivation | -.08 | .71 | .27 | .79 | .02 | .69 | -.31 | .65 | -.10 | .78 | 1.00 | -.13 | -.02 | .64 | -.02 | .86 |
| Surface Strategy | .08 | .67 | .28 | .80 | -.08 | .59 | .15 | .57 | .22 | .47 | .69 | .19 | -.02 | .76 | .01 | .84 |
| Deep Motivation | .67 | -.06 | .84 | -.19 | .67 | .16 | .60 | .05 | .51 | .21 | .43 | .52 | .68 | -.08 | .70 | .19 |
| Deep Strategy | .85 | -.07 | .84 | -.26 | .88 | -.21 | .67 | .02 | .91 | -.14 | -.06 | .89 | .83 | -.23 | .81 | -.14 |
| Achieving Motivation | .41 | .23 | .71 | .17 | .43 | .50 | .13 | .58 | .31 | 1.44 | -.06 | .24 | .48 | .32 | .62 | .31 |
| Achieving Strategy | .79 | -.02 | .83 | -.20 | .70 | .01 | .64 | -.01 | .66 | .09 | .14 | .75 | .37 | .08 | .76 | -.26 |

Source: see Note 2.

factors but rather be associated with the approach which was more likely to succeed in that context: thus the United Arab Emirates and Hong Kong students sampled clearly associated both the AM and AS scales with a deep approach to learning. Interestingly, there was a tendency in the remaining countries for achieving strategies to be strongly associated with a deep approach but this trend was weaker for the corresponding motivation scale whose loadings tended to be divided between the two factors. Confirmatory factor analysis of responses to the LPQ, which shares the same underlying motive/strategy model as the SPQ, by 10 samples of school students from six different countries also confirmed the two basic factors of deep and surface approach (Wong, Lin, & Watkins, 1996).

### Correlations with other learning questionnaires

There are several questionnaires tapping scales parallel to those of the SPQ. These include the Approaches to Study Inventory (ASI) (Entwistle, Hanley, & Hounsell, 1979), the Cognitive Styles Inventory (CSI) (Moreno & DiVesta, 1991) and the Inventory of Learning Processes (ILP) (Schmeck, Ribich & Ramanaiah, 1977). Unfortunately there appear to be few studies which have used the SPQ and one or more of these other inventories but those few studies are encouraging. For example, Wilson, Smart and Watson (1996) found correlations for two samples of Australian psychology students between the SPQ and ASI to be .45 and .61 for Deep Approach, .44 and .62 for Surface Approach, and .46 and .46 for Achieving Approach (all $p<.001$). In the unpublished South African study (Watkins & Akande, 1994) referred to above, correlations between these same approach scales were .41, .40, and .34 for Black students and .26, .18, and .31 for White students (all $p <.01$). Moreover, as would be predicted, the CSI's Integrating Strategy and the SPQ's Deep Strategy scales correlated .28 and .42 for the White and Black South African students, respectively (both $p <.01$).

## Between-construct validity

### Correlates with academic grades

It would be expected that students' approaches to learning would influence their academic performance. In particular, we would predict that a surface approach would be significantly negatively correlated while the other two approaches would be positively correlated.

TABLE 6.4   Summary of research reporting correlations between SPQ scales and academic achievement

| Country | Subjects | Surface Approach | Deep Approach | Achieving Approach |
|---|---|---|---|---|
| Australia[a] (1) | 815 CAE students | -.18* | .22* | .23* |
| Australia[a] (2) | 1550 university students | -.10* | .22* | .21* |
| Australia (3) | 269 university students | -.18* | .06 | .10 |
| Australia[a] (4) | 249 university students | -.25* | .24* | .18* |
| Hong Kong | 162 university students | -.23* | .20* | .23* |
| Nepal | 342 university students | -.10* | .06 | .06 |
| United Arab Emirates | 246 university students | -.27* | .25* | .36* |
| USA (1) | 524 university students | -.11* | .16* | .14* |
| USA (2) | 202 university students | .02 | .11 | .27* |
| Overall mean correlations | 4359 university students | -.16 | .17 | .20 |

* correlation is significantly different from zero at .05 level
a these correlations are based on self-estimates of academic performance
Source: see Note 3.

Table 6.4 reports the correlations between approaches to learning and academic achievement for nine samples of 4359 university students from five countries. It can be seen that 21 of the 27 correlations were statistically different from zero and in the predicted direction. Over all the nine samples the mean correlations were: -.16, .17, and .20 for the surface, deep, and achieving approaches, respectively. These means are pulled down by the Nepalese data which also has the lowest SPQ scale reliabilities. It is also likely that the correlations are a reflection that university grades are often not a true indicator of the quality of learning outcomes (Tang & Biggs, 1996). However, while the correlations obtained may seem disappointingly small it must be kept in mind that in fact few variables consistently show correlations of above .20 with achievement across a number of studies (Fraser, Walberg, Welch & Hattie, 1987), let alone across a diverse range of countries as here.

### Correlations with self-esteem and locus of control
It is to be expected that students who are more self-confident, particularly with their academic abilities, and who accept greater responsibility for their own learning outcomes are more likely to adopt deeper, more achieving approaches to learning which require them to rely more on their understanding of course materials rather

TABLE 6.5   Summary of research reporting correlations between SPQ approach scales and both self-esteem and internal locus of control

| Country | Subjects | Surface Approach | Deep Approach | Achieving Approach |
|---|---|---|---|---|
| **Self-esteem** | | | | |
| Australia | 386 Teacher Education, Nursing & Liberal Studies First Years | .01 | .20* | .32* |
| Hong Kong | 162 Nursing, Radiography & Communication First Years | -.13 | .25* | .22* |
| Kenya | 88 Undergraduates | -.14 | .20 | .30* |
| Nepal | 398 Arts & Science Postgraduates | -.02 | .54* | .30* |
| South Africa | 179 White Psychology Undergraduates | -.03 | .17* | .10 |
| | | -.07 | .18* | .09 |
| South Africa | 184 Black Psychology Undergraduates | -.04 | .43* | .32* |
| Sweden | 149 Education Undergraduates | | | |
| **Internal Locus of Control** | | | | |
| Australia | 83 Teacher Education & Nursing First Years | -.18 | .22* | .18 |
| Hong Kong | 162 Education, Nursing, & Liberal Studies First Years | -.34* | .00 | .24* |
| Indonesia | 90 Social Science Undergraduates | -.18 | .16 | .15 |
| Nepal | 129 Undergraduates | -.18* | .10 | .20* |
| Nepal | 342 Postgraduates | -.10* | .24* | .21* |
| USA | 202 Psychology Undergraduates | -.04 | .06 | .20* |
| **Overall Mean Correlations** | | | | |
| Self-esteem | 1546 Students | -.05 | .29 | .24 |
| Internal locus of control | 1007 Students | -.17 | .13 | .20 |

* correlation is significantly different from zero at .05 level

Source: see Note 4.

than being overly-dependent on the teacher or textbook. Table 6.5 summarises the correlations found between measures of both self-esteem and locus of control and approaches to learning as measured by the SPQ. It can be seen that, based on correlations from 1546 students from seven cultures, self-esteem as predicted correlated moderately highly both with Deep (overall $r = .29$) and Achieving (overall $r = .24$) approaches; locus of control also correlated with the SPQ approach scales generally as predicted (if weakly) with overall correlations, based on six samples of 1007 students, of -.17, .13, and .20 for Surface, Deep, and Achieving approaches, respectively.

### Scalar equivalence

The above cross-cultural evidence of conceptual equivalence of the SPQ scales is only partially supportive whereas evidence of the reliability and within- and between-construct validity is encouraging. However, cross-cultural comparisons of raw SPQ scale scores should be carried out with caution. This is because of evidence of cross-cultural differences in ways subjects respond to questionnaires such as the SPQ: in particular in response sets such as social desirability, acquiescence, and extreme responding (Hui & Triandis, 1989; Watkins & Cheung, 1995). The influence of such response sets on learning questionnaires in any culture has seldom been examined but two recent studies have suggested that for school students from Hong Kong (Watkins, 1996) and India (Watkins & Singh-Sengupta, 1996) responses to LPQ scales may be significantly contaminated by social desirability response set. Problems with scalar equivalence can also occur in within-country studies. For example, in an as yet unpublished study in which the author is involved with Dr. Akande, the means of Black South African students were statistically higher than those of their White peers on all six SPQ scales. This makes interpretation in terms of ethnic differences in learning motivation and strategy rather difficult! The traditional method of standardising within subjects before conducting statistical analysis advocated by cross-cultural methodologists (Hui & Triandis, 1985) can, unfortunately, also remove real differences between groups.

### SUMMARY

To sum up, while the SPQ may be reliable and valid for use for research and perhaps other purposes *within* many cultures, there may be exceptions such as Nepal. Moreover, doubts have been raised about the use of raw SPQ scores for comparisons across cultures. It will also be argued below that appropriate uses of the SPQ and similar instruments are already adding to our understanding of student learning in non-Western cultures.

## APPLICATIONS OF THE SPQ

### UNDERSTANDING STUDENT LEARNING

The SPQ can be, and has been, used to explore individual differences in approaches to learning. For example, Wilson, Smart and Watson (1996) used it and the ASI to investigate gender differences in the approaches to learning of Australian psychology students. Research with these instruments generally has found that gender differences are much smaller than disciplinary differences; with Arts students tending to report greater use of meaning-oriented learning strategies than Science students (Hayes & Richardson, 1995; Watkins, 1982; Watkins & Hattie, 1985).

Research in Australia, the United Kingdom, and Hong Kong, using questionnaires such as the SPQ, has also indicated aspects of the learning context which are both controllable and encourage superficial learning strategies. These factors include assessment methods which are perceived as rewarding reproduction of facts (Thomas & Bain, 1984; Tang & Biggs, 1996); formal teaching methods (Ramsden, 1984); excessive workloads (Lee, 1993); and a restrictive learning environment (Chan & Watkins, 1994; Ramsden, 1984). The SPQ can also be used to explore causal models linking personality factors, approaches to learning, and learning outcomes in different cultures (see, for example, Drew & Watkins, in press; Murray-Harvey & Keeves, 1994).

### STAFF DEVELOPMENT

As Ramsden (1992) makes clear, to be most effective a university teacher needs to understand how his or her students learn. One of the problems which has been identified with the teaching of Chinese students both at home and abroad is that their lecturers often mis-perceive these students as rote learners (Watkins & Biggs, 1996). Balla, Stokes and Stafford (1991) report how the responses of City University of Hong Kong students to the SPQ could be used in workshops to highlight such mis-perceptions leading to improved approaches to teaching. The provision of SPQ and LPQ norms for Australian (Biggs, 1987) and Hong Kong students allows the individual teacher to compare his or her students' approaches to learning to typical students in the same educational system. This writer has also used the SPQ in a class as a tool to allow students to explore their own approaches to learning and to realise that other students may be using a different approach.

## EVALUATING TEACHING EFFECTIVENESS

While the SPQ could be used as an element of formal evaluation procedures for formative or summative staff decisions, it has been mainly used to examine the effects of changes in educational evaluations such as a change in the assessment system (Tang & Biggs, 1996). Recently in Hong Kong, repeated applications of the SPQ have been used to monitor the progress of innovations in a formative way to decide what further changes may be necessary in the spirit of action research as well as providing objective evidence of the effectiveness of the innovations for summative purposes (Kember, Charlesworth, Davies, McKay & Stott, in press). Kember et al. point out that the SPQ should be used as one element of an evaluation package and not relied on as sole indicator.

Because questionnaires such as the SPQ tap approaches to learning which reflect how students are adjusting to the learning environment they are encountering, they can be used as an indicator of teaching effectiveness at various levels. (Kember et al., in press).

### *University-wide level*

Longitudinal studies have tracked students' approaches to learning at two universities in Hong Kong (Gow & Kember, 1990; Stokes, Balla, & Stafford, 1989). Both studies used the SPQ to show rather disappointingly that deep and achieving motives and strategies tended to decrease as the students progressed through their tertiary studies. Similar results were found in Australia using the ASI (Watkins & Hattie, 1985) and the SPQ (Biggs, 1987) and for nursing students in Hong Kong (Chan & Watkins, 1995). Such findings can prove a useful focus for a university considering the quality of learning they are providing. Results can easily be provided for different faculties or departments and thus possibly highlight areas where further staff development may be necessary.

### *Course level*

The SPQ can also be used to reflect the influence of a particular course on student learning. If used in this way the respondents should be asked to answer each item with respect to the course of interest to the investigator, rather than their approach in general (the normal instructions for the SPQ).

## LANGUAGE OF INSTRUCTION

An important policy issue for a number of non-Western countries is whether students should be taught in their native language or some other language, usually English. The SPQ can be used to investigate the effect of the choice of the language of instruction on student approaches to learning. Gow, Kember and Chow (1991) have shown that Hong Kong students with low proficiency in English are likely to adopt a surface approach while high proficiency is likely to increase the likelihood of adopting a deep approach. A study by Watkins, Biggs and Regmi (1991) confirmed these findings for both Hong Kong and Nepalese students.

## CONCLUSIONS

This chapter has provided evidence that the SPQ, like its school equivalent the LPQ, can be used validly to assess student learning in a number of countries differing in terms of cultural values, ethnicity, and educational systems. Hong Kong is one non-Western country where the SPQ has been widely used in both applied and more theoretical research to aid our understanding of student learning and teaching effectiveness. In these days of calls for demonstrating the value of a university education as a whole and the effectiveness of individual teachers, in particular, world wide, the SPQ offers a tool for directly assessing the quality of learning processes students are using which are known to have a strong impact on the quality of learning outcomes they can achieve. Further work is needed to fully justify cross-cultural comparisons of student learning; in particular the possibility of cross-cultural differences in social desirability responding, and any impact on responses to the SPQ needs further investigation. Moreover, it may be necessary to modify the SPQ for Nepalese (and perhaps other) students for whom the underlying concepts and the current SPQ items seem to be of dubious validity. Even for Hong Kong students for whom the extensive SPQ reliability and validity evidence is encouraging, it may be possible to tailor the items to reflect differences from Western students in terms of both motives for learning and the use of memorising and understanding strategies, as discussed earlier.

## Notes

1  The source references for the data reported in Table 6.2 (*Reliability*) and from which further details can be obtained are as follows: Australia (Biggs, 1987); Brunei (Watkins & Murphy, 1994); Hong Kong (1) (Biggs, 1993); Hong Kong (2) (Drew & Watkins, in press); Hong Kong (3) (Chan & Watkins, 1995); Indonesia (Hotma Ria, 1993, personal communication); Kenya and South Africa (Watkins & Akande, unpublished research), Nepal (1) and (2) (Watkins & Regmi, as yet unpublished research); South Africa (Watkins & Akande, as yet unpublished research); Sweden (Dahlin & Watkins, 1996); and United Arab Emirates (Albaili, 1995).

2  The source references in Note 1 are also for the data reported in Table 6.3 (*Responses to the SPQ*).

3  The source references for the data reported in Table 6.4 (*Correlations with achievement*) and from which further details can be obtained are as follows: Australia (1) and (2) (Biggs, 1987); Australia (3) and (4) (Murray-Harvey & Keeves, 1994, and personal communication); Hong Kong (Drew & Watkins, 1996); Nepal (Watkins & Regmi, 1990); United Arab Emirates (Albaili, 1995). USA (1) and (2) (Rose, Hall, Bollen & Webster, 1996; and Bollen, personal communication).

4  The source references for the data reported in Table 6.5 (*Correlations with self-esteem and locus of control*) and from which further details can be obtained are as follows: Australia (Murray-Harvey, personal communication); Hong Kong (Drew & Watkins, 1996); Indonesia (Hotma Ria, 1993, personal communication); Nepal (Watkins & Regmi, 1990, and unpublished research); South Africa (Watkins & Akande, unpublished research); Sweden (Dahlin & Watkins, 1996); and USA (Rose et al., 1996).

5  The writer would like to thank Hotma Ria, Ros Murray-Harvey and Larry Bollen for providing unpublished data.

## References

Albaili, M.A. (1995). An Arabic version of the Study Process Questionnaire: Reliability and validity. *Psychological Reports, 77*, 1083–1089.

Altbach, P., & Selvaratnam, V. (Eds.). (1989). *From dependence to autonomy: The development of Asian universities.* Dordrecht: Kluwer.

Balla, J., Stokes, M., & Stafford, K. (1991). *Using the Study Process Questionnaire to its full potential: A Hong Kong view*, (Technical Report No. 1). Educational Technology Centre, City University of Hong Kong.

Berry, J. (1989). Imposed emics-derived etics. The operationalisation of a compelling idea. *International Journal of Psychology, 24*, 721–735.

Biggs, J.B. (1987). *Student approaches to learning and studying*. Melbourne: Australian Council for Educational Research.

Biggs, J.B. (1993). What do inventories of students' learning processes really measure? A theoretical review and clarification. *British Journal of Educational Psychology, 63*, 3–19.

Chan, Y-Y.G., & Watkins, D. (1994). Classroom environment and approaches to learning: An investigation of the actual and preferred perceptions of Hong Kong secondary school students. *Instructional Science, 22*, 233–246.

Chan, Y-K.C.A., & Watkins, D. (1995). How do Hong Kong hospital-based student nurses learn? *Educational Research Journal, 10*, 54–59.

Cronbach, L.J., & Meehl, P.E. (1955). Construct validity in psychological tests. *Psychological Bulletin, 52*, 281–302.

Dahlin, B., & Watkins, D. (1996). *Assessing study approaches in Sweden: A cross-cultural perspective*. Manuscript submitted for publication.

Drew, P-Y., & Watkins, D. (in press). Affective variables, learning approaches and academic achievement: A casual modeling investigation with Hong Kong Chinese tertiary students. *British Journal of Educational Psychology*.

Ehindero, O.J. (1990). A discriminant function analysis of study strategies, logical reasoning ability and achievement across major teaching undergraduate curricula. *Research in Education, 44*, 1–11.

Enriquez, V. (1982). *Decolonising the Filipino psyche*. Quezon City: Philippine Psychology Research House.

Entwistle, N.J., Hanley, M., & Hounsell, D. (1979). Identifying distinctive approaches to studying. *Higher Education, 8*, 365–380.

Entwistle, N.J., & Ramsden, P. (1983). *Understanding student learning*. London: Croom Helm.

Fraser, B.J., Walberg, H.J., Welch, W.W., & Hattie, J.A. (1987). Synthesis of educational productivity research. *International Journal of Educational Research, 11*, 145–252.

Gonzales, A. (1989). The Western impact on Philippine higher education. In P. Altbach, & V. Selvaratnam (Eds.), *From dependence to autonomy: The development of Asian universities*. Dordrecht: Kluwer.

Gow, L., & Kember, D. (1990). Does higher education promote independent learning? *Higher Education, 19*, 307–322.

Gow, L., Kember, D., & Chow, R. (1991). The effects of English language ability on approaches to learning. *Regional English Language Centre Journal, 22*, 49–68.

Hayes, K., & Richardson, J.T.E. (1995). Gender, subject, and context as determinants of approaches to studying in higher education. *Studies in Higher Education, 20*, 215–221.

Hui, C.H. & Triandis, H.C. (1985). Measurement in cross-cultural psychology: A review and comparison of strategies. *Journal of Cross-Cultural Psychology, 16,* 131–152.

Hui, C.H., & Triandis, H.C. (1989). Effects of culture and response format on extreme response style. *Journal of Cross-Cultural Psychology, 20,* 296–309.

Kember, D. (1996). The intention to both memorise and understand: Another approach to learning? *Higher Education, 31,* 341–354.

Kember, D., Charlesworth, M., Davies, H., McKay, J., & Stott, V. (in press). Establishing the effectiveness of educational innovations: Using the Study Process Questionnaire to show that meaningful learning occurs. *Studies in Educational Evaluation.*

Kember, D., & Gow, L. (1991). A challenge to the anecdotal stereotype of the Asian student. *Studies in Higher Education, 16,* 117–128.

Kim, V., & Berry, J.W. (Eds.). (1993). *Indigenous psychologies: Research and experience in cultural context.* London: Sage.

Lee, A. (1993). Coping with workload and time constraints. In J. Biggs, & D. Watkins (Eds.), *Learning and teaching in Hong Kong: What is and what might be.* Hong Kong: Education Paper No. 17, University of Hong Kong.

Marton, F., Dall'Alba, G. & Beaty, E. (1993). Conceptions of learning. *International Journal of Educational Research, 19,* 277–300.

Marton, F., Hounsell, D., & Entwistle, N.J. (Eds.). (1984). *The experience of learning.* Edinburgh: Scottish Academic Press.

Marton, F., & , Säljö R. (1976). On qualitative differences in learning – I: Outcome and process. *British Journal of Educational Psychology, 46,* 4–11.

Moreno, V., & DiVesta, F.J. (1991). Cross-cultural comparisons of study habits. *Journal of Educational Psychology, 83,* 231–239.

Murray-Harvey, R., & Keeves, J. (1994). *Student learning processes and progress in higher education.* Paper presented at the annual meeting of the American Educational Research Association, New Orleans.

Nunnally, J.C. (1978). *Psychometric theory* (2nd ed.). New York: McGraw Hill.

Omokhodion, J.O. (1989). Classroom observed: The hidden curriculum in Lagos, Nigeria. *International Journal of Educational Development, 9,* 99–110.

Ramsden, P. (1984). The context of learning. In F. Marton, D. Hounsell, & N. Entwistle (Eds.), *The experience of learning.* Edinburgh: Scottish Academic Press.

Ramsden, P. (1988). *Improving learning: New perspectives.* London: Kogan Page.

Ramsden, P. (1992). *Learning to teach in higher education.* London: Routledge.

Rose, R.J., Hall, C.W., Bollen, L.M., & Webster, R.E. (1996). Locus of control and college students' approaches to learning. *Psychological Reports, 79*, 163–171.

Salili, F. (1996). Accepting personal responsibility for learning. In D. Watkins, & J. Biggs (Eds.), *The Chinese learner: Cultural, psychological, and contextual influences.* Hong Kong/Melbourne: Comparative Education Research Centre/Australian Council for Educational Research.

Schmeck, R. (Ed.). (1988). *Learning strategies and learning styles.* New York: Plenum.

Shmeck, R., Ribich, F., & Ramanaiah, N.V. (1977). Development of a self-report inventory for assessing individual differences in learning processes. *Applied Psychological Measurement, 1*(3), 413-431.

Stokes, M., Balla, J,. & Stafford, K. (1989). How students in selected degree programmes at CPHK characterise their approaches to study. *Educational Research Journal, 4*, 85–91.

Tang, C., & Biggs, J. (1996). How Hong Kong students cope with assessment. In D. Watkins, & J. Biggs (Eds.), *The Chinese learner: Cultural, psychological, and contextual influences.* Hong Kong/Melbourne: Comparative Education Research Centre/Australian Council for Educational Research.

Thomas, P., & Bain, J. (1984). Contextual differences in learning approaches: the effects of assessment. *Human Learning, 3*, 227–240.

Triandis, H.C. (1972). *The analysis of subjective culture.* New York: Wiley.

Watkins, D. (1982). Identifying the study process dimensions of Australian university students. *Australian Journal of Educational Research, 26*, 76–85.

Watkins, D. (1996). The influence of social desirability on learning process questionnaires: A neglected possibility? *Contemporary Educational Psychology, 21*, 80–82.

Watkins, D., & Akande, A. (1994). Approaches to learning of Nigerian secondary school children: Emic and etic perspectives. *International Journal of Psychology, 29*, 165–182.

Watkins, D., & Biggs, J. (Eds.). (1996). *The Chinese learner: Cultural, psychological, and contextual influences.* Hong Kong/Melbourne: Comparative Education Research Centre/Australian Council for Educational Research.

Watkins, D., Biggs, J., & Regmi, M. (1991). Does confidence in the language of instruction influence a student's approach to learning? *Instructional Science, 20*, 331–339.

Watkins, D., & Cheung, S. (1995). Culture, gender and response bias: An analysis of responses to the Self-Description Questionnaire. *Journal of Cross Cultural Psychology, 26*(5), 490–504.

Watkins, D., & Hattie, J. (1985). A longitudinal study of the approaches to learning of Australian tertiary students. *Human Learning, 4,* 127–141.

Watkins, D., & Murphy, J. (1994). Modifying the Study Process Questionnaire for ESL students. *Psychological Reports, 74,* 1023–1026.

Watkins, D., & Regmi, M. (1990). An investigation of the approach to learning of Nepalese tertiary students. *Higher Education, 29,* 459–469.

Watkins, D., & Regmi, M. (1992). How universal are student conceptions of learning? A Nepalese investigation. *Psychologia, 35,* 101–110.

Watkins, D., & Regmi, M. (1995). Assessing approaches to learning in non-Western cultures: A Nepalese conceptual validity study. *Assessment and Evaluation in Higher Education, 20,* 203–212.

Watkins, D., Regmi, M., & Astilla, E. (1991). The Asian-learner-as-a-rote-learner stereotype: Myth or reality? *Educational Psychology, 11,* 21–34.

Watkins, D., & Singh-Sengupta, S. (1996). Social desirability and the Learning Process Questionnaire: An investigation with students in India. *Psychological Reports, 79,* 181–182.

Wilson, K.L., Smart, R.M., & Watson, R.J. (1996). Gender differences in approaches to learning in first year psychology students. *British Journal of Educational Psychology, 66,* 59–72.

Wong, N-Y., Lin, W-Y., & Watkins, D. (1996). Cross-cultural validation of models of approaches to learning an application of confirmatory factor analysis. *Educational Psychology, 16,* 317–327.

## PART THREE

# CHAPTER 7

# The Solo Model: Addressing Fundamental Measurement Issues

*John Hattie and*

*Nola Purdie*

The SOLO model, developed by Biggs and Collis (1982), proposes a structure of learning outcomes, and thus provides a clear basis for a technology of testing within learning and test theory. Chapter 9, by Gillian Boulton-Lewis, clearly demonstrates the applicability of the SOLO model to teaching and learning in all spheres of higher education. The primary purpose of this chapter is to illustrate the power of the SOLO model with particular reference to measurement issues confronted by students in teacher education programs in universities. We provide practical examples, drawn from teachers' work with primary and secondary school students, of how the model can be used in the classroom to guide lesson plans, model how students learn, model how effectively teachers teach, and construct any form of test item. We believe in the potential to improve the quality of teaching and learning in schools by devising teacher education programs that provide students with a sound understanding of the theoretical basis of the SOLO model, and practical examples of how the model can be implemented in classrooms.

## THE SOLO TAXONOMY

Biggs and Collis (1982) developed their model from a study of learning outcomes in various school subjects and found that students learn quite diverse material in stages of ascending structural complexity that display a similar sequence across tasks. This led to the formulation of the SOLO taxonomy (Structure of the Observed Learning Outcome). The taxonomy makes it possible, in the course of learning a subject, to identify in broad terms the stage at which a student is currently operating. In this consistent sequence, or cycle, the following stages occur:

*Prestructural* – there is preliminary preparation, but the task itself is not attacked in an appropriate way.

*Unistructural* – one aspect of a task is picked up or understood serially, and there is no relationship of facts or ideas.

*Multistructural* – two or more aspects of a task are picked up or understood serially, but are not interrelated.

*Relational* – several aspects are integrated so that the whole has a coherent structure and meaning.

*Extended abstract* – that coherent whole is generalised to a higher level of abstraction.

Biggs and Collis (1982) based their model on the notion that in any 'learning episode, both qualitative and quantitative learning outcomes are determined by a complex interaction between teaching procedures and student characteristics' (p. 15). They emphasised the roles played by: the prior knowledge the student has of the content relating to the episode; the student's motives and intentions about the learning; and the student's learning strategies. They noted that 'power' factors, such as general ability, operate across the board and thus have little prescriptive value. While quantitative aspects of evaluating learning are well understood and applied, qualitative aspects have not been researched or applied to nearly the same extent. Such qualitative learning develops in a hierarchy of levels of increasing structural complexity. Biggs and Collis (1982) claimed their model was the 'only instrument available for assessing quality retrospectively in an objective and systemic way that is also easily understandable by both teacher and student' (p. xi).

The levels are ordered in terms of various characteristics: from the concrete to the abstract; an increasing number of organising dimensions; increasing consistency; and the use of organising or relating principles. It was developed to assess the qualitative outcomes of learning in a range of school and college situations, in most subject areas, hence the title of the taxonomy: Structure of the Observed Learning Outcome. The model is premised on four factors:

*Capacity*: Each level of the SOLO taxonomy refers to a demand on amount of working memory or attention span. For example, at the unistructural and multistructural levels, a student need only encode the given information and may use a recall strategy to provide an answer. At the relational or extended abstract level, a student needs to think about more things at once.

*Relationship*: Each level of SOLO refers to a way in which the question and the response interrelate. A unistructural response involves generalising only in terms of one aspect and thus there is little or no relationship involved. The multistructural level involves relationship in terms of a few limited and independent aspects. At the relational level, the student needs to generalise within a given or experienced context, and at the extended abstract level, the student needs to generalise to situations not experienced.

*Consistency and closure*: These refer to two opposing needs felt by the learner. On the one hand, the student wants to come to a conclusion and thus answer the question. But on the other hand, the student wants to be consistent so that there is no contradiction between the question and answer. Often when there is a greater need for closure, then less information is utilised, whereas a high level of need for consistency is required to utilise more information when conceiving an answer. At the unistructural level, the student often seizes on immediate recall information, but at the extended abstract level, the student leaves room for inconsistency across contexts.

*Structure*: The unistructural response takes one relevant piece of information to link the question to the answer. The multistructural response takes several. The relational response makes more use of an underlying conceptual structure and the extended abstract requires more structure so that the student can demonstrate that he or she can deduce answers beyond the original context.

On the basis of the sequencing of student learning according to levels of structural complexity, Collis and Biggs (1982) proposed that there are clear implications for how schools develop programs that enable students to accommodate to the culture of school learning as opposed to that of learning for everyday life. They argue that the 'school program must take into account, among other things, the sequence of four major transitions within the concrete-symbolic mode which define particular educational tasks in content areas determined within the context of the general aims' (p. 193, see also Biggs & Collis, 1989). Students should be assisted to advance in the following way.

*From pre-structural to unistructural*: They argued that the curriculum needed to help students 'join the game' with its new rules and its different way of conceptualising reality. For example, when teaching to read, it is worthwhile to take advantage of the children's iconic mode; that is, to use their interest in listening to stories and extracting meaning from pictures.

*From unistructural to multistructural*: The curriculum needs to concentrate on consolidating and automating the unistructural knowledge and skills, building a store of concrete symbolic knowledge, and encouraging students 'to do more' with their knowledge base.

*From multistructural to relational*: The task involves more than 'getting to know more about a topic or being adept at following through a sequence of procedures; it includes understanding or integrating what is known into a coherent system wherein the parts are inter-related. This interrelationship comes about as a result of an ability to form an overviewing principle which can be derived from the information given' (p. 196).

*From relational to extended abstract*: This process involves a shift to the formal mode of operating and typically requires dedicated hard work to master abstract concepts and relationships which form the basis of an academic discipline.

## SOLO AND LEARNING PROCESSES

An important underlying assumption of the SOLO model is the learning processes used by students when addressing content materials and learning new information. Biggs has published extensively on the development of such learning processes (Biggs, 1985, 1987, 1990). He argued that 'reproducing' or surface approaches depend on an intention that is extrinsic to the real purpose of the task, they usually require investing minimal time and effort consistent with appearing to meet requirements, invoke relating already understood information, and rarely go beyond the surface of the content. These approaches can increase one's knowledge, and involve memorisation and reproducing as well as the application of facts and procedures in different contexts. The unistructural and multistructural levels are at these surface or reproducing levels. The term 'transforming' or deep approach reflects an intention to gain understanding by relating to the task in a way that is personally meaningful, or that links up with existing knowledge. The relational and extended abstract levels are at these transforming or deep levels, where the aim is to understand, see something in a different way, and/or change as a person.

This continuum can be traced to Marton and Säljö (1976) who formulated two major levels of learning: surface and deep. A surface approach involves minimum engagement with the task and typically focuses on memorisation or applying procedures that do not involve reflection, but aim merely to gain a passing grade. The contrasting deep approach involves an intention to understand and impose meaning. The student focuses on relations between various aspects of the content, formulates hypotheses or beliefs about the structure of the problem, and relates more to obtaining an intrinsic interest in learning and understanding. High quality learning outcomes are associated with deep approaches, whereas low quality outcomes are associated with surface ones (see Biggs, 1987; Entwistle, 1988; Harper & Kember, 1989; Marton & Säljö, 1984). There is much evidence that teachers (both in schools and universities) can also adopt a surface or a deep approach to teaching, and this has consequential effects on what and how students learn (Boulton-Lewis, 1995; Boulton-Lewis, Dart & Brownlee, 1995; Boulton-Lewis, Wilss & Mutch, 1996 ).

Three examples are provided to illustrate more fully the four SOLO levels and the value of the underlying model. The first is found in a meta-analysis of study skills programs by Hattie, Biggs and Purdie (1996). A major issue in that study was the power of the SOLO method to classify interventions. A unistructural study skills intervention was based on one relevant feature or dimension, such as an intervention focused on a single point of change, like coaching on one algorithm, training in underlining, using a mnemonic device, or anxiety reduction. The target parameter may be an individual characteristic or a skill or technique. The essential feature is that it alone is the focus, independently of the context, or its adaptation to or modification by content. A multistructural intervention involved a range of independent strategies or procedures, but without any integration or orchestration concerning individual differences, or content or contextual demands. Examples would include typical study skills packages taught directively, without a metacognitive or conditional framework. A relational intervention occurred when all the components were integrated to suit the individual's self-assessment, were orchestrated to the demands of the particular task and context, or involved a degree of self-regulation in learning (e.g. metacognitive interventions emphasising self-monitoring and self-regulation, and many attribution retraining studies). An extended abstract intervention occurred when the integration achieved in the previous category was generalised to a new domain.

Unistructural and multistructural programs were highly effective with virtually all students when studying material requiring only low level cognitive involvement (e.g. memorisation of specific information). Multistructural approaches were most effective with younger rather than older students. Relational programs, integrating the informed use of strategies to suit the content, and used for near transfer in context, were highly effective in all domains (performance, study skills, and affect) over all ages and ability levels, but were particularly useful with high ability students and older students.

A second example of the power of the SOLO taxonomy is its use to classify the behaviour of teachers in classrooms. Hattie, Clinton, Thompson and Schmidt-Davis (1997) observed elementary school teachers who had been certified as 'Highly accomplished' by the National Board for Professional Teaching Standards. This certification was as a consequence of extended performance evaluations of a large number of teachers and the setting of high and rigorous standards, but did not involve any classroom observations. Hattie et al. visited teachers in their classrooms and, among an array of measures, they were interested in the effects of the teaching on the students. Many researchers have emphasised the importance of 'knowledge' when differentiating experts from novices (Shulman, 1987) and have observed that knowledge that is useful for experts may hold little meaning for novices (deGroot, 1965). Of more importance are the differences in the way knowledge is used in teaching situations. As Chi, Feltovich and Glaser (1981) noted with physicists, experts were more sensitive to the deep structures of the problems they dealt with, whereas novices were sensitive to surface structures.

Given the well known problems of using achievement outcomes as indicators of teaching effectiveness (Haertel, 1986), Hattie et al. used the four levels of the SOLO taxonomy to code students' work as artefacts of the teacher's lesson. Such coding related more to the depth of understanding that the teacher could accomplish, rather than the typical breadth of knowledge assessed by many traditional achievement tests. The following student essay (from a student in one of the classes observed for this study) would be classified as multistructural, as it only contains a series of unrelated ideas:

> If I could be any tree I would be a Redwood. A Redwood tree can live 4000 years. They are very strong and tall. They even name a forest after me. I think a redwood is a good tree to be. I would be the state tree of my state. I would be known all the way across the state. When somebody cut me down I would fall down real hard on the ground.

The student essay below would be classified as at least relational, as the major contributions are the series of related ideas that demonstrate a degree of integration and higher levels of abstraction:

> I think I would be a willow tree, because I go with the flow like a willow's limbs in the wind. I'm strong to stand up to in hard times and I come out OK. Like a willow in a storm, only the hardest things can get me down. I'm calm and easy going, part of nature, and cannot be missed.

Along with many other attributes, the students of teachers who received certification at the level of 'Highly accomplished' were most likely to exhibit the deep levels of SOLO (47 per cent of the artefacts from the passing teachers versus 27 per cent from the failing teachers were classified as relational or extended abstract). Hattie et al. concluded that

> expert teachers are more likely to lead students to deep rather than surface learning. These teachers will structure lessons to allow the opportunity for deep processing, set tasks that encourage the development of deep processing, and provide feedback and challenge for students to attain deep processing. (1997, p. 54)

A third example is the evaluation of gifted programs by Maguire (1988). He used the SOLO taxonomy as part of an evaluation of programs for bright and gifted students in elementary and junior high school. The students in the program often pursued the objectives of the program by working independently on projects, working together in small groups, or participating in a mentorship program.

> [This] diversity in learning activity may lead to uneven levels of knowledge about a particular content domain, in spite of the fact that levels of attainment of higher order objectives such as critical thinking may be uniformly high. In many situations the content provides a vehicle for instruction and may differ across students. It is not easy to find instruments that are relevant to program objectives, flexible enough to capture the creativity and divergence expected in performance from these kinds of students, yet at the same time possess utility and validity. (Maguire, 1988, p. 10)

Thus, to evaluate the program, Maguire devised two writing and three mathematics tasks, and the answers to these questions were coded into the SOLO levels. It was expected that the students in the gifted program would have a more positively skewed distribution (that there would be more in the higher levels) compared with students of similar ability not in the program.

Maguire argued that the SOLO approach seemed to tap a complex of deep understanding, motivation, and intuition as applied to a particular task, thus it was appropriate to assess complex achievements, deep understanding, higher order skills, and strategic flexibility (c.f. Snow, 1989). He found that students operating at the higher levels of the SOLO taxonomy (i.e. relational and extended abstract) tended to have higher scores on deep and achieving styles. Students who gave higher level responses to the SOLO writing tasks were also students who were more deeply engaged in their learning, while students who produced lower level products seemed to have more superficial approaches. When he compared the SOLO profiles from the students in the gifted program with a group of students in the regular classrooms identified as being gifted, and another group identified by the teachers as 'potentially gifted', there were no discernible differences. As Maguire concluded, the results provide 'a picture of a program that is not yet succeeding' (p. 9). The use of the SOLO levels, however, allowed this researcher to 'put outcomes on a common base while at the same time avoiding the confinement of standardized instruments. ...(SOLO) has been a very useful tool for detecting problem areas' (p. 9).

These three examples illustrate the diversity of situations where SOLO can be used. They demonstrate the power of SOLO for assessing interventions, teachers or any observational studies, and for evaluating programs. An under-utilised use of SOLO is in assessing item construction and test analysis.

## SOLO AND TEST ITEM CONSTRUCTION

A powerful advantage of the SOLO taxonomy is that it can readily be used to devise test items. There are three ways that items can be constructed according to SOLO. Either the questions are worded in an attempt to elicit particular SOLO level-type responses, or answers are scored depending on the evidence at the appropriate SOLO level, or a combination of these methods. For all three methods, the items can be analysed using traditional psychometrics, or by the classical model approach whereby estimates of reliability, difficulty and discrimination (e.g. point-biserials) are calculated and items are thereby dropped or improved. The alternative item response models can also be used whereby invariant estimates of the difficulty, discrimination and/or guessing can be estimated and items that maximise the desired test information functions are retained.

Each level of the taxonomy provides a working principle for an item. (Prestructural is not considered as it involves inappropriate processing that leads to incorrect solutions.) Either a set of up to four items (a testlet), or a series of items that can be coded into one of the four levels can be written (see Biggs, Holbrook, Ki, Lam, Li, Pong & Stimpson, 1989).

*Unistructural* – Contains one obvious piece of information coming directly from the stem. An answer is based on only one relevant aspect of the presented evidence, so that the conclusion is limited and likely to be dogmatic.

*Multistructural* – Requires using two or more discrete and separate pieces of information contained in the stem.

*Relational* – Uses two or more pieces of information each directly related to an integrated understanding of the information in the stem. Most or all of the evidence is accepted, and attempts are made to reconcile. Conflicting data may be placed into a system that accounts for the given context.

*Extended abstract* – Requires use of an abstract general principle or hypothesis that can be derived from, or suggested by, the information in the stem. There is recognition that the given example or question can lead to a more general case.

This item (Figure 7.1) illustrates the power of the SOLO taxonomy to provide students and teachers with a structure and a process for developing their own questions. In the first question, only a single piece of information is required. It is close to the recall sense of 'knowledge'. In the second question, the student is required to use two separate pieces of information (the position of Venus to the sun, and the position of Mars to the sun) to work out the answer. In the third question, it is necessary that the student sees the connection between the movement of a planet to the sun with the phenomenon of night and day. Finally, in the fourth question, the student has to go beyond the information provided in the item to deduce a more general principle as to the effects of the Earth's position to the sun and the effects on the climates and seasons.

Although the questions in the example above are open-ended, there is no requirement that a particular form of question is more advantageous at any of the levels of SOLO. Nor is there a requirement that every level of the SOLO taxonomy must be present in

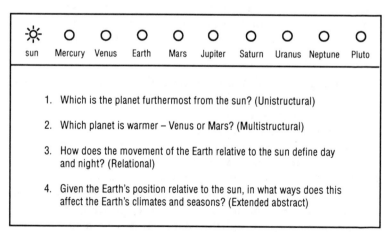

FIGURE 7.1 An item constructed according to SOLO
Source: see Note 1.

What is the value of D in the following statement? Show all working.

(84 / 42 ) * 7 = (84 * 7) / (D x 7)?

a.  42
b.  14
c. 294
d.  6

The answers, and reasons are:

| | | | |
|---|---|---|---|
| a. | 42 | Unistructural | There is no 42 on the right side; 2(84/42) = 42 |
| b. | 14 | Unistructural | The student has only calculated the left side where there is all information. In a and b, the student has only sought one piece of information. |
| c. | 294 | Multistructural | A step by step calculation, 2 * 7 = 588 / (D * 7) = 294. The student has used information [incorrectly] on both sides of the equation. |
| d. | 6 | Relational Extended abstract | Step by step calculation carried out correctly, or Balancing $\underline{84 * 7} = \underline{84 * 7}$ <br> $\phantom{Balancing\ }42 \qquad D * 7$ |

FIGURE 7.2    A SOLO multiple choice item

every question. Consider the multiple choice item in Figure 7.2.

In this item, the highest scored level could be Relational (if 6 is chosen), or the work provided may allow the teacher to score the item at either the Relational or Extended Abstract levels.

SOLO items can also be constructed in sets. As in many of the examples (e.g. the relation between the sun and planets), there is one stem, and several items aiming at progressively higher SOLO levels. Thus, there may be context effects as the student is forced to progress through a predetermined path of increasing complexity. The items are grouped into what Wainer and Kiely (1987) called 'testlets'. That is, 'a testlet is a group of items related to a single content area that is developed as a unit and contains a fixed number of predetermined paths that an examinee may follow' (p. 190). As a consequence, the item at each level is embedded in a testlet, and thus is context bound.

There are many advantages when using the testlet approach. First, if the total score of the student is then a score on each testlet (calibrated by either classical or IRT methods), then more stable information is gained (as the testlet score is based on a series of items) and there is information not only relating to the student's proficiency on the content matter but also relating to the depth or complexity level of the student's processing proficiency.

Second, testlets can improve the computer adaptive testing procedures (CAT). In CAT situations the computer program chooses an item to administer to the student depending on his or her performance on previous items. One approach may be to choose items at the multistructural level first, and then choose items at SOLO levels depending on the student's response to this multistructural item (of course, there can then be multiple alternative items at each level relating to the same stem). Such a sequential strategy may be most advantageous when the CAT covers materials across diverse subject areas (such as in tests of scholastic aptitude). It may, for example, be advantageous for the test developer to ensure that every student is given items across certain content areas. The differing length of the CAT could then be a function of the number of items within each testlet (i.e. the level of complexity would change, but the coverage of content may be more or less fixed).

Third, the items within each testlet can be investigated separately to ensure that they follow the desired patterning, and thus information can be gained about items, the performance of the items within the testlet, the performance of the item within the total test, and the performance of the testlet within the total test (e.g. see Rosenbaum, 1988). This can greatly improve the available diagnostics for developing excellent tests.

Several procedures for the analysis of SOLO-based test items have been suggested. Wilson (1989) recommended using the one-parameter partial credit model to analyse SOLO items. Using five in biology and five in chemistry (from Romberg, Collis, Donovan, Buchanan & Romberg, 1982; Romberg, Jurdack, Collis & Buchanan, 1982) he reported that this model displayed excellent fit for both persons and items. The levels of the SOLO taxonomy were ordered by item difficulty. Over the total number of items, students with low estimates of ability tended to get the unistructural correct, whereas with increased ability there was a tendency to get higher SOLO level items correct (see Figure 7.3). For example, on Item 2 (from the biology test), persons with low ability on the test (-2 to-1 on the total score scale, in logits (see Note 2)) tended to get only the

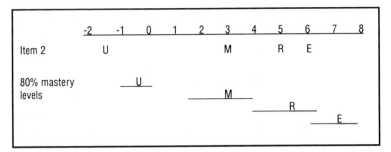

FIGURE 7.3 Ability and success on a SOLO item
Source: Adapted from Wilson, 1989.

Unistructural item correct, whereas those with 'middle' ability (3 logits) tended to also get the Multistructural item correct. As you move up the overall ability level, the probability of passing the higher SOLO levels increases.

A second very useful interpretation procedure was also suggested by Wilson (1989). The '80% mastery levels' at the bottom of Figure 7.3 indicate the region where the student is expected to master the questions of a given level in the taxonomy. Thus, if a student's ability is within a mastery level (say the score is 5) they have an 80 per cent probability of succeeding at all Unistructural and Multistructural items, and an 80 per cent chance of failing on the Extended Abstract items. This student would be expected to be in the Relational area of learning in biology.

Wilson (1989) also demonstrated how fit-statistics could be used to ascertain which items students are not performing to the expected level of their learning capabilities, and demonstrated the paucity of information that is derived when using a Guttman scalogram analysis. In a related paper, Wilson and Masters (1993) illustrated how the partial credit model could be used when there were null categories. For example, a test developer may create a SOLO testlet that does not include an item assessing extended abstract, and thus in the total test there are a series of testlets with most including items at all four levels, and some with a reduced number of levels. Thus, for these latter testlets, there is a 'logically null level'. Wilson and Adams (1993) introduced the ordered partition model, which is akin to the partial credit model, for the analyses of data (like SOLO) in which item responses are categorised and then scored in ordered levels (see also Biggs, 1990; Lam & Foong, 1996; Wilson & Iventosch, 1988).

A final application of the SOLO taxonomy in the realm of testing is its ability to classify items within a published test, regardless of whether it is constructed using the SOLO methods. For example, the questions on an achievement test (like the SAT or a teacher-made achievement test) can be classified into the four SOLO levels and this information used to either re-score the test or to ascertain the depth of learning that the teacher is aiming to assess (or maybe has aimed to teach). Further, we have participated in a school wide evaluation plan based on such an analyses. The principal wished to know the depth of learning in mathematics in his elementary school (Mort, personal communication). He first analysed the items that were being administered at each grade level to ensure that they covered the four levels of SOLO. The responses to these items were scored according to their SOLO level and a profile graph of each class compiled to show the percentage of students at each level (he also investigated content coverage). The principal and the teachers not only found this most informative, they also then set goals as to percentages desired at each level (and the teachers also profiled each student and set appropriate goals). The effect was a re-focusing of teaching away from exclusive content aims, towards more depth of processing aims, and a consequential leap in the percentage of students at the higher levels of SOLO.

## SOLO COMPARED WITH THE MAJOR ALTERNATIVE: BLOOM'S TAXONOMY

Modern test theory is at a crossroads. The traditional model is rooted in classical test theory and more recently in item response theory. Both theories involve applying mathematical models to 'true scores' or to 'expected responses' from a sample of test items. These hypothetical constructs aim to represent traits or the proficiency of students to answer various items. As Mislevy (1996) has stated, these theories attend to

> the problem stimulus strictly from the assessor's point of view, administering the same tasks to all examinees and recording outcomes in terms

of behavior categories applied in the same way for all examinees. Behavior constitutes direct evidence about behavioral tendencies. (p. 391)

A more defensible model is derived from cognitive psychology which makes claims such as: we interpret experience and solve problems by mapping them to internal models; these internal models must be constructed; and the constructed models result in situated knowledge that is gradually extended and decontexualised to interpret other structurally similar situations (Mislevy, 1996, p. 389). Thus, we need measurement models that acknowledge that different knowledge structures can lead to the same behaviour, where observed behaviour constitutes indirect evidence about cognitive structure, and we need to assess the degree or depth to which the students understand or process. The most dramatic example of a test writing technology based on the earlier 'behavioural tendency' models is Bloom's taxonomy, whereas an excellent example of a test writing technology based on the cognitive processing model is Biggs and Collis's SOLO taxonomy.

For the past four decades the development of most measures of cognition and achievement have been based on Bloom's taxonomy of educational objectives (Bloom, Engelhart, Furst Hill, & Krathwohl, 1956). This model proposes six levels: knowledge, comprehension, application, analysis, synthesis and evaluation. Knowledge refers to those behaviours and test situations that emphasise the remembering, either by recognition or recall, of ideas, material, or phenomena. Comprehension involves translation, interpretation or extrapolation of knowledge. Application requires the student to know an abstraction well enough that he or she can correctly demonstrate its use when asked to do so. Analysis emphasises the breakdown of material into its constituent parts and detection of the relationships of the parts and of the way they are organised. Synthesis involves the putting together of elements and parts to form a whole. Evaluation is defined as the making of judgements about the value, for some purpose, of ideas, works, solutions, methods, materials, etc. (definitions are taken from Bloom et al., 1956).

The taxonomy was published in 1956, has sold over a million copies, has been translated into several languages, and has been cited thousands of times. The Bloom taxonomy has been extensively used in teacher education to suggest learning and teaching strategies, has formed the basis of many tests developed by teachers (at least while they were in teacher training), and has been used to evaluate many tests. It is thus remarkable that the taxonomy has been subject to so little research or evaluation. Most of the evaluations are philosophical treatises noting, among other criticisms, that there is no evidence for the invariance of these stages, or claiming that the taxonomy is not based on any known theory of learning or teaching (Calder, 1983; Furst, 1981).

There are many similarities between the Bloom and SOLO taxonomies. It is necessary when using both taxonomies to know the context of learning, and it is expected that the questions asked follow from some form of instruction or prior exposure to the information required. There is also the premise that the concepts in the instruction are hierarchical, although SOLO is less affected by this assumption.

There are also fundamental differences between the Bloom and SOLO taxonomies. The Bloom taxonomy presupposes that there is a necessary relationship between the questions asked and the responses to be elicited (see Schrag, 1989), whereas in the SOLO taxonomy both the questions and the answers can be at differing levels. Whereas Bloom separates 'knowledge' from the intellectual abilities or process that operate on this 'knowledge' (Furst, 1981), the SOLO taxonomy is primarily based on the processes of understanding used by the students when answering the prompts. Knowledge, therefore, permeates across all levels of the SOLO taxonomy.

Bloom has argued that his taxonomy is related not only to complexity but also to an order of difficulty such that problems requiring behaviour at one level should be answered more correctly before tackling problems requiring behaviour at a higher level. Although there may be measurement advantages to this increasing difficulty, this is not a necessary requirement of the SOLO method. It is possible for an item at the relational level, for example, to be constructed so that it is less difficult than an item at the unistructural level. For example, an item aiming to elicit relational responses might be 'How does the movement of the Earth relative to the sun define day and night'. This may be easier (depending on instruction, etc.) than a unistructural item that asks 'What does celestial rotation mean?' Thus, there can be certain aspects of knowledge that are more complex than aspects of analyses or evaluation. Other writers also have noted that activities aimed at a lower level of Bloom's taxonomy may activate mental operations placed in the higher levels. For example, Pring (1971) claimed that comprehension of principles must include the ability to apply principles to new situations (see also Furst, 1981).

Bloom's taxonomy is not accompanied by criteria for judging the outcome of the activity (Ennis, 1985), whereas SOLO is explicitly useful for judging the outcomes. Take, for example, a series of art questions suggested by Hamben (1984).

*Knowledge*: Who painted Guernica?
*Comprehension*: Describe the subject matter of Guernica.
*Application*: Relate the theme of Guernica to a current event.
*Analysis*: What compositional principles did Picasso use in Guernica?
*Synthesis*: Imagine yourself as one of the figures in Guernica and describe your life history?
*Evaluation*: What is your opinion of Picasso's Guernica?

When using Bloom's taxonomy, the supposition is that the question leads to the particular type of Bloom response. There is no necessary relationship, however, as a student may respond with a very deep response to the supposedly lower order question: 'Describe the subject matter of Guernica'. Similarly, a student may provide a very surface response to 'What is your opinion of Picasso's Guernica?'. When using the SOLO taxonomy, either the questions would be written in a different manner, or the test scorer would concentrate on classifying the responses only. An example of rewriting to maximise the correspondence between the question asked and the answer expected is:

*Unistructural*. Who painted Guernica?
*Multistructural*. Outline at least two compositional principles that Picasso used in Guernica.
*Relational*. Relate the theme of Guernica to a current event.
*Extended Abstract*. What do you consider Picasso was saying via his painting of Guernica?

The greatest criticism of the Bloom taxonomy is that there is little evidence supporting the invariance and hierarchical nature of the six levels. Let us recall that Bloom claimed these six levels 'represent something of a hierarchical order of the different classes of objectives. As we have defined them, the objectives in one class are likely to make use of and be built on the behaviors found in the preceding classes in this list' (1956, p. 18). A prior condition of the hierarchy is that there is common understanding of the various levels. Ennis (1985) argued that analysis relates to many levels.

> Analysis of a chemical compound, analysis of an argument, analysis of a word, analysis of an opponent's weaknesses in a basketball game, and analysis of the political situation in South Africa seem like such different activities that we might very well wonder just what we are supposed to teach under the label 'analysis'. (p. 45)

Calder (1983) was much more critical of all Bloom's levels, and provided illustration of the conceptual morass that followed from a 'classification filled with nebulous terms (which) makes it impossible to detect similarities in objectives in different subject areas, and frustrates efforts to develop precise principles of teaching and testing bearing on sharply delineated objectives' (p. 297). As an example, he considered the notion of 'knowledge', which includes cases where the student *relates* definitions of terms to specific instances as well as *recalls* definitions verbatim. This first instance could be confused with 'relating abstractions to concrete instances' which is defined by Bloom as 'Comprehension'. Further, he claimed that 'too many categories contain a pantechnicon assortment of skills' (Calder, 1983, p. 298). Such conceptual confusions make it difficult to expect there to be a hierarchy.

Kropp and Stoker (1966) used a simplex analysis and found on one test (relating to Atomic Structure) that synthesis and evaluation were placed between knowledge and comprehension. However, on other tests related to Glaciers and to Economic Growth synthesis was located between knowledge and comprehension, and on a test related to Earthquakes, the levels of Bloom's taxonomy were as expected. Analysing the same data, Smith (1968) found support for the order of comprehension, application and analysis only, Miller, Snowman and O'Hara (1979) found Evaluation to follow Comprehension rather than Synthesis, and Madaus, Woods and Nuttall (1973) concluded that their results did not support the cumulative hierarchy of the model (see also Gall et al., 1978; Kropp, Stoker & Bashaw, 1966; Klein, 1972; Kunen, Cohen, & Solman 1981; Ryan 1973, 1974; Seddon, 1978). Instead, Madaus et al. proposed a

Y-shaped structure, in 'which the stem of the Y originates at Knowledge and goes to Comprehension, one branch of the Y goes from Comprehension to Application to Synthesis, and the other branch goes from Comprehension to Analysis' (p. 73). The Kropp and Stoker data were analysed using structural equation modeling by Hill and McGaw (1981) who concluded that knowledge did not fit into the hierarchy at all.

A possible reason for the 'mis'placement of synthesis is that many evaluation activities or processes require less constructive or extensive semantic activity than do the synthesis tasks. As Kunen, Cohen & Solman (1981) claimed,

> evaluative activities are more connected with considering the value, worth, or appropriateness of given information than on the construction of new information, as is the goal in Synthetic tasks. Evaluative skills may not represent the most efficacious level to use to orient students to instructional material when the goals are acquisition and retention of information. Tasks that tap synthetic or creative activities appear to be more effective in promoting learning. (p. 208)

## APPLICABILITY OF SOLO TO VARIOUS CONTENT DOMAINS

A particular feature of the SOLO model is its applicability across content domains, clearly demonstrated in the many tests that have been written across a range of school subject areas. Biggs and Collis deliberately started with poetry, when they devised SOLO, as that was considered one of the more difficult domains in which to write questions. It is important to note, however, that the SOLO model does not claim to be content or value free. Such neutrality is not possible (Furst, 1981; Ormell, 1974). The Bloom taxonomy is more attentive to the outcomes than the process of learning and instruction, whereas the SOLO taxonomy delineates processes of thinking rather than end-states of processing knowledge. These processes may vary markedly across subject domains.

A major criticism of Bloom's taxonomy is that the taxonomy is premised on a distinction between process and content. Furst (1981), for example, was particularly trenchant in his criticism of Bloom and brought together an arsenal of writers from Wittgenstein (1953), Hirst (1974) and Ormell (1974) to illustrate the problem. In more modern writings, Shulman (1987) has written extensively on the importance of embedding curricula developments within the context of the subject matter. The SOLO levels are premised on 'understanding' whereas Bloom's taxonomy excludes this category. Such 'understanding' can be content-specific. Ormell (1974, 1979) was particularly critical of Bloom for excluding understanding, and claimed that the test for understanding is whether the student can answer a connected range of 'if ... then ...' questions about some situation, preferably a hypothetical one. This is akin to at least the relational and certainly the extended abstract levels.

Bloom's taxonomy is more applicable to educational objectives formulated in precise and specific terms. As Bloom stated 'it cannot be used to classify educational plans which are made in such a way that ... the student behaviors cannot be specified' (p. 15). As Krathwohl, Bloom & Masia (1964) claimed, the taxonomy is concerned only with the behavioural repertoire of students, that is, with their abilities and inclinations. Popham (1987) has traced the evolution of Bloom's taxonomy to the behavioural objectives movement, such that they 'became part of the lexicon employed by those who worked with educational objectives' (p. 35).

The SOLO taxonomy can be adapted to each content domain, although performances on the SOLO, certainly more so than for Bloom, can be summed across content domains to form an easily generalisable statement about an individual's level of processing or depth of understanding. As with many aggregations, much information can be lost. The following examples serve to illustrate how teachers can use the taxonomy in several different content areas.

*In Poetry*: unistructural items can ask about a relevant feature such as a comment on rhyme, a concrete point made by the poem, a repetition form of the poem involving no interpretation. Multistructural items can ask for several concrete points supportive of one interpretation, one or more substantive points together with comments on a structural aspect of the poem, or a paraphrase of the poem involving substantive interpretations of independent points. Relational items can require a more coherent framework for interpreting most or all of the poem, but typically such items are limited to the context set by the poet. Extended abstract items concern more universal statements of the poem, alternative explanations of the poem, and/or reference to more abstract structures or features inherent in the poem.

*In History*: Biggs and Collis (1982) argued that there were at least six major types of processes involved in understanding history. They then provided examples of questions that can elicit responses at either of the four levels. The six major types of historical processing are:

1 Drawing conclusions from a display of information, such as providing answers to the question 'What reasons did the squatters have for defying the government's regulations?'
2 Making value judgements about an historical event, such as providing a passage about William the Conqueror and asking, 'Do you think William was cruel?'
3 Reconciling conflicting evidence from different sources, such as providing two extracts about life in the colonies, and asking 'Do you think the colonists were well off?'
4 Constructing a plausible interpretation from incomplete data, such as providing information about Stonehenge and asking 'Do you think Stonehenge must have been a fort and not a temple? Why do you think that?'
5 Understanding historical terms and social concepts, such as 'What is a king?'
6 Inducing meaning of a concept from a context, such as providing an historical text and asking what a particular concept means.

To illustrate the SOLO procedure, consider the question 'What is a king?' A unistructural response could be 'The King lives at Buckingham Palace'; a multistructural response could be 'A king is very important and rich, and a famous man from a royal family'. A relational response could be 'A king is a ruler of a country'. An extended abstract response could be: 'A king is a male sovereign ruler of an independent state'.

*In Mathematics*: Collis and Romberg (1992) have published a test called the 'Collis-Romberg Mathematical Problem Solving Profiles' (see also Collis, 1983). The aim is to provide a profile so that teachers can quickly and accurately determine a 9- to 17-year-old student's progress through a range of mathematical problem solving skills. There are five testlets or, as Collis and Romberg call them, super-items for each domain: algebra, chance and data, measurement, number, and space. Within each testlet there are four questions, one aimed at each SOLO level. A profile can then be drawn of the student's SOLO level across the five domains. Collis and Romberg provide an excellent set of instructional suggestions for advancing the student along each one level.

*In Geography:* SOLO items can relate to interpreting a map and drawing conclusions, accounting for change in several characteristics from a written description, or explaining natural phenomena (see Courtney, 1986; Stimpson, 1989). For example:

Why does it get dark at night?

*Unistructural:* Because the sun goes to the other side of the world.

*Multistructural:* Because the earth is spinning and the sun is going round the earth.

*Relational:* It gets dark at night because the sun goes around the earth once for 12 hours and for the other 12 hours it is day as the sun is around the opposite side of the earth.

*Extended abstract:* The earth is spherical in shape and rotates about its north-south axis. As it rotates, at any one time the half of the Earth's sphere facing the sun will be in light while the opposite half will be in shadow. As the earth is rotating continuously, a point on the earth's surface will pass alternately through the lighted half and the shaded half.

Two examples of items in *Languages* are:

Translate: 'sa table de nuit', 'il avait raison'

| | | |
|---|---|---|
| *Unistructural:* | His table of the night | He had a reason |
| *Multistructural:* | His table at night | He had a reason |
| *Relational:* | His night table | He was right |
| *Extended abstract:* | His bedside table | It was just as well |

Other examples can be found in science (Collis & Davey, 1986), economics (Pong, 1989), chemistry (Holbrook, 1989), computer studies (Ki, 1989), and assessing attitudes towards teenage pregnancy (Kryzanowski, 1988).

## ADVANTAGES OF THE SOLO MODEL FOR EVALUATION OF STUDENT LEARNING

There are several advantages of the SOLO model over the Bloom taxonomy in the evaluation of student learning. These advantages concern not only item construction and scoring, but incorporate features of the process of evaluation that pay attention to how students learn, and how teachers devise instructional procedures to help students use progressively more complex cognitive processes. Unlike the Bloom taxonomy, which tends to be used more by teachers than by students, the SOLO can be taught to students so that they can learn to write progressively more difficult answers or prompts. There is a closer parallel to how teachers teach and how students learn. Both teachers and students often progress from more surface to deeper constructs and this is mirrored in the four levels of the SOLO taxonomy. There is no necessary progression in the manner of teaching or learning in the Bloom taxonomy.

Items can be easily written at all levels, across all subjects, and there is no requirement that a student reaches a certain level of capability before they can answer items at the highest levels. The notion of extended abstract, for example, can be interpreted relative to the proficiency of the students. Six-year-old students can be taught to derive general principles and suggest hypotheses, though obviously to a different level of abstraction and detail than their older peers. Using the SOLO method, it is relatively easy to construct items to assess such abstractions.

The SOLO taxonomy not only suggests an item writing methodology, but the same taxonomy can be used to score the items. The marker assesses each response to establish either the number of ideas (one = unistructural; $\geq$ two = multistructural), or the degree of interrelatedness (directly related or abstracted to more general principles). This can lead to more dependability of scoring. The model allows for partial knowledge, as progressively, deeper questions can be asked. It may be important, for the assumptions of some test models, to ensure that the answer to a more difficult question is not premised on getting a more surface item correct. The SOLO taxonomy also resolves many of the issues relating to whether global or analytical marking should be used. The items can be written as testlets such that a mixture of analytical marking (particularly at the first two levels) and global marking (at the last two levels) can be effectively combined. It is rare to see scores reported at the six levels of the Bloom's taxonomy, whereas scoring at each level of SOLO is not only possible but most informative (e.g. see in previous examples related to mathematics).

Unlike the experience of some with the Bloom taxonomy (Anderson, 1994; Fairbrother, 1975), it is relatively easy to identify and categorise the SOLO levels. For example, Biggs and Collis (1982) used two judges to code a series of history questions and reported a 79 per cent agreement in categorising the responses into the correct level, 11 per cent at one level difference, and only 9 per cent at more than one level difference. In one study, Hattie and Purdie (1994) asked 30 teachers to classify 19 multiple choice items taken directly from Bloom et al. (1956). Half the group classified the items into Bloom levels and then into SOLO levels; the other half did the same but in counterbalanced order. The average accuracy was 60 per cent correctly allocated into the exact SOLO levels and 96 per cent at the level of one level difference, and 40 per cent into the exact Bloom levels and 75 per cent at the level of one level difference. While neither accuracy rate is at a level that inspires confidence, the figure does suggest a greater 'user friendliness' of the SOLO taxonomy.

SOLO can also be used to address many vexing issues in measurement. For example, items in an 'item bank' can be classified according to the various levels of SOLO. Such information can assist in computer adaptive tests for choosing appropriate items to be administered, for ensuring that sufficient items at each level have been presented prior to stopping the adaptive testing, and for scoring such adaptive tests.

Similarly, teachers could be encouraged to use the 'plus one' principle when choosing appropriate learning material for students. That is, the teacher can aim to move the student one level higher in the taxonomy by appropriate choice of learning material and instructional sequencing.

SOLO can be used for operationalising the quality of learning and standards for teachers and students to aim for with respect to particular tasks. For example, the teacher could prescribe a minimum of $r$ per cent unistructural, $s$ per cent multistructural, $t$ per cent relational, and $u$ per cent extended abstract for a particular course, class, or school. Further, SOLO can be used to match students to instruction. Each SOLO level is a metric of the complexity of the material, and thus it is easier for a test developer/test user to select a test relevant to the performance of the students.

## CONCLUSIONS

One of the major reasons why Bloom's taxonomy has survived is that there have been few alternative models. There have been some minor variants (for example, Miller, Williams & Haladyna, 1978; O'Neil, 1979; Roid & Haladyna, 1982) and there have been taxonomies based on learning theories (for example, Ausubel & Robinson, 1969; Gagne, 1977; Merrill, 1971), but none have had the impact or lasting influence of Bloom's taxonomy. We believe the SOLO taxonomy offers teachers of students at all levels an alternative tool that can be used not only as a basis for selecting items for a test (as was the original intention of the Bloom taxonomy), but which also can provide a structure to help teachers devise appropriate instructional processes, engage in curriculum and task analysis, make judgements about the quality of learning that takes place in the classroom, and instigate appropriate remedial procedures where necessary.

As Anderson (1994) has noted, 'teachers may have beliefs about teaching and learning that are inconsistent with using the (Bloom) taxonomy' (p. 140). The testing movement seems to value higher order thinking but then confuses this with 'above knowledge'. Whereas the Bloom levels reflect a teacher-imposed view of what it means to have achieved full mastery in a given task (i.e. to know, to comprehend, to apply, to analyse, to synthesise, and to evaluate), the SOLO levels arise from an understanding of the process of student learning, and a concern to develop 'qualitative criteria of learning that have formative as well as summative value' (Biggs & Collis, 1982). The power of the SOLO taxonomy to evaluate the quality as well as the quantity of learning is a feature absent from many of the procedures typically used by teachers to make judgements about student learning. In this respect we have provided numerous examples, broad in scope, of the capacity of the SOLO model to form the basis of criterion-referenced measures of the quality of student learning. The examples we have given have been drawn mainly from work with primary and secondary school students. As amply illustrated by the work of Boulton-Lewis (1995, and this volume), however, the relevance of the SOLO taxonomy to the shaping and assessing of learning in higher education can be demonstrated just as easily. Moreover, if we can help tertiary students in Education (both pre-service and in-service) to understand and be competent users of the SOLO model, we believe we will have teachers who are better equipped to provide quality learning experiences for their students and to evaluate the outcomes of those experiences.

A feature of the SOLO model that we have highlighted in this chapter is the way in which it reflects the complexity of human learning. Unlike the assumptions on which the Bloom taxonomy has been predicated, there is no separation between content and context, and there is a recognition of the role of both the student and the teacher in student learning. The level at which the student is operating can be assessed, and the teacher can plan lessons and classroom activities aimed at helping students progress from simple unistructural responses to more complex ones involving relational and abstract thinking. We have provided examples from various content domains demonstrating the applicability of the SOLO taxonomy to a range of teaching aspects. In this chapter we have not been able to outline the full range of possibilities of the use of SOLO in the various subject domains. Biggs and Collis (1992), however, provide many examples of how teachers can use the taxonomy not only to assess content knowledge, but to assist students to explore the full range of possibilities related to a given task. In poetry, for instance, teachers can use the taxonomy just as easily to explore students' knowledge of the structural features of a poem as they can to evaluate students' grasp of its metaphorical meaning, or to explore students' affective reactions. No less possible is the ability of a teacher of mathematics to use the taxonomy to devise instructional methods aimed at developing reasoning, creativity and positive attitudes in their subject.

There is a clear distinction in the SOLO model of learning between learning and development, as is evident in the hierarchy of stages (prestructural, unistructural, multistructural, relational, and extended abstract). Learning theories based on Piagetian stages of development proceed from assumptions of a stable, linear, and irreversible sequence of steps that lead to prescriptions about what should be taught, when, and how. On the other hand, SOLO extends the notion of 'readiness' by shifting the focus of attention from an assumed stage of development of the student to the quality of the response the student gives to a particular task. Nevertheless, it is clear from many of the examples we have cited that there is a hierarchy of levels in the SOLO taxonomy such that students move from the simple to the more complex in terms of their responses to a task. The challenge for teachers, according to Biggs and Collis (1992), is to attend to the transition of students from one level to the next by using the principle of 'plus one'.

In the conclusion to their book, Biggs and Collis (1982) noted that 'If these frankly speculative suggestions are ultimately supported by research, then what started out as a descriptive model for a circumscribed context – school learning – might contain within it the seeds of a theory of learning with a wide range of application.' Fifteen years hence, there is ample evidence to demonstrate the power of the SOLO model in educational contexts in which age, subject matter, and instructional processes are widely varied. In this chapter we have presented tangible evidence of the capacity of the SOLO model to inform the practice of educators at all levels of student learning.

## Notes

1  We thank Jackie Bolt, a trainee teacher, for suggesting this item.
2  A logit is a unit of measure, used in Rasch analysis of test data, that indicates the degree of difficulty of an item when compared to other items in the same test. For more information about Rasch models, see, for example, Wright & Masters, 1982.
3  This chapter was written with the support of a grant from the Australian Research Council.

## References

Anderson, L.W. (1994). Research on teaching and teacher education. In L.W. Anderson, & L.A. Sosniak (Eds.), *Bloom's taxonomy: A forty-year retrospective. Ninety-third Yearbook of the National Society for the Study of Education: Part II* (pp. 126–145). Chicago: University of Chicago Press.

Ausubel, D.P., & Robinson, F.G. (1969). *School learning: An introduction to educational psychology*. New York: Holt, Rinehart & Winston.

Biggs, J.B. (1985). *Learning Processes Questionnaire*. Melbourne: Australian Council for Educational Research.

Biggs, J.B. (1987). *Student approaches to learning and studying*. Melbourne: Australian Council for Educational Research.

Biggs, J.B. (1990). Asian students' approaches to learning: Implications for teaching overseas students. In M. Kratzing (Ed.), *Eighth Australian Learning and Language Conference* (pp. 1–51). Queensland University Technology Counselling Services.

Biggs, J.B., & Collis, K.F. (1982). *Evaluating the quality of learning: The SOLO taxonomy (Structure of the Observed Learning Outcome)*. New York: Academic.

Biggs, J.B., & Collis, K.F. (1989). Toward a model of school-based curriculum development and assessment using the SOLO taxonomy. *Australian Journal of Education, 33,* 151–163.

Biggs, J.B., Holbrook, J.B., Ki, W.W., Lam, R.Y.H., Li, W.O., Pong, W.Y., & Stimpson, P.G. (1989, November). *An objective format for evaluating the quality of learning in various secondary subjects.* A symposium presented to the sixth annual Conference of the Hong Kong Educational Research Association. Hong Kong: City Polytechnic of Hong Kong.

Bloom, B.S., Engelhart, M.D., Furst, E.J., Hill, W.H., & Krathwohl, D. (1956). *Taxonomy of educational objectives: The cognitive domain.* New York: McKay.

Boulton-Lewis, G.M. (1995). The SOLO taxonomy as a means of shaping and assessing learning in Higher Education. *Higher Education Research and Development, 14,* 143–154.

Boulton-Lewis, G.M., Dart, B., & Brownlee, J. (1995). Student teachers' integration of formal and informal knowledge of learning and teaching. *Research and Development in Higher Education, 18,* 136–142.

Boulton-Lewis, G.M., Wilss, L., & Mutch, S. (1996). Teachers as adult learners: Their knowledge of their own learning and implications for teaching. *Higher Education, 32,* 89–106.

Calder, J.R. (1983). In the cells of Bloom's taxonomy. *Journal of Curriculum Studies, 15,* 291–302.

Chi, M., Feltovich, P., & Glaser, R. (1981). Categorization and representation of physics problems by experts and novices. *Cognitive Science, 5,* 121–152.

Collis, K.F. (1983). Development of a group test of mathematical understanding using superitem/SOLO technique. *Journal of Science and Mathematics Education in Southeast Asia, 6,* 5–14.

Collis, K.F., & Biggs, J.B. (1982). Developmental determinants of qualitative aspects of school learning. In G.T. Evans (Ed.), *Learning and teaching cognitive skills.* Melbourne: Australian Council for Educational Research.

Collis, K.F., & Davey, H.A. (1986). A technique for evaluating skills in high school science. *Journal of Research in Science Teaching, 23,* 651–663.

Collis, K.F., & Romberg, T.A. (1992). *Collis-Romberg mathematical problem solving profiles.* Melbourne: Australian Council for Educational Research.

Courtney, T.D. (1986). The significance of the SOLO taxonomy for learning and teaching in geography. *Geographical Education, 5,* 47–50.

deGroot, A.D. (1965). *Thought and choice in chess.* The Hague: Mouton.

Ennis, R.H. (1985). A logical basis for measuring critical thinking skills. *Educational Leadership, 43*(2), 45–48.

Entwistle, N.J (1988). Approaches to learning and perception of the learning environment. *Higher Education, 22,* 201–204.

Fairbrother, R.W. (1975). The reliability of teachers' judgments of the abilities being tested by multiple-choice items. *Educational Research, 17,* 202–210.

Furst, E.J. (1981). Bloom's taxonomy of educational objectives for the cognitive domain: Philosophical and educational issues. *Review of Educational Research, 15,* 175–198.

Gagne, R. (1977). *Conditions of learning.* New York: Holt, Rinehart & Winston.

Gall. M.D., Ward, B.A., Berliner, D.C., Cohen, L.S., Winne, P.H., Elashoff, J.D., & Stanton, G.C. (1978). Effects of questioning techniques and recitation on student learning. *American Educational Research Journal, 15,* 175–198.

Haertel, E. (1986). The valid use of student performance measures for teacher evaluation. *Educational Evaluation and Policy Analysis, 8,* 45–60.

Hamben, K. (1984). An art criticism questioning strategy within the framework of Bloom's taxonomy. *Studies in Art Education: A journal of issues and research, 26,* 41–50.

Harper, G., & Kember, D. (1989). Interpretation of factor analyses from the Approaches to Studying Inventory. *British Journal of Educational Psychology, 59,* 66–74.

Hattie, J.A., Biggs, J., & Purdie, N. (1996). Effects of learning skills intervention on student learning: A meta-analysis. *Review of Research in Education, 66,* 99–136.

Hattie, J.A., Clinton, J.M., Thompson, M., & Schmidt-Davis, H. (1997). *Identifying 'Highly accomplished teachers': A validation study.* Greensboro, NC: National Board for Professional Teaching Standards, Technical Analysis Group, Center for Educational Research and Evaluation, University of North Carolina-Greensboro.

Hattie, J.A., & Purdie, N. (1994). *Using the SOLO taxonomy to classify test items.* Unpublished manuscript, The University of Western Australia, Graduate School of Education, Western Australia.

Hill, P.W., & McGaw, B. (1981). Testing the simplex assumption underlying Bloom's taxonomy. *American Educational Research Journal, 18,* 93–101.

Hirst, P.H. (1974). *Knowledge and the curriculum: A collection of philosophical papers.* London: Routledge and Kegan Paul.

Holbrook, J.B. (1989). *Writing chemistry items using the SOLO taxonomy.* A symposium presented to the sixth annual Conference of the Hong Kong Educational Research Association. Hong Kong: City Polytechnic of Hong Kong.

Ki, W.W. (1989). *Computer studies.* A symposium presented to the sixth annual Conference of the Hong Kong Educational Research Association. Hong Kong: City Polytechnic of Hong Kong.

Klein, M.F. (1972). Use of taxonomy of educational objectives (cognitive domain) in constructing tests for primary school pupils. *The Journal of Experimental Education, 40*, 38–50.

Krathwohl, D.R. Bloom, B.S., & Masia, B.B.(1964). *Taxonomy of educational objectives: The classification of educational goals: Handbook II: Affective domain.* New York: David McKay.

Kropp, R.P., & Stoker, H.W. (1966). *The construction and validation of tests of the cognitive processes as described in the taxonomy of educational objectives.* Tallahassee, FL: Florida State University. (ERIC Document Reproduction No. ED 010 044)

Kropp, R.P., Stoker, H.W., & Bashaw, W.L. (1966). The validation of the taxonomy of educational objectives. *Journal of Experimental Education, 34*, 69–76.

Kryzanowski, E.M. (1988). *Attitudes towards adolescent pregnancy and parenthood.* Unpublished doctoral dissertation. Department of Educational Psychology, University of Alberta.

Kunen, S., Cohen, R., & Solman, R. (1981). A levels-of-processing analysis of Bloom's taxonomy. *Journal of Educational Psychology, 73*, 202–211.

Lam, R., & Foong, Y.Y. (1996). *Rasch analysis of math SOLO taxonomy levels using hierarchical items in testlets.* ERIC Documentation Reproduction ED 398 271.

Madaus, G.F., Woods, E.M., & Nuttall, R.L. (1973). A causal model analysis of Bloom's taxonomy. *American Educational Research Journal, 10*, 253–262.

Maguire, T.O. (1988, December). *The use of the SOLO taxonomy for evaluating a program for gifted students.* Paper presented at the Annual Conference of the Australian Association for Research in Education, University of New England, Armidale, NSW.

Marton, F., & Säljö, R. (1976). On qualitative differences in learning: I. Outcome and process. *British Journal of Educational Psychology, 46*, 4–11.

Marton, F., & Säljö, R. (1984). Approaches to learning. In F. Marton, D. Hounsell, & N. Entwistle (Eds.), *The experience of learning* (pp. 36–55). Edinburgh, Scotland: Scottish Academic Press.

Merrill, M.D. (1971). Necessary educational condition for defining instructional outcomes. *Educational Technology, 11*, 34–39.

Miller, H.G., Williams, R.G., & Haladyna, T.M. (1978). *Beyond facts: Objective ways to measure thinking.* Englewood Cliffs: Educational Technology

Miller, H.G., Snowman, J., & O'Hara, T. (1979). Application of alternative statistical techniques to examine the hierarchical ordering in Bloom's taxonomy. *American Educational Research Journal, 16*, 241–248.

Mislevy, R.J. (1996). Test theory reconceived. *Journal of Educational Measurement, 33*, 379–416.

O'Neil, H.F., Jr. (1979). *Procedures for instructional systems development*. New York: Academic Press.

Ormell, C.P. (1974). Bloom's taxonomy and the objectives of education. *Educational Research, 17*, 3–18.

Ormell, C.P. (1979). The problem of analyzing understanding. *Educational Research, 22*, 32–38.

Pong, W.Y. (1989). *Economics*. A symposium presented to the sixth annual Conference of the Hong Kong Educational Research Association. Hong Kong: City Polytechnic of Hong Kong.

Popham, W.J. (1987). Two-plus decades of educational objectives. *International Journal of Educational Research, 11*, 31–41.

Pring, R. (1971). Bloom's taxonomy: A philosophical critique. *Cambridge Journal of Education, 1*, 83–91.

Roid, G.H., & Haladyna, T.M. (1982). *A technology for test-item writing*. New York: Academic Press.

Romberg, T.A., Collis, K.F., Donovan, B.F., Buchanan, A.E., & Romberg, T.A. (1982). *The development of mathematical problem-solving superitems* (A Report of NIE/ECS item development project). Madison, WI: Center for Educational Research.

Romberg, T.A., Jurdak, M.E., Collis, K.F., & Buchanan, A.E. (1982). *Construct validity of a set of mathematical superitems* (A report of the NIE/ECS item development project). Madison, WI: Center for Educational Research.

Rosenbaum, P.R. (1988). Item bundles. *Psychometrika, 53*, 349–360.

Ryan, F.L. (1973). Differentiated effects of levels of questioning in student achievement. *Journal of Experimental Education, 41*, 63–67.

Ryan, F.L. (1974). The effects of social studies achievement in multiple student responding to differentiated levels of questioning. *Journal of Experimental Education, 42*, 91–95.

Schrag, F. (1989). Are there levels of thinking? *Teachers College Record, 90*(4), 529–533.

Seddon, G.M. (1978). The properties of Bloom's taxonomy of educational objectives for the cognitive domain. *Review of Educational Research, 48*, 303–323.

Shulman, L.S. (1987). Knowledge and teaching: Foundations of the new reform. *Harvard Educational Review, 19*(2), 4–14.

Smith, R.B. (1968). An empirical examination of the assumptions underlying the 'Taxonomy of educational objectives for the cognitive domain'. *Journal of Educational Measurement, 5*, 125–127.

Snow, R.E. (1989). Toward assessment of cognitive and cognitive structures in learning. *Educational Researcher, 18*, 8–14.

Stimpson, P. (1989). *Viability of the SOLO test format: The case of geography*. A symposium presented to the sixth annual Conference of the Hong Kong Educational Research Association. Hong Kong: City Polytechnic of Hong Kong.

Wainer, H., & Kiely, G.L. (1987). Item clusters and computerized adaptive testing: A case for testlets. *Journal of Educational Measurement, 24*, 185–201.

Wilson, M. (1989). A comparison of deterministic and probabilistic approaches to measuring learning structures. *Australian Journal of Education, 33*, 127–140.

Wilson, M., & Adams, R.J. (1993). Marginal maximum likelihood estimation for the ordered partition model. *Journal of Educational Statistics, 18*, 69–90.

Wilson, M., & Iventosch, L. (1988). Using the partial credit model to investigate responses to structural sub-tests. *Applied Psychological Measurement, 1*, 319–334.

Wilson, M. & Masters, G.N. (1993). The partial credit model and null categories. *Psychometrika, 58*, 87–99.

Wittgenstein, L. (1953). *Philosophical investigations*. Oxford: Basil Blackwell.

Wright, B.D. & Masters, G.N. (1982). *Rating scale analysis*. Chicago, IL: MESA.

# CHAPTER 8

# Towards a Theory of Quality in Higher Education

*Ference Marton*

## INTRODUCTION

I have always been obsessed with views and the best view I know is that of the harbour and the mainland from the hills of Hong Kong Island, where the University of Hong Kong is located, in the upper part of the Western District. Robert Black College, where visitors of the University reside, is in the corner of the area which is closest to Victoria Peak, the highest point in Hong Kong. Although trees and tall buildings block much of the view, if you are fortunate enough to get one of the rooms on the left-most side looking downhill on the complex, you will discover a view just as stunning at night as it is in daylight. When the darkness has fallen, one of the busiest ports in the world is lit up by the lights of big ships, small fishing boats, ferries and various other vessels. When visiting Hong Kong University at the end of October 1994 I had the good fortune to get one of those rooms in the left wing of Robert Black. Moreover, it was a suite, two rooms with a bathroom and a corridor between them.

The reader might think: 'Good on you mate, but what on earth does this have to do with quality in higher education?' Well, the thing is that not long before my arrival in Hong Kong, my very dear old friend John Biggs (not very old, but very dear) had formed a consortium together with a number of colleagues from different institutions of Higher Education in Hong Kong. They had received a most substantial grant aimed at boosting quality in the tertiary sector of the Hong Kong system of education, and, as I was responsible for quality issues at my own university in Sweden since more than a year back, I was invited to give a seminar on 'Quality in Higher Education'. I was happy with the invitation, as there were indeed quite a few issues I was keen on discussing with colleagues who – like myself – were relative newcomers in 'quality circles'.

The year I took charge of quality issues at my university, that is 1993, coincided with a reform implemented in Swedish higher education, in connection with which there was quite a bit of discussion about the possible linking of the distribution of resources by the Government to some form of quality assessment of the universities themselves. Both direct and indirect linkages were discussed. After some debate it was eventually decided that there should be no direct link, but that grants should be allocated during a period of three years to the universities for the improvement of quality and for developing systems for quality assurance and self-evaluation. A central agency was also set up for carrying out an evaluation of the efforts made by the universities to develop and monitor these systems for developing and assuring quality.

As an unforgivably naive novice in the field I assumed that in order to improve quality you have to have some idea of what it is and then work in the direction your idea of quality suggests. This did not turn out to be at all obvious in quality circles, however. Indeed, as I later came to learn, in line with Vroeijenstijn's (1991) argument that it is a waste of time trying to define quality, the reverse applied. This is also supported by Diana Green who, in an edited book *What is quality in Higher Education?* (Green, 1994), in the introductory chapter drew the conclusion that as there are different interests and hence different perspectives (e.g. those of students, teachers, employers, politicians, citizens at large) of relevance to the path higher education is taking in a country, 'there is no single definition of quality that is right to the exclusion of all the others' (Green, 1994, p. 17).

Although this all sounds pretty fair and democratic, I felt somewhat disturbed. 'Quality control', 'Quality management', 'Quality assurance', 'Quality assessment', 'Quality audit', and so on, what is all the fuss about? I very much felt the sentiment conveyed by the Australian writer Roy Cambell, as quoted by Margetson (1994, p. 3), commenting on an appraisal that had been made of certain novelists, when looking for some substance in the notion of 'quality':

> You praise the firm restraint with which they write
> I'm with you there, of course:
> They use the snaffle and the curb all right,
> But where's the bloody horse?

While undoubtedly there can be many different and disparate views of quality, if you want to improve it you have to take a stance and define your own view which you are then obliged to argue for.

I thought that issues related to quality in higher education should be dealt with by using an approach inherent in the culture of the University. This would be a theoretical approach, where a theory for me is simply an elaboration of our understanding of the nature of the phenomenon in question and an attempt to clarify both how different component parts are related to each other and how the phenomenon is related to other phenomena. So, trying to improve quality in higher education meant to me deciding what the quality of what we wanted to improve was, to make explicit what we think better quality of that is, having an idea of how it can be achieved and bringing together the different aspects of the issue in a theory-like statement.

In accordance with this, I chose the same title for my seminar at the University of Hong Kong in October 28, 1994, as for the present chapter two years later and it is here that the harbour view from Robert Black College is relevant. During the night before the seminar I was sitting by the desk in my room looking at the lights on the water and trying to come up with a first formulation of what could possibly be developed into a theory of the quality of higher education. As I had a suite I could walk over to the other room when I got excited – or tired. And of course I had the same view from there. Occasionally I switched on the TV for a couple of minutes, made some coffee and went on working. Next morning I presented the fruits of my deliberation at a seminar chaired by John, and I find it very appropriate now, two years later, when trying to push the project further, to be writing a chapter for a book dedicated to him.

## THE IDEA OF THE UNIVERSITY

The conjunction of teaching and research is now probably seen as the most distinctive aspect of the University, a societal institution that has survived for some eight and a half centuries. In it teaching is supposed to contribute to the students' learning, and research is about developing knowledge which is new in an absolute sense, in that nobody has been aware of it previously. But learning is not only – and probably not even mainly – a function of teaching. Rather, the students develop knowledge by different means, knowledge which is of course new for them, but not necessarily new for others, for their teachers for instance. But also entirely new knowledge coming about is a learning experience for those involved in its development. This process is both different and the same in research and student learning. In research, human knowledge in its entirety is widened and humanity learns, so to speak, such that we can see research as resulting in learning on the collective level as compared to what the students are doing, where the focus is on individual learning. We can then talk about two forms of knowledge formation, learning on the individual and collective level, and can then try to find the nature of the relationship between them instead of looking for the relationship between teaching and research.

Now, if the University is about the two forms of knowledge formation, learning at the individual and at the collective level, quality in higher education has necessarily to do with the quality of learning in these two senses. And if the two are related then our answers to the question 'What is quality in these two cases?' should be related as well. So let us start with learning on the individual level, referring to it simply as 'learning' in the subtitle of the next section.

## LEARNING

Perhaps the most frequent and most important forms of learning come about almost as by-products without specific arrangements being made. For instance, we learn our native language by interacting with others and gradually entering the language with which the world surrounding us is imbued; we develop motor capabilities by interacting with the physical world; and we develop social capabilities by interacting with the social world. Even developing professional competence can be seen more or less as a by-product of becoming a member of a professional group. Necessary skills and knowledge are acquired as parts of the growing familiarity with ways of being, ways of thinking, ways of seeing the world characterising the group and the context we gradually and increasingly inhabit.

This is also highlighted in an excellent but sadly little known book by Christie (1985), in which he compares what he calls 'white learning' with 'Aboriginal learning' in Australia and shows that whereas the latter is an intrinsic part of life, the former is separated and institutionalised. This view is also put forward by Jean Lave (1996), an anthropologist, who by studying tailor apprentices in Liberia became aware of the occasional nature of learning in the technical sense (becoming capable of producing cloth, for instance) and who in a sense helped lay the ground for the apprentice almost emerging as the prototypic learner during the 1990s. This came about as a result of the convergence of the interest for learning in natural (as opposed to institutional) settings, the interest in the socio-historical school of psychology and the post-modern zeitgeist. The idea was then developed further by Lave and Wenger (1991) where learning as a by-product of socialisation is regarded as part of a transition from being 'a legitimate peripheral' to a less peripheral participant in a particular field of social practice. Such a view was also implied earlier by Brown, Collins and Duguid (1989) in a highly influential article contemplating the implications of such a view of learning for schools.

What these seemingly diverse orientations have in common is the emphasis on the cultural, social, linguistic and contextual embeddedness of human thought and human action (and hence human learning as well). 'Cognitive apprenticeship' has become the term aimed at capturing their central idea of learning that the meaningful learning of concepts, ideas, principles, and so on, has to be situated in authentic practices where these concepts, ideas and principles are functional and where they constitute discursive resources for the learners.

However convincing though this may seem, it focuses only on the conditions of learning, its nature and the question of how it is taking place and not on the nature of the capabilities – in a more narrow sense – which learning is supposed to result in. Furthermore, institutional learning lacks as a rule the characteristics of 'authentic practices'; characteristics which are seen by the proponents of the social-historical-contextual-discursive view as desirable or even as necessary pre-conditions for learning. The question is: should the practices of institutional learning be transformed into something which more closely resemble practices of non-institutional learning, and, if we feel so, then to what extent can this be attained?

There is a basic dilemma of institutional learning that we have always been confronted by, although it has become more problematic and more obvious recently. This is, that institutions are certain kinds of contexts with certain kinds of practices, but their main function is to prepare learners for other contexts with other practices. The reason why this is becoming more obvious and more problematic is that the contexts which the educational institutions aim at preparing the students for are becoming increasingly variable and increasingly unknown. And how do you prepare people for the unknown by means of the known? The latter refers to knowledge, the societal heritage which the institutions are supposed to be responsible for.

However urgent this question might seem, it is not novel; it is the question of learning for school versus learning for life, the question of how something we have learnt in one situation can be made use of in another, the question of 'transfer', and is by no means specific for institutional learning. Indeed, to varying degrees it is relevant to all kinds of learning; where the more 'situations of applications' differ from 'the situation of acquisition' the more intriguing it is. This is because if we have learnt and done something in one situation and if we can do something different in another situation, then we must have learnt something which is not identical with what we seemingly learnt in the first situation. This has important implications. Instead of, as is more common, trying to examine conjectures about possible mechanisms of transfer, the genuine problem of learning should be posed in terms of the question of 'What is learned?' (c.f. Smedslund, 1953). This can be illustrated as follows.

Let us look at such a fundamental capability as the mastery of mother tongue. We can make sense of what is said with a wide range of variation in pitch, tone, loudness, pronunciation, mode of expression, style, etc. So how can that be? We assume that we see, hear, feel the world through our previous experiences and we assume that we can deal with varying experiences because we have had varying experience in the past. Let us contemplate a chilling thought experiment. If all the linguistic experience a little baby was exposed to – God forbid – originated from a voice synthesiser speaking with exactly the same pitch, tone, loudness and so on all the time, she would fail to notice those aspects corresponding to dimensions of potential variation and hence subsequently have great difficulties in understanding speech which differed from what she has been used to (if she could understand it at all).

So my suggestion for an answer to the question 'What is learned?'

is that it is the variation that is learned. As far as mother tongue is concerned, for instance, the regularities, the invariances we learn – because we surely learn those too – are embedded in a great number of dimensions of variation. This can be said differently: the dimensions and the relationships constituted between them are the invariants. Or moderating the claim slightly: they are invariants. And because we have learnt the variation we can deal with not only what we have encountered previously but also that which we have not. We can make sense of new situations in terms of their critical features. These critical features are dimensions of variation constituted by the new situation and the previous ones which it resembles in critical respects. The thesis is that we will be capable of dealing with varying (and novel) situations in the future because we have experienced varying (and novel turned known) situations in the past.

Again, this can be said in other words, in a more straightforward way perhaps. When we encounter something new we are simultaneously aware of both this and that which we have experienced earlier. It is this simultaneous awareness of what is here and now and what was there and then, that is the meaning of the phrase that 'we see the world through our previous experiences' (see Marton & Booth, 1997). 'The new' is then seen with 'the old' and we make sense of the former in terms of the dimensions of variation that it constitutes together with other instances experienced earlier. What this implies is that 'applying something that we have learned' is not so much using what we have learned again and again in an unaltered form, or superimposing it on the new. 'Application' is every time a novel, simultaneous experience of 'the old' and 'the new'.

Sometimes, however, 'the new' differs in a striking respect from everything that we have experienced earlier. That is a start for the constitution of a new dimension of variation. We become aware of 'language', 'skin colour' or 'nationality', for instance, when we discover that there are more than one of each.

What makes this thesis interesting is the fact that the variation that we have experienced in the past and the variation we are going to face in the future do not have to be identical in terms of actual 'values' in the dimensions of variation. Rather, the condition is only that we can make sense of situations in the future in terms of dimensions of variation established in the past. And even this condition can be transcended: completely novel features imply that the new situation differs in some important respect from everything we have ever experienced. Such a crucial difference would open up a new dimension of variation and thus a new way of seeing something.

This line of reasoning applies presumably to capabilities that are fostered in educational institutions. If the students are dealing with a narrow range of problems in their studies, the likelihood of their being able to deal with other kind of problems in relation to which their studies are potentially relevant would be much less than if they had encountered more variation. In order to be able to make use of what one has learned in a course of studies, a new situation has to be seen by the individual in such a way that certain knowledge and certain skills appear relevant, and what we can make use of and apply depends on how we see, interpret and define the situation. This also makes the most fundamental form of learning into learning to see, learning to experience and learning to understand certain things in certain ways, as for instance when a scientist develops a scientific way of seeing scientific phenomena, a lawyer develops a juridical way of seeing legal problems or a physician develops a medical way of listening to heart-beats, seeing x-ray pictures, and so on.

In consequence, learning to see, hear, experience something in a new way is tantamount to discerning certain aspects of a particular phenomenon or a particular class of situations and being focally aware of them (i.e. the aspects are simultaneously figural in one's awareness). The mastery of simple arithmetic, for instance, takes a particular way of experiencing and understanding numbers, where one has to be aware of their 'manyness', sequential ordering, part-whole relationships and the units they consist of simultaneously. An important element of understanding Newtonian mechanics is, for instance, the discernment of a frame of reference from which a moving body is seen as a critical aspect, a dimension of potential variation (Marton & Booth, 1997).

## RESEARCH

Just as we can argue that developing the capability of seeing certain situations and certain phenomena in new ways is the most important form of learning, we can argue that the most important forms of research add to our collective understanding of the world by introducing new ways of seeing and experiencing it or different aspects of it. However, just as not all learning is of this kind, not all research is either. As a matter of fact most research is not. But just as the most important forms of learning do contribute in these ways, the most important forms of research do alter our way of seeing certain parts or certain aspects of reality. This is probably one of the two most fundamental ways in which learning and research (or individual and collective learning) are related. Through research, new ways of seeing things in the world (including seeing ourselves, of course) are introduced, and through learning they are propagated.

The other most fundamental aspect of the relationship has to do with the idea of continuity between advanced scientific thinking and more mundane forms of thought, like those the students are supposed to engage in. Where although some argue that there is a profound difference in kind, others maintain that one grows out of the other. This latter position can also be derived from one of the most basic ideas underlying the phenomenological school of thought, according to its founder Edmund Husserl, which posits that all scientific knowledge develops from our experience of the life-world. Reflection originates in the pre-reflective experience, the sophisticated grows from the mundane and the world as experienced spontaneously is the soil from which the most advanced forms of scientific thinking spring (see for instance, Gurwitsch, 1974; Husserl, 1970).

Piaget's genetic epistemology, which rests on the assumed parallelism between onto- and phylogenesis, that is on the conjecture that individual (intellectual) development resembles collective historical development, offers a less explicit, but still pretty straightforward support of the idea of continuity (between different forms of thinking). The changing ideas the child develops about the physical world for instance, more or less follow the order of the appearance of those ideas in the history of humankind. Aristotelian ways of thinking are followed by Galilean ways of thinking, which are followed by Newtonian ways of thinking, just to take one example (see Piaget & Garcia, 1988).

## WAYS OF SEEING THE WORLD

There are thus classical formulations which explicitly or implicitly support the idea of continuities between learning and research and between the students' and the scholars' ways of thinking. We referred to two such formulations and there are others. We will now develop this idea further, but from another angle.

By and large during two decades from the mid-1970s onwards, there has been a strong research orientation within the study of school related learning, called 'conceptual change', a major inspiration for which was Piagetian constructivism. In this vein, when applied to different subjects and domains studied in school, researchers focused on the learners' varying ways of understanding central concepts and central phenomena. They pictured learning as content-specific conceptual development within different areas of knowledge and very much in terms whereby one way of understanding the concept or the phenomenon is replaced by another more advanced understanding of the same thing. Cognitive conflict was seen as the chief mechanism by which such a change was brought into being. This paradigm has generated a most impressive amount of research, although it has recently been subject to criticism (see for instance, Linder, 1993). One of the issues raised was whether the idea of replacing one understanding with another is a reasonable description of learning and development. It is instead now argued to be more accurate to say that in the course of learning, the learner is widening the range of possible understandings or increasing her repertoire, so to speak.

Supporting the latter ideas are the recent disclosures of a longitudinal study of pupils' understandings of ecological processes carried out by Helldén (1995), who followed a group of children from age 9 to 15 and interviewed them individually several times. He found that although there was considerable conceptual development of their understanding taking place with respect to the issues of interest, there was also a very strong element of continuity in the sense that the pupils had individual and sometimes idiosyncratic themes which they elaborated on further. These individual themes were frequently based on certain concrete personal experiences which they went back to again and again, mostly without remembering that they had related to the same event at the previous interviews as well. Indeed this was not understood until the last interview when they were 15 and listened to how they had answered the same questions when they were 9 years old. That is, the pupils often revealed particular and concrete experiences which they implicitly referred to independently (without being aware of the connections) at different points in time (at different ages) such that if the conceptual changes are seen as changes in form, in ways of thinking, the enduring personal themes were the substance, that which the thinking was about. In fact Helldén also discovered that the stuff of which increasingly sophisticated explanation was made was frequently – in fact mostly – anthropomorphic and teleological (and in that sense 'not very scientific') but that these naive 'unscientific' images were highly instrumental in the development of more advanced, scientific understandings. As a means of illustration, let us consider how Oscar answered the question 'What makes the leaves fall from the trees in Autumn?'

> Age 11: They don't have the strength to remain sitting there. They must jump off.
>
> Age 13: They fall at autumn and they want much sun. Well, perhaps the tree doesn't have the strength to carry them any longer. It has enough to do getting nourishment itself and it drops the leaves.
>
> Age 15: Well ... during winter the tree cannot give nourishment to the leaves and itself, so it drops the leaves. It closes the supply of nourishment to the leaves, doesn't it. Then they die and drop. (Helldén, 1995, p. 5)

These quotes seem to follow on from each other in spite of the fact that there are two years between each and Oscar did not remember what he said from a previous interview on any one subsequent occasion. That is, there are clear links between them ('the strength to hold' between the first and the second interview and 'getting/giving nourishment' between the second and the third interview, for instance) and there is an anthropomorphic flavour running through all three interviews ('not having the strength', 'must jump off', 'closing the supply'). However, there is still a clear development taking place from 'leaf centred' to 'tree-centred' views, and from explanations phrased in terms of physical efforts to those phrased in terms of physiological needs.

As a second support we can call upon Nemirovsky, Tierney and Wright (1995) who carried out a similar kind of study but in an entirely different time scale. Two girls of 10 and 9 years old respectively, used a motion detector in the context of individual interviews and the first 22 and 35 minutes of their acquaintance with the tool respectively were the objects of the researchers' interest. The detector measured the distance between a tower and a button that the girls were holding in their hands, such that by moving closer or further away from the tower, the girls could monitor a time and distance graph on a computer screen. Approaching the tower from a distance of say three metres at a steady rate holding the button in one hand generated a descending line (the distance decreased as a function of time), where the slope of the line indicated the velocity by which the girl was moving (the faster the movement, the steeper the slope).

In order to be able to monitor the graph the girls had to find out what aspects of their (or rather the button's) movement were significant and co-varied in a systematic manner with aspects of the graph. One girl thought initially that the vertical co-ordinates of the graph reflected how high above the ground she held the button (high-high and low-low). The other girl assumed initially that the vertical co-ordinates reflected the speed by which the button was moved (fast-high and slow-low). However, through interacting with the apparatus they developed a grasp of the correlation between their movements and properties of the graph. Their occasional use of the graphs as drawings (and generating bird-like shapes, for instance) turned out to be instrumental for improving their understanding of the behaviour of the graph.

This result parallels Helldén's (1995) observation that an anthropomorphic understanding of ecological processes could make up the substance out of which scientific understandings are developed. However, a second highly interesting observation was made by Nemirovsky et al. when, after the two girls participating in the experiment had mastered the relationships between aspects of movement and aspects of the graph (distance-from-tower <=> vertical co-ordinates, velocity of movement <=> slope of graph), the conditions were altered and one of the girls was asked to monitor two graphs by holding two buttons, one in each hand, while the other was asked to monitor the graph by operating a little electric train on which the button was placed. These changes made both girls revert to their initial understandings. The first girl tried to create two separate graphs by holding the two buttons at different heights above the ground (but at the same distance from the sensor), the second girl tried to make the graph go downwards by slowing down the train and she tried to make the graph go upwards by speeding it up.

This means that in both cases the girls selected and focused on aspects of the situations which they selected initially under the first conditions and then abandoned in favour of other aspects that were indeed systematically related to aspects of the graph. So what could be seen as learning or even as conceptual change, turned out to be reversible. Nemirovsky et al. (1995) suggest that this happened because the lived-in space, that is, the space experienced by the subject, is constituted through her acts, such that what may seem to the reader like fairly small changes actually transformed the space in which the acts were performed. In the first case, by introducing the one-button-in-each-hand problem, the relation between the two hands becomes the object of focal awareness for the girl (and not so much the relation between her and the sensor). In the second case, where the girl is controlling the speed of the train, she is very much focused on not letting it bump into things and thus less focused on her relationship to the sensor. Both girls are acting in new spaces when the conditions are changed and thus they start with their habitual understanding of the vertical co-ordinates of the graph as position above ground and as speed, respectively.

In an unpublished study, Neuman and Renström have also come up with some fairly striking demonstrations of reversibilities of these kinds, in their case, though, concerning how highly trained adults can revert back to their childhood way of understanding something if conditions force constraints on them, similar to ones they experienced then. This study followed on from Neuman's analysis of the distinctively different ways in which young children (about 6 years old) experience numbers (Neuman, 1987), where she had been able to demonstrate that while children can discern different aspects of numbers such as unit, part-whole relations, their sequential ordering and their 'manyness', they have difficulties experiencing the various aspects simultaneously and may focus on one – or some of them – at a time, and that although their answers to arithmetic problems may at times appear pretty erratic, their understanding is in this sense more partial than wrong (according to interpretation of Neuman's findings by Marton & Booth, 1997). For instance, if they focused on the sequential ordering and not on the 'manyness' of numbers they were likely to use numbers as 'names', where the name of the first object counted is 'one', the name of the second is 'two' and so on, and where furthermore the child learns that the name of the last object is the name of all the objects counted. This is so because every time she has to determine the number of a set of objects, the last numeral uttered is emphasised (e.g. Adult: 'How many apples are there in the basket Lisa?' Lisa: 'One, two, three, four. Adult: Four, you are right!').

Now, if numbers are seen as names and the sequential ordering and the one-to-one correspondence (between 'names' and objects) are not combined with a sense of 'manyness', children may come up with quite surprising answers to simple arithmetic problems. For instance there are 6- to 7-year-old children (not many of them admittedly) who claim that they have five fingers on one hand (usually the left hand) and ten on the other (see Neuman, 1987). This, as they start counting their fingers on the first hand: 'one, two, three, four five ... there are five' and then on the second hand: 'six, seven, eight, nine, ten ... there are ten'. In accordance with the same way of understanding numbers, when asked the question 'If you have two kronor and want to buy an ice-cream for 9 kronor, how many more kronor do you need?', they may say '9'. They might imagine the first krona is called 'one' and the second is called 'two' and then you have to add a couple, the last one of which is called '9' (because 9 is what you have to come up with). Hence all those you add are called '9' together.

A group of highly educated adults were subjects in Neuman and Renström's study, in which the experimenter pointed to a set of different coins and said: 'This is A this is B, this is C and so on. How much is D plus F? Or G minus C? If you have B and you want I, what more do you need?', and so on. The subjects were generally puzzled and they asked questions like 'When you say C do you mean this one (C) or these together (A, B, C)?', to which the experimenter replied 'Well, this is for you to decide'. The idea was to let the subjects face the same situation, the same difficulties as children are facing in their early use of numbers: the ambiguity between the two aspects: sequential ordering and 'manyness', the difficulty with co-ordinating the two, the difficulty with developing a sensuous understanding of 'manyness' (e.g. 'How can we experience the "sevenness" of seven?', or (in the experiment) 'How can we experience the "G-ness" of G?' When facing difficulties resembling those experienced by children, the highly educated adults seemed to handle the situation in ways which closely resembled those shown by children.

In this experiment the efforts of the adult subjects to occasionally try to translate letters into numerals were blocked by the experimenter. They could then use letters as 'names' and often said things like, 'If you have B and you want I then you need I more'. They could also use letters as 'estimates' (focusing on the approximate 'manyness') and often then said something like 'D and E is H together', and sometimes they tried to engage in pretty hopeless double-counting procedures such as when trying to determine how much D+J is by saying 'D, E-A, F-B', and using the second letter to keep track and stopping when they got to J.

## CONTINUITY WITHIN AND BETWEEN INDIVIDUALS

The studies referred to in the above section point to the continuity between different ways of seeing the world, where one evolves from the other, not by replacing it but by adding a further possibility to it, and where earlier ways of seeing the world are the stuff which later ways are made of. And this stuff does not disappear. When conditions change we may keep changing our ways of seeing accordingly. And when we encounter the same difficulties, the same constraints, the same demands as at an earlier stage, it is very likely that we will experience things in a similar way as we did then.

This line of reasoning is thus relevant in relation to the question of what is variable and what is invariant in the individual case, what is the nature of continuities and discontinuities there. Although the argument was put forward earlier that one of the two most important links between research and learning rests with the resemblance between the most fundamental forms of both – introducing a new way of seeing something on the one hand and acquiring or developing a new way of seeing something on the other – the question as to whether the individual continuity argument illuminates further the relationship between learning and research remains. However, the examples that were discussed above also dealt with continuity between less and more advanced – or more complex – ways of seeing the world, even though they do not include research achievements – the introduction of universally novel ways of thinking about a phenomenon.

Such arguments can be found, however, in case stories of major figures in the history of the development of human knowledge where in a great number of instances we find that the full-blown scientific achievements were foreshadowed by ideas and ways of understanding appearing early in the individuals life. The life and work of Robert Burns Woodward (1917–1974), one of the greatest chemists of this century who was awarded the Nobel prize in 1965 for his 'meritorious contributions to the art of organic synthesis', illustrates this excellently. His major achievement, the synthesis of various organic substances, was made possible by his remarkable ability

> ...for visualising three-dimensional molecular structures. It was as though he could move, in his mind, among these structures, viewing them from all angles, even foreseeing their transformations, as he effected, step-by-step, their pathways toward new possibilities and eventual targets. (C.E. Woodward, 1989, pp. 241-242)

As a matter of fact Woodward began thinking about and trying to 'dream up' synthesis as early as at the age of 12, when he worked out a synthesis for quinine, an outstanding scientific achievement.

In this case we find a perfect case of continuity within the individual, ranging from the very young boy's first ideas about chemical compounds to him finding his orientation and his idiosyncratic style as a researcher in his early teens and his stunning scientific career. However, in Woodward's case we can find the link between learning and research not only in the individual but also in the social or pedagogical sense. In 1948 Woodward, who was American, visited Europe for the first time and gave one of his electrifying lectures at Imperial College in London. Derek Barton, who received the Nobel prize for his work on conformational analysis in 1969, was there and commented on it later thus:

> It was a brilliant demonstration of how you could take facts in the literature which seemed obvious and just by thinking about them, as he so ably did, interpret them and obtain the results and then go into the laboratory and prove it was the right result. That we thought was the work of genius ... Ten years later (at Imperial College) our second year undergraduate students could do that problem, and ... about 25% of them could get it right. Now, does that mean that in 1958 we had 25% mini-Woodwards in the second year class? No, of course it didn't. What it meant was that Woodward had taught us organic chemists how to think. (Barton, 1981, p. 240, cited in Woodward, 1989)

## THE SPACE OF VARIATION

Quality in higher education has been dealt with here mostly from a point of departure in ways of experiencing various phenomena and situations. This has been seen as the most fundamental aspect of learning as well as of research, hence linking the two together. But the capability of experiencing or seeing something in a certain way is highly relevant in relation to other questions as well. Indeed, although the capability of seeing something in a certain way could be understood almost literally in Woodward's case, mostly the expression should have a metaphoric interpretation. The question is, how can we characterise 'experiencing something in a certain way' in more general terms?

This question is fundamentally relevant in relation to the issue of what kind of competence universities are supposed to nurture in their students. As pointed out above, the basic dilemma of educational institutions is that they are expected to bring about learning at certain points in time in certain situations, where what is learned then and there will enable the learners to deal with situations in an unknown future, in unknown places, in situations which cannot be defined in advance. There are degrees of uncertainty, where the less 'situations of application' resemble 'situations of acquisition' the higher is the uncertainty and where the more diverse, more changing, more dynamic the society is, the less we know about the situations the students of today will encounter. In order to find out what knowledge or skills are applicable you have to see the situation in such a way that certain knowledge, certain skills appear relevant. Again, ways of seeing and experiencing are the most basic capabilities, the most fundamental aspects of the competence the students develop at the university. And – in accordance with the above line of reasoning – they are some of the most fundamental aspects of research achievements as well.

The title of this chapter suggests that there should be some conjectures about possible ways of improving quality in higher education and theories are also frequently expected to have some corollaries for practice. However, up to this point I have mainly tried to single out capabilities for experiencing, seeing certain things in certain ways as a key issue – *the* key issue, in fact – as far as quality in higher education is concerned. I have also argued that capabilities reflect continuity both within and between individuals. Now, I will briefly elaborate on some ideas about the nature of those capabilities and will deal with some possible practical implications – even more briefly – where I will draw on more detailed accounts given elsewhere (primarily by Marton & Booth, 1997) to illustrate.

From the flux of the seemingly chaotic flow of an ever changing reality we discern and delimit phenomena and situations, and within these we delimit and discern parts and part-part as well as part-whole relations. However, we also relate the phenomena and the situations thus discerned to other phenomena and other situations and, most importantly, we discern aspects which distinguish or relate one phenomenon from or to others and aspects that distinguish or relate situations from or to other situations, and parts from parts, parts to parts, parts from wholes, parts to wholes and so on. That is, these aspects or dimensions of variation imply actualities and potentialities. For instance, discerning velocity as an aspect of a phenomenon implies not only that it has a certain velocity but also that it could have had another velocity, and focusing on the fact that someone is tall implies height as a figural aspect in our awareness, that is we see a person's tallness in the light of the variation in height we have experienced previously among people.

Experiencing something or someone in a certain way implies discerning a limited number of critical aspects and being focally and simultaneously aware of them. This is the structural side of 'a way of experiencing something' and it is dialectically intertwined with the referential side, with the global meaning the phenomenon has for someone. The different parts delimited, related to each other and to the whole, the different aspects discerned and held in focal awareness simultaneously specify a particular entity (person, phenomenon, situation) which has a certain meaning for someone. It is an object of awareness, something that in principle can be experienced in different ways. Even in imagination, like Woodward's molecules or Entwistle and Marton's (1994) 'knowledge objects', it can be 'rotated' in thought – literally sometimes, metaphorically mostly. However, because there is a limited number of critical aspects that can be constituted in the relationship between human subjects and a certain kind of object (see Marton & Booth, 1997), there is also a limited number of qualitatively different ways in which a certain phenomenon or a certain class of situations can be understood. Different combinations of those aspects define the different ways in which the phenomenon is experienced. The set of aspects is finite at every historical point in time, but open in the sense that there are always other aspects that can be introduced. The last word can never be said about the nature of any phenomena.

In other words, a phenomenon is always an experienced phenomenon where subject and object are not independent and it can be understood as a complex of all the possible ways in which it can be experienced, where the more one is aware of the range of variation, the better understanding one has of the phenomenon. Included in this is the fact that each possible way of experiencing a phenomenon can be seen as a combination of dimensions of variation. A similar line of reasoning is assumed to apply to the question of how we can prepare students in advance for novel situations which are impossible to define in advance through the experiences they have during their studies, through what they learn there. Again: 'How can we prepare people for the unknown by means of the known?' Or, 'How does what one learns in one situation contribute to one's capability of handling another – and more or less different – situation?' As mentioned above, Smedslund (1953) pointed out more than four decades ago that the concept of transfer is obsolete. If we can answer the question of 'What is learned?' then we can also make sense of what class of situations that which is learned applies to and in what respect.

I suggested above that a general answer to the question of 'What is learned?' is *variation*. We learn to know people, mother tongue, phenomena, situations through variation in appearance, sound-pattern, perspectives, important parameters. As we learn the variation we also learn about situations that we have never encountered and about phenomena in ways we have never seen them – they can be made sense of in terms of the variation that we have learned as not-as-yet-realised potentialities. Could it not be the case that we may be able to discover new dimensions of variation constituted between the new that we have encountered and previous experiences, relevant in other respects. This is how new ways of seeing come into being. And if we can develop a capability for appropriating new ways of seeing, that is opening new dimensions of variation, then we have developed a capability for learning to learn in a fundamental sense of the word. And in consequence with the above, this can only be achieved through experiencing variation between dimensions of variation. What follows from this is that the more narrow the range of situations, problems, appearances of phenomena, points of view, perspectives, that we have encountered in our studies are, the less likely it is that we will be capable of dealing with novel situations, new appearances, other points of view, other perspectives. What we learn are contingencies of variation, constituting a space, representing the range of phenomena, situations, aspects and appearances we are capable of dealing with. The larger, the richer, the more differentiated and integrated this space is, the better equipped we are to face the future. This space can only be built out of experience. In order to become capable of dealing with a varying future we must have met a varying past.

## A BLUEPRINT FOR EXCELLENCE

The idea I have tried to promote here is that any concern about quality in higher education should start by exploring the nature of quality in learning and research, because if we have a reasonably good idea of what this is then we are better off when it comes to efforts to improve quality. I make this suggestion on the basis of a conviction that the distinctly different ways in which we experience and understand the world make up the most important aspects both of learning and of research. The quality of the latter can be seen in terms of the extent to which it contributes to enriching our collective understanding of the phenomena researched, whilst quality of the former can be seen in terms of the extent to which it contributes to enriching the individual student's understanding of the phenomena studied. Underlying this line of reasoning is the notion that knowledge does not exist ready-made, out there, waiting to be discovered, to be acquired. Rather, knowledge, in the sense of understanding the world around us, is constituted as intrinsic person-world relations, on the ground of previously constituted person-world relations. Seen from the collective point of view, there is an ever ongoing historical, cultural, social constitution of human knowledge. Research and learning are two different, but closely related, forms of knowledge formation. When engaged in studies or in research we are oriented towards the knowledge to be gained or towards the object about which knowledge is to be gained. Thus, in order to improve quality, in the above sense of the word, we should focus not only on knowledge and on the objects of knowledge, but also on the acts and processes of knowledge formation.

The aspects of learning and research that are seen as central in the present context, ways of experiencing and understanding the world around us, have been described above as complexes of variation, where it is argued that if variation is what is learned, then understanding can be widened and made more broadly applicable through experiencing greater variation in more dimensions. This is in accordance with the non-dualistic ontological stance, where person and world are not seen as separate from each other. A phenomenon can be made sense of as a complex of all the different possible ways in which it can be experienced and understood, and understanding a phenomenon can be seen as a combination of different dimensions of variation and enhanced by widening their range (that both within and between dimensions). Different ways of experiencing and understanding a phenomenon are different contingencies of variation and a further grasp of a phenomenon is achieved by encountering and hence becoming aware of other ways of experiencing and understanding it. (This should be true within certain limits, of course. Understanding – and variation – have both range and structure.)

This means simply that we can learn from each other, not only students from teachers, but also teachers from students (they have to, as a matter of fact, in order to be good teachers), teachers from teachers, students from students, researchers from researchers. We can also learn about the historical variation – how disciplinary knowledge has evolved, and about the cultural and contextual embeddedness of knowledge (variation across cultural and contextual boundaries). This means, of course, that we pay attention also to ways of experiencing and understanding which are incorrect when measured against the yardstick of the received view, based on current scholarly standards. As was argued above, understandings which are deemed incorrect represent, as a rule, partial understandings and there is a continuity between different ways of understanding a phenomenon; one develops from the other. This is true both on the individual and on the collective level. And how can we contribute to developing ways of understanding the world if we are ignorant of what there is to be developed?

By becoming aware of other ways of understanding a certain phenomenon, our own understanding becomes visible to us and appears exactly as *a* way of understanding. In this way it becomes much easier to change, and develop, our way of understanding that phenomenon. When teachers become aware of the students' ways of understanding of what *they* (the students) take for granted, they become aware of what *they* (the teachers) have taken for granted – and should not take for granted.

In the process of being confronted with other ways of understanding a phenomenon it becomes more and more fully constituted as the object of our experience. In the context of studies we become more knowledgeable of current and past understandings of the object of our studies. In the context of research, by arriving at a novel understanding, we are also enhancing the likelihood of arriving at a fuller, richer one as well. That is, by becoming aware of other ways of experiencing and understanding phenomena of interest, the collective consciousness of the knowledge organisation, the university, will grow as knowledge is then framed by our becoming conscious of how it is formed. I believe this is one way in which quality in higher education can be raised.

## AT LAST

The ideas put forward in this chapter are obviously far from fully developed as yet. But I feel a strong sense of direction and I do hope that this chapter points to ways in which things can be dramatically improved at universities. Yes, the chapter is meant to be a pointer. Nothing more and nothing less.

In the introduction I mentioned how I was preparing the first version of these ideas, overlooking Hong Kong harbour lights. Now, little more than two years later, I am sitting at home in Sweden. It is Christmas and the world through our window is completely white. It is beautiful too – in a different way.

## Acknowledgments

During the last two years I have had excellent opportunities for discussing issues of quality in higher education. One context for the exchange of ideas has been the Swedish-British research group headed by professors Marianne Bauer and Maurice Kogan, conducting comparative studies of the recent developments in higher education in the two countries with financial support from The Swedish Council for Studies of Higher Education. Another context is the ongoing efforts for improving the quality of learning and research at my own university, in Göteborg. Some of the ideas dealt with in this chapter have been presented earlier by Marton and Rovio-Johansson (1995) in that connection. The third context is my co-operation with professor John Bowden at the Royal Melbourne Institute of Technology in Australia. It is our intention to include some of the issues discussed here in a more comprehensive framework and develop them further (Bowden and Marton, forthcoming).

## References

Bowden, J., & Marton, F. (forthcoming). *The university of learning. Beyond quality and competence.* London: Kogan Page.

Brown, J. S., Collins, A., & Duguid, P. (1989). Situated cognition and the culture of learning. *Educational Researcher, 18,* 32–42.

Christie, M.J. (1985). *Aboriginal perspectives on experience and learning: The role of language in Aboriginal education.* Malvern: Deakin University Press.

Entwistle, N., & Marton, F. (1994). Knowledge objects: Understandings constituted through intensive academic study. *British Journal of Educational Psychology, 64,* 161–178.

Green, D. (Ed.). (1994). *What is quality in higher education?* Ballmoor: Society for Research in Higher Education & Open University Press.

Gurwitsch, A. (1974). *Phenomenology and the theory of science.* Evanston, Ill.: Northwestern University Press.

Helldén, G. (1995). *Aspects of the development of pupils' ideas about decomposition in nature.* Paper presented at the European Conference on Research in Science Education, University of Leeds, Leeds.

Husserl, E. (1970). *The crisis of European sciences and transcendental phenomenology.* Evanston, Ill.: Northwestern University Press.

Lave, J. (1996). Teaching, as learning, in practice. *Minds, culture, and activity, 3,* 149–164.

Lave, J., & Wenger, E. (1991). *Situated learning: Legitimate peripheral participation.* New York: Cambridge University Press.

Linder, C.J. (1993). A challenge to conceptual change. *Science Education, 77,* 293–300.

Margetson, D. (1994). Quality assurance, management, etc – All harness and no horse? In G. Foster (Ed.), *Questions of quality* (pp. 1–14). The Tertiary Education Institute, The University of Queensland.

Marton, F., & Booth, S. (1997). *Learning and awareness.* Mahwah, N.J.: Lawrence Erlbaum.

Marton, F., & Rovio-Johansson, A. (1995).Vad är universitet till för? In Marianne Bauer (Ed.), *Universitetet: Ett framtidstema med variationer – röster om Göteborgs universitet* (The idea of the university) (pp. 11–16). Göteborg: Göteborgs universitet, Informationsavdelningen.

Nemirovsky, R., Tierney, C., & Wright, T. (1995). *Body motion and graphing.* Paper presented at the Annual Conference of the American Educational Research Association.

Neuman, D. (1987). *The origin of arithmetic skills. A phenomenographic approach.* Göteborg: Acta Universitatis Gothoburgensis.

Neuman, D., & Renström, L. Unpublished study.

Piaget, J., & Garcia, R. (1988). *Psychogenesis and the history of science.* New York: Columbia University Press.

Smedslund, J. (1953). The problem of 'What is learned?'. *Psychological Review, 60,* 157–158.

Vroeijenstijn, T.S. (1991). *External quality assessment: Servants of two masters?* Paper presented to the Conference on Quality Assurance in Higher Education, 15–17 July, Hong Kong. (Cited by Green, 1994.)

Woodward, C.E. (1989). Art and elegance in the synthesis of organic compounds: Robert Burns Woodward. In D.B. Wallace, & H.E. Gruber (Eds.), *Creative people at work* (pp. 227–253). New York: Oxford University Press.

# Applying the SOLO Taxonomy to Learning in Higher Education

*Gillian Boulton-Lewis*

The SOLO taxonomy developed by John Biggs and Kevin Collis has been applied to describing levels of expected learning outcomes in a range of subject areas in secondary education and more recently in primary education. This chapter is a discussion of the current and potential use of the SOLO (Structure of Observed Learning Outcomes) taxonomy (Biggs & Collis, 1982, 1989; Biggs, 1991, 1992a, 1992b; Boulton-Lewis, 1992, 1994) as a means of facilitating and assessing learning in higher education. It complements the work of Hattie and Purdie in this volume (Chapter 7) who describe the use of SOLO as an alternative to Bloom's taxonomy. This chapter includes a summary of the research and use of SOLO to date as a means of: finding out what students know and believe about their own learning; assessing entering knowledge in a discipline; presenting examples of structural organisation of knowledge in a discipline; providing models of levels of desired learning outcomes; and, in particular, assessing learning outcomes. Suggestions are made for further application and research.

Barnett (1990) proposed that :

> an educational process can be termed higher education when the student is carried on to levels of reasoning which make possible critical reflection on his or her experiences, whether consisting of propositional knowledge or of knowledge through action. These levels of reasoning and reflection are "higher", because they enable the student to take a

view (from above, as it were) of what has been learned. Simply, "higher education" resides in the higher-order states of mind. (p. 202)

## LEARNING AND TEACHING IN HIGHER EDUCATION

The belief about higher education underlying this chapter is in keeping with the quotation from Barnett. Higher education should lead ideally to higher order thinking for most graduates. That is, they should acquire necessary declarative (propositional) and procedural (action) knowledge in their discipline areas, understand it and be able to reflect on it critically. This means that the preferred learning outcomes for students completing university education should be understanding, integration and potential application of the crucial aspects of their discipline. It follows that lecturers should teach to facilitate such outcomes. This would require a conception of teaching, at least, as one of facilitating knowledge but preferably as 'an activity aimed at changing students' conceptions or understanding of the world (Samuelowicz & Bain, 1992). The outcome of such teaching should be students who have deeper knowledge and more sophisticated levels of reasoning than those with which they began university study, and who are beginning to think in a manner similar to an expert in their area. To facilitate such thinking lecturers need to utilise strategies that will cause students to learn in such a way. It is suggested here that the use of adaptations of the SOLO taxonomy is one such way of influencing and assessing learning outcomes to facilitate higher order thinking.

### HIGHER ORDER THINKING

One of the goals of higher education is surely to produce graduates who can be involved in rational decision making and leadership roles in society. This entails teaching students so that they understand the content and structure of their chosen disciplines and can apply these effectively in further development of knowledge and in vocational situations. Such behaviour requires something like critical thinking as Norris (1989) defined it. Critical thinkers are those who seek reasons, attempt to be well informed, use and acknowledge credible sources, consider alternatives and other points of view, withhold judgement until they have sufficient evidence and seek to be as precise as possible. In order to think in such a manner it is necessary to possess requisite declarative, procedural and theoretical knowledge, at least, as described below and to value critical thinking. Possession also of conditional and metatheoretical knowledge would enhance the decision making process.

Declarative knowledge consists of factual knowledge of a discipline, represented in symbols, and the way in which it is structured for retrieval. Procedural knowledge is that which allows the purposeful manipulation of declarative knowledge to undertake a task, solve problems, make decisions, understand and so on. It also includes some generalisable cognitive skills (Lehman, Lempert & Nisbett, 1988). Conditional knowledge includes knowing when to use certain procedures and access appropriate content, that is 'knowing how and why' (Biggs, 1992a). Biggs (1992a) also described theoretical and metatheoretical knowledge, which are at higher levels of abstraction than declarative knowledge. He asserted that in higher education we have traditionally aimed at teaching theoretical and metatheoretical knowledge but have found difficulty in teaching procedural and conditional knowledge effectively. Of course this does not mean that we always teach theoretical or metatheoretical knowledge well either.

It is asserted that critical thinking must rest on deep rather than surface learning approaches and hence deep learning outcomes as described by Marton and Säljö (1976a, 1976b, 1984). A deep approach to learning is one in which the student is interested, intends to understand the material, and hence to relate parts to a whole, to integrate it with existing knowledge and to apply it in real world situations (c.f. Biggs & Moore, 1993). Deep learning outcomes occur when a student is successful in such intentions. Critical thinking would also assume qualitative conceptions of learning as described by Marton, Dall'Alba and Beaty (1993) because a deep approach is related to such conceptions. Qualitative conceptions include understanding, seeing something in a different way and ultimately perhaps changing as a person. These three qualitative conceptions subsume and build on quantitative conceptions of learning which Marton et al. described 'as increasing one's knowledge, memorising and reproducing and applying'. Marton, Watkins and Tang (1997) proposed a two-dimensional outcome space to describe learning based on work with Asian students. The first dimension consists of four ways of experiencing learning (committing words to memory, committing meaning to memory, understanding meaning, and understanding a phenomenon). The second dimension consists of the temporal facets of acquiring, knowing and making use of learning in each of the four ways of experiencing it. Whilst these conceptions of learning are derived specifically from research with Chinese high school students in Hong Kong, the category 'relating', which is making use of learning at the 'understanding phenomenon' level, is the kind of learning that one would expect of university graduates. It seems to be similar to the relational level of learning in the formal mode described for the SOLO taxonomy below. In order to think critically in a discipline, it is posited therefore that it is necessary to acquire knowledge (words, meanings, understanding of meaning and phenomena) memorise, know and then be able to apply it. Such outcomes would allow the student to evaluate, challenge and perhaps extend knowledge to a new area. It is important also to determine the conceptions that students hold about learning because they shape the approach that a student takes to learning in most situations (Prosser & Millar, 1989) providing the context of learning is congruent with a particular conception (Dart, Chapter 10 in this volume). If students' conceptions of learning are not congruent with the desired outcomes then that is also important to know so that learning contexts can be created that will, if necessary, cause students to change their conceptions and approach to learning.

There is a great deal of evidence that most students graduate from universities with little but surface declarative knowledge of their disciplines and that they do not learn to think like experts in their areas of study (Ramsden, 1988). In short, their conceptions of learning are probably quantitative and so are the learning outcomes. They acquire information from lectures, and texts and may be able to apply it routinely, but do not necessarily understand it nor become critical thinkers. Such outcomes may be not only a result of students' lack of knowledge about learning or lack of motivation. They could also be the result of lecturers' knowledge of learning (or lack of it) and their expectations, strategies, and course organisation.

## THE SOLO TAXONOMY

The SOLO taxonomy developed by Biggs and Collis (Biggs & Collis, 1982, 1989) is a taxonomy of the structure of learning outcomes for which SOLO is an acronym. It can be applied to different content areas to provide descriptions of the structural organisation of knowledge at increasingly more complex levels across increasingly more abstract modes of learning. Biggs and Collis described five levels of the structure of observed learning outcomes. These ranged, on the basis of the structural organisation of the knowledge in question in a particular mode, from incompetence to expertise in hierarchical order as follows: prestructural (incompetence, nothing is known about the area); unistructural (one relevant aspect is known); multistructural (several relevant independent aspects are known); relational (aspects of knowledge are integrated into a structure); and extended abstract (knowledge is generalised to a new domain). As a person develops, and learns more about a discipline, levels of structural organisation of knowledge recur in a cyclical fashion, for increasingly more formal modes of learning, from sensorimotor through iconic, concrete-symbolic, formal-1 and then formal-2 (later described as postformal) modes of knowing. Biggs and Collis (1989) and Biggs (1991) proposed that the concrete-symbolic mode was typical of most secondary school learning, that the formal-1 (formal) mode was typical of early university learning, and that the formal-2 (or postformal) mode should be achieved in postgraduate study. The formal mode of learning entails declarative, procedural and theoretical knowledge and the postformal mode, in addition, entails metatheoretical and conditional knowledge. These formal modes of learning, particularly those at the postformal level, should underpin the ability to think critically in a discipline area.

Biggs and Collis (1982) provided examples of SOLO levels for a range of secondary school subject areas. Recently, levels of learning in the iconic and concrete symbolic modes of functioning for aspects of mathematics in the primary school have been described in detail (e.g. Campbell, Watson & Collis, 1992; Watson, Campbell & Collis, 1993). There are also some examples of levels of outcomes in some discipline areas for tertiary education and these are described in this chapter. It is suggested that further examples can be generated or derived from students' work in university discipline areas.

In summary, ideally students in undergraduate study at the tertiary level should develop knowledge in their discipline areas that is organised structurally at the relational or extended abstract level in the formal mode and in postgraduate study at the postformal mode

(Biggs & Collis, 1989; Biggs, 1991, 1992a). It is posited, however, that in discipline areas that are new to them some students may only be performing in the concrete-symbolic mode and hence only acquire declarative and procedural knowledge in that mode. That is, they may be acquiring knowledge of their discipline in a mode such that they are memorising words and concepts (perhaps understanding them) and relating them to concrete situations, organising them perhaps at the relational or extended abstract level in that mode but are not really able to theorise about the ideas. The challenge to lecturers is to determine, if possible, at what level and in which mode students are operating and to facilitate movement to higher modes and levels. The SOLO taxonomy can be used in part to do this.

## THE 3P MODEL OF LEARNING

Biggs (1993) presented a 3P model of learning (developed in earlier publications and discussed elsewhere in this book). The purpose of considering it here is to relate the use of the SOLO taxonomy to the 3P model. It is suggested that the SOLO taxonomy as a tool can be utilised in each of the three Ps of the model, that is in presage, process and product. In the 3P model, presage includes *student* factors such as prior knowledge, abilities, ways of learning, value and expectations, and *teaching* factors such as curriculum, teaching method, climate and assessment (Biggs, 1993). In relation to presage, the SOLO taxonomy can be useful as a means of determining students' prior knowledge of their own learning and of their knowledge of the content and its structural organisation in a discipline. It can also be used in the teaching context to provide models of desired learning outcomes. In the process part of the model, use of target examples at the desired SOLO level in the formal mode could be used explicitly to attempt to shape the product and perhaps to facilitate effective approaches to learning. Most importantly, aspects of the SOLO taxonomy can be used in the product part of the model for assessment, where the intention is to measure both the mode of knowing and the level of structural organisation of the content in a discipline area. In summary, aspects of SOLO can be used to influence all parts of the 3P model and in particular to assess the mode and level of structure of the outcomes of teaching and learning. This chapter is an examination of its application to date mainly to the presage and product aspects of the model.

## TEACHING, LEARNING AND THE SOLO TAXONOMY

If it is intended that students acquire qualitative conceptions of learning and adopt approaches that will lead to deep learning and hence critical thinking, then teaching and assessment must be directed to that end. In order to do this it is important to determine student presage factors. In particular it is important to understand what students know and believe about their own learning, because that will largely determine the approach that they take to learning. It is also important to determine the level of knowledge in a discipline that students possess when they enter a course. The latter will allow lecturers to help students to take a relational view of learning (Ramsden, 1988). That is, to assist them to relate the new knowledge to their existing knowledge. For example, if a discipline is new to students one can assume that they will know very little in a formal sense and will need to become familiar first with jargon and factual details or, in other words, requisite declarative knowledge and basic procedural and theoretical knowledge before they can engage in higher order learning requiring conditional and metatheoretical knowledge.

McKeachie, Pintrich, Lin and Smith (1990) cited research which indicated that if material is presented in a structured way it helps students to organise course content. Entwistle and Entwistle (1992) found that students appreciate structure in material presented by lecturers but suggest that, paradoxically, too much structure may relieve students of the need to derive their own personally intelligible forms of a discipline. Probably the less students know about a discipline the more structure they need initially. Examples of learning outcomes at the desired level, that is, in the relational or extended abstract levels in the formal mode of SOLO, could be used to provide students with some structure, and as a guide to the level of organisation that they should aim to achieve.

A search of the literature provides examples of the use of SOLO in tertiary teaching for a range of presage purposes. These include determining what students know and believe about their own learning and their entering knowledge of content in the discipline area of learning. This will enable the lecturer to develop appropriate teaching approaches for desired learning outcomes.

Boulton-Lewis (1992, 1994; Boulton-Lewis, Wilss & Mutch, 1996) proposed, as a modification and extension to the SOLO taxonomy, examples of levels in the formal mode that could be used as models to assess and describe students entering and changing knowledge of their own learning as they progressed through courses in higher education. An illustrative example of a SOLO response at each level is given in Table 9.1 taken from Boulton-Lewis (1994). A further set of examples is to be found in Boulton-Lewis, Wilss and Mutch (1996). Responses at each level ranged from weak to strong, depending on the inclusion of relevant information about the learning process, as well as on the structure. Except for the example at the prestructural level, which may reflect lack of interest, the examples given represent strong responses at each level in the formal mode.

Analysis of SOLO levels by motives and strategies as measured by the Study Process Questionnaire (SPQ) (Biggs, 1987) showed that as the structural organisation of knowledge of learning increased then the concern with surface motives declined and deep motives and deep strategies assumed more importance (Boulton-Lewis, 1994).

Boulton-Lewis, Wilss and Mutch (1996) asked qualified, experienced teachers who were undertaking an in-service subject in adult learning to write statements about learning. They were asked to do this so that the lecturers could use the information to teach them, and subsequent students, more effectively. The responses were categorised at SOLO levels in the formal mode, based on their structural organisation, and the content at each of the SOLO levels was analysed. Eighty per cent of these students gave responses at the multistructural level. This indicated that they had knowledge of many aspects of learning but could not explain it in an integrated and coherent way that would allow them to apply the knowledge flexibly to their own and others' learning.

It was notable from the content analysis of these responses that very little mention was made of factors typical of adult learning. None of the students stated that they knew what they wanted to learn despite the fact that they had enrolled in this as an elective subject. They believed that their attitudes and the relevance of the subject were important to their learning. None of them stated that they should be responsible for their own learning. They were not as well informed about learning processes as one would expect, although they generally knew what motivated them. Prior learning and satisfaction with learning outcomes were considered important.

TABLE 9.1    Examples of responses at each level of the SOLO taxonomy for knowledge of learning

**Prestructural**
No idea.

**Unistructural**
Real learning is what you remember, that is, important values and lessons, even information you remember from schooling in the years after it. That is how I have found it. You remember it and in your later years it is amazing the data you can recall.

**Multistructural**
Learning is to have real understanding about a particular subject, whether through actual experience or through other sources such as text books etc.

This belief was probably acquired through the conservative thinking of the education system I was brought up with. I know that I can learn easily and quickly if there is a teacher who teaches in a methodological planned way; where I can see the plan and know where I am heading. I usually go about learning by reading, memorising, by applying to my actual experiences or knowing about other peoples' experiences. By applying it to reality it becomes simpler. Other peoples' espoused opinions and beliefs and values influence how I learn, and sometimes make it difficult to learn. By this I mean, I sometimes want to hold my own 'opinion' but other people try to sway me to their belief. I know that I have learnt something when I feel satisfied. I also know when I use the knowledge years later.

**Relational**
Learning involves the sharing of knowledge to facilitate personal growth and a greater understanding of the world around me. This perception of learning is based entirely on my own subjective value judgements and could not be considered a view that I have acquired within the education system which, in the most part, focuses on a relatively utilitarian approach, i.e. producing skilled people for the work force. Learning for me is facilitated by my being able to gain further insight into why I am here, how I fit into the society I live in, and why certain attitude and belief systems exist in that society. I know I have learnt something when I reach a greater understanding of myself as a person and the complex interrelationships that mould the society in which I live.

**Extended abstract**
First of all, learning for me is a body of information that's there to be acquired. But I don't think that body of information should be taken in and just regurgitated to others. So often in our society people think learning is about how 'well' or 'good' you can regurgitate it. I believe in the synthesis of information and one's own life experience, that is, applying your own experience to the information that you learn, and looking for the sense or reasoning contained within that melting pot of 'experience and information'. This is the only way we make sense of our world. In order to feel confident in the world we live in we need to have understanding and knowledge of ourselves, others, and the things around us. If we know how something works and understand it, it gives us confidence which I believe is a virtue. However, it only becomes really virtuous when we use that knowledge and understanding for the good of mankind. And this is where moral implications come into play. Knowledge and understanding of something involved with law and order, or more specifically 'justice', is what constitutes 'good learning'.

Source: Boulton-Lewis, 1994.

Most of them conceived of learning as quantitative rather than qualitative and stated that desired outcomes were facts and skills. This suggested that these teachers needed to learn more about their own learning in order to become the independent self-directed learners that statements in the literature about adult learning would lead one to expect. The simple process of asking them to write a statement about learning provided us with a great deal of insight into their beginning knowledge and its organisation. The conclusion was that we needed to organise teaching to facilitate the development of the learning behaviour one would expect of adults with some knowledge of the discipline rather than, as we might have done, assume the knowledge existed.

Boulton-Lewis (1992; Boulton-Lewis & Dart, 1994) used presentation and discussion of SOLO levels and examples as part of the teaching process, in an attempt to shape students' learning outcomes in courses in adult learning. Students, who in each case were experienced educators, were introduced to the SOLO taxonomy, discussed it as part of the content of the course and were told that their work would be assessed for content and structure at SOLO levels. The results in terms of improving students' structural organisation of knowledge were disappointing in both studies. The majority of students were, and remained, multistructural at the formal level although they did improve in terms of content knowledge within levels in most cases. These results probably did not match expectations because the approach was confined to one subject in a 13 week semester. Dart (Chapter 10 in this volume) subsequently reported results from a study where more substantial changes in SOLO levels, inter alia, were brought about by improved learning activities.

## ASSESSMENT AND SOLO

The major purpose of assessment is to determine whether teaching is accomplishing its goals for student learning in terms of the objectives and principles of instruction. If the intention is that students become critical thinkers, it is necessary to use assessment procedures to assess the level of structural organisation as well as knowledge of the content of the discipline to measure such learning outcomes. Nickerson (1989) asserted that a major criticism of tests constructed for the purposes of determining student grades is that they 'tend to emphasize recall of declarative or procedural knowledge and provide little indication of either the level at which students understand subject matter or of the quality of their thinking (Fleming & Chambers, 1983; Morgenstern & Renner 1984)' (p. 3). He goes on to say that if the major goal of education is higher order cognitive functioning then it is regrettable that we lack adequate tools for assessing such functioning. Because of increasingly large numbers of students in core subjects in university courses, resort is often made to assessing, at least in part, their knowledge of content through short answer or multiple choice tests. It is possible for multiple choice questions to be designed so that they measure some aspects of higher order thinking (Nickerson, 1989; Norris, 1989; Collis & Romberg, 1992). An example of a way of ordering the outcomes for a mathematics item in a test in the concrete-symbolic mode is cited in Biggs (1992, taken from Biggs, Balla, Lam & Ki, 1988). With careful thought similar examples could be generated for responses to tests in the formal mode at university level. For Table 9.2, toothpicks were used to make one box, two boxes joined (i.e. with one side in common) and three boxes (i.e. with two sides in common). Underneath the boxes the statement is made that 'Toothpicks are used to make this pattern. Four are used to make

TABLE 9.2   Ordering the outcomes for mathematics items in a test

| | |
|---|---|
| **UNISTRUCTURAL** | **a.** How many toothpicks are used to make three boxes? |
| **MULTISTRUCTURAL** | **b.** How many more toothpicks are used to make 5 boxes than are used to make 3 boxes? |
| **RELATIONAL** | **c.** Calculate how many boxes can be made with 31 toothpicks? |
| **EXTENDED ABSTRACT** | **d.** If I have made *y* boxes, how many toothpicks have I used? |

Source: Biggs, 1992 from Biggs et al., 1988.

one box, seven to make two boxes, etc.' Success with the questions below indicates the level of the student's knowledge in this mode:

However, despite the examples described above, short answer and multiple choice tests, unless very carefully designed, usually only measure declarative and theoretical information. Most tests demand surface rather than deep knowledge (Marton & Säljö 1976a, 1976b). Objective tests and examinations generally emphasise low level skills, facts, and memorisation of procedures, and these are not the aspects of knowledge that constitute the higher order thinking needed for generating arguments and solving problems (Frederickson & Collins, 1989). In order to test for higher order thinking, assessment procedures are required that measure declarative and theoretical content as well as procedural, conditional and metatheoretical knowledge.

Entwistle and Entwistle (1992) proposed that when students study they frame their preparation strategies in line with the 'form' of understanding they perceive will meet requirements. They described five such forms, four of which are assessment driven (from repeating lecture notes to personal restructuring of course material), with only one form addressing the development of an individual conception of the discipline. They concluded that the form of understanding developed in an academic course often represents an uneasy compromise between desire for understanding and the constraints of the course and assessment procedures. Nickerson (1989) suggested that because there is a causal function between assessment and instruction we should make a virtue of a perceived vice, direct tests at the outcomes of learning that we want for students and teach for those. Dart (1994) found that 'the way in which learners interpret the learning environment determines to an important degree the goal orientation they pursue which, in turn, influences the learning strategies they employ' (p. 467). He also found support for the possibility that students could hold both learning and performance goals simultaneously. That is, they want both to understand the subject and to produce work that is assessed highly. Assessment procedures therefore, as part of the learning environment, need to be carefully designed, made explicit, and implemented so that they encourage and recognise the development of those aspects of learning that lead to higher order thinking, if that is the intended outcome.

McKeachie et al. (1990) described a range of procedures for assessing the cognitive structure of a student's knowledge. These included both direct and indirect approaches derived from studies of knowledge structures at both the high school and college level. They stated that data gathering (hence testing) procedures for these approaches should include a definition of key concepts, the appropriateness of responses to be elicited, clear instructions for the subject and an adequate scoring procedure. The direct approaches, which seem to be more relevant to assessing knowledge of structure and course content, include such tasks as tree construction, concept mapping, concept structuring analysis technique (a combination of free sorting and interview) and other similar alternatives. They concluded that all these techniques for assessing and inferring representations of cognitive structure have limitations when considered for practical applications for the following reasons. Representations of cognitive structure are limited in advance when key concepts are defined, most of the representations access static propositional declarative knowledge, the cognitive structure as described by the tester may be the consensus of experts but may differ from the individual's cognitive structure, there are difficulties with transforming cognitive structure into diagrams and finally, and perhaps most importantly, there is the impracticality of using such complicated techniques for general assessment purposes. It is proposed here, therefore, that probably the most effective means in many disciplines of assessing deep learning outcomes and critical thinking is through essay-style (long or short) answers that require students to provide examples of their level of understanding, based on the organisational structure and extent of their content knowledge, and, if relevant, its application to a problem or situation. Such a procedure has the advantage that it does not limit the concepts that the students might present, the responses do not need to be static, they are potentially individual and, if properly moderated, challenge students to present conditional and metatheoretical knowledge if they possess it.

Grading procedures for essays have been criticised on the basis of subjectivity, however checklists for marking, such as that of Cawley (1989, cited in Ramsden, 1992), can obviate such problems. Biggs (1992b) proposed that such responses can be assessed effectively for content and structure using the SOLO taxonomy

(Biggs, 1992b). He described a procedure for using the SOLO taxonomy for assessment in higher education and argued that it would convey appropriate messages about learning by addressing higher level cognitive outcomes and be seen by students to be doing so. In essence, he proposed a category system based on letter grades A, B, C, D and F, for example, each of which would describe a qualitatively different kind of performance. These performances would be ordered along a scale of increasing acceptability with F being unacceptable and A outstanding. The grade of F would be multidimensional and account for failure to learn or moral or administrative problems. The other grades all relate to a formal level of SOLO as follows: D, unistructural, the student has only understood one or a few aspects of the course; C, multistructural, the student has understood or used several aspects of the course; B, relational, aspects of the student's response form a coherent whole (he suggests that most questions or assignment topics should require this structure); and A, extended abstract, high level of abstract thinking, generalisations to new contexts or original conclusions. Biggs also suggested that there be three levels within each category which indicate that the student has met the level minimally, adequately, or very well. He described procedures for combining grades with the caveat that these are qualitative scores and ideally should be treated as such.

A search of the literature provides some examples of the use of SOLO in tertiary teaching for assessing learning outcomes, assessing beliefs about a course and assessing learning on specific tasks.

Boulton-Lewis (1992) and Boulton-Lewis and Dart (1994) used the SOLO taxonomy to grade students' work in postgraduate courses in teaching and learning. A similar system to that described by Biggs (1992b) was evolved to assess students' assignments based on levels and content of responses. Students' work was assessed by the lecturer as EA (Extended abstract), R (Relational), M (Multistructural), and U (Unistructural) at those levels or at '+' or '–' those levels depending on mastery and kind of content at each level. Grades were returned to students as, for example, HD (High Distinction), HD+ or HD–, if they were EA, EA+ or EA–, in order to conform with the University's grading system. These were treated as qualitative grades in determining the final composite grade. Regrettably it was also necessary to give the final grade a nominal percentage to conform with the university grading system. Boulton-Lewis and Dart

(1994) also compared written responses, categorised according to SOLO, with concept maps as an alternative way for students to demonstrate their knowledge and structural organisation of course content. Concept maps were assessed quantitatively and also at SOLO levels. There was 75 per cent agreement between SOLO levels for concept maps and written material at the end of the subject. Concept maps, however, have a minor disadvantage when compared to textual material in that their use must be taught separately as a technique.

Tang and Biggs (1995) described an innovative procedure, the letter to a friend technique (LTF), influenced by the work of Trigwell and Prosser (1990). The assessment portfolio for the course below included letters (LTF) written early and late in the course and allowed analysis of conceptual change. The objectives in the 'Nature of Teaching and Learning' course for in-service primary and secondary teachers were formulated in terms of the target levels of cognitive complexity for instruction. The categories of objectives could also be used for grading purposes in a manner similar to that suggested by Biggs (1992). The LTFs were assessed for content and SOLO structure. The final grades were taken as criteria of change and 'roughly one third produced evidence ... that reflective decision making had occurred'. The SOLO structure of the second LTF was more likely to be relational. The task of writing a letter would seem to provide a better stimulus to describe changed conceptions than the straight statements about learning and teaching requested by Boulton-Lewis.

Galenza (1993) described the teaching and assessment of three courses in introductory psychology where the desirability of achieving high level responses was addressed explicitly and facilitated by practice and discussion. Questions, for example for the experimental group in one study, were designed at each SOLO level for four exams during the semester and the students were informed that the final exam would be marked according to SOLO. This consistent approach produced better results only for students who were described as middle level learners (and hence probably needed more assistance with structure).

Van Rossum and Schenk (1984) used the SOLO taxonomy to assess the learning outcomes, as expressed in answers to open questions, for a sample of 69 first year psychology students who were asked to study a text. They categorised most of the learning outcomes at either the multistructural or relational levels. They found a strong relation between a surface approach to learning and multistructural responses, and between a deep approach to learning and responses at the relational level. Watkins (1983) used the SOLO taxonomy to assess the level of learning outcomes as determined by the quality of students' explanations of a learning task they had worked on recently in class. The sample consisted of 60 students, chosen to represent the 10 highest scores on the meaning orientation scale and the 10 highest scores on the reproducing orientation scale of Entwistle's (Entwistle & Ramsden, 1983) Approaches to Study Inventory, from each of a faculty of arts, science and economics. Watkins found it hard to distinguish between relational and extended abstract responses but obtained high interjudge agreement when these responses were categorised as high and responses at the multistructural level and below as low. There was a strong relationship between high SOLO ratings and deep processing and low SOLO ratings and surface processing. They give examples of responses at different levels in the discipline areas.

Trigwell and Prosser (1991) and Prosser and Trigwell (1991) used the SOLO taxonomy to assess qualitative differences in overall understanding of the purpose of a course, in first year nursing communications, in response to a question asking students to describe what the course was about. They found that responses could be classified as either relational or multistructural and an example at each of these levels was provided. The results suggested a positive relationship between the Deep and Relating Ideas approaches to learning (derived from an adaptation of the Approaches to Study Inventory, Entwistle & Ramsden, 1983) and higher level qualitative outcomes as assessed by SOLO at the course level.

In summary, the use of the SOLO taxonomy for assessment indicates that it is an effective means for distinguishing between relational and multistructural responses at least. The finer differences between responses and hence gradings probably need to be determined on the kind and extent of knowledge in the responses.

## CONCLUSION

The research described above suggests that the SOLO taxonomy is a potentially useful tool in higher education both to shape and assess learning. There are some examples of how modifications have been used already to find out what students know about their learning, to assess entering knowledge in a discipline, to present examples and models of structural organisation of content in a discipline area, to illustrate acceptable learning outcomes, to shape learning through assessment and, most important of all, to assess learning outcomes. Other examples could be generated or collected by lecturers specifically for their discipline areas.

It also appears that there is a relationship, though not necessarily causal, between SOLO levels and deep approaches to learning and between SOLO levels and conceptions of learning. This is indicated by results that show that as the structural organisation of knowledge of learning improves, as demonstrated by higher SOLO levels presumably in the formal mode, then the concern with surface motives declines and deep motives and deep strategies assume more importance (Boulton-Lewis, 1994; Trigwell & Prosser, 1991; Van Rossum & Schenk, 1984; Watkins, 1983). Dart (Chapter 10 in this volume) also found a strong relationship between constructive (qualitative) conceptions of learning and SOLO responses at the multistructural and relational levels; and between reproductive (quantitative) conceptions of learning and SOLO responses at the unistructural and multistructural levels.

It is acknowledged that use of the SOLO taxonomy is only one way of assessing the extent of a student's content knowledge in a discipline and of its structural organisation. McKeachie et al. (1990) described a range of alternative methods as discussed above. However, the SOLO taxonomy has the advantage that it can also be used as a model to challenge students to engage in deep learning and to organise and present their knowledge in their own way to demonstrate understanding. It is not difficult or too time consuming to use and there are suggested models for grading responses. It requires some creative thinking on the part of lecturers, however, to generate models in their own disciplines and to then collect a range of examples from students. It also involves some explicit teaching of desired levels of structural organisation of knowledge.

It seems that further research in the adaptation and use of the SOLO taxonomy to improve the quality of learning in tertiary education is warranted. It could be used in the ways described above, examples could be generated in further discipline areas and the outcomes could be researched and documented. SOLO could be used in conjunction with other strategies which challenge students to become critical thinkers. This would include situations that require students increasingly to take control of their own learning by reading, summarising, presenting and discussing material with their peers, taking responsibility for searching the literature themselves and drawing out implications for practice. Students would also be encouraged to write, discuss and rewrite material, individually and in groups, until their descriptions reach at least the relational level in the formal mode. Finally, it would be made clear to students, in descriptions of objectives and assessment procedures, that their work would be assessed according to the level of its structural organisation as well as the nature and depth of the knowledge presented.

## Notes

1   This chapter is based on and expanded from Boulton-Lewis, 1995.

## References

Barnett, R. (1990). *The idea of higher education.* Buckingham: The Society for Research into Higher Education and Open University Press.

Biggs, J.B. (1987). *The Study Process Questionnaire (SPQ) users' manual.* Melbourne: Australian Council for Educational Research.

Biggs, J.B. (Ed.). (1991). *Teaching for learning: The view from cognitive psychology.* Melbourne: Australian Council for Educational Research.

Biggs, J.B. (1992a). Modes of learning, forms of knowing, and ways of schooling. In A. Demetriou, M. Shayer, & A. Efklides (Eds.), *Neo-Piagetian theories of cognitive development* (pp. 31–51). London: Routledge.

Biggs, J.B. (1992b). A qualitative approach to grading students. *HERDSA News, 14*(3), 3–6.

Biggs, J.B. (1993). What do inventories of students' learning processes really measure? A theoretical review and clarification. *British Journal of Educational Psychology, 63*, 3–19.

Biggs, J.B., & Collis, K.F. (1982). *Evaluating the quality of learning: The SOLO taxonomy.* New York: Academic Press.

Biggs, J.B., & Collis, K.F. (1989). Towards a model of school-based curriculum development and assessment: Using the SOLO taxonomy. *Australian Journal of Education 33*, 149–161.

Biggs, J.B., & Moore, P. (1993). *The process of learning* (3rd ed.). New York: Prentice Hall.

Boulton-Lewis, G.M. (1992). The SOLO taxonomy and levels of knowledge of learning. *Research and Development in Higher Education, 15,* 482–489.

Boulton-Lewis G. M. (1994) Tertiary students' knowledge of their own learning and a SOLO Taxonomy. *Higher Education, 28,* 387–402.

Boulton-Lewis, G.M. (1995). The SOLO Taxonomy as a means of shaping and assessing learning in higher education. *Higher Education Research and Development, 14*(2), 143–154.

Boulton-Lewis, G.M., & Dart, B.C. (1994). Assessing students' knowledge of learning: A comparison of data collection methods. In G. Gibbs (Ed.), *Improving student learning: Theory and practice.* OCSD: Oxford.

Boulton-Lewis, G.M., Wilss, L., & Mutch, S. (1996). Teachers as adult learners: Their knowledge of their own learning. *Higher Education, 32,* 89–106.

Campbell, K.J., Watson, J.M., & Collis, K.F. (1992). Volume measurement and intellectual development. *Journal of Structural Learning and Intelligent Systems, 11,* 279–298.

Collis, K.F., & Romberg, T.A. (1992). *Collis-Romberg mathematical problem solving profiles.* Melbourne: Australian Council for Educational Research.

Dart, B.C. (1994). A goal-mediational model of personal and environmental influences on tertiary students' learning strategy use. *Higher Education, 28,* 453–470.

Entwistle, A., & Entwistle, N. (1992). Experiences of understanding in revising for degree examinations. *Learning and Instruction, 2,* 1–22.

Entwistle, N., & Ramsden, P. (1983). *Understanding student learning.* London: Croom Helm.

Fredrickson, J.R., & Collins, A. (1989). A systems approach to educational testing. *Educational Researcher, 18*(9), 27–31.

Galenza, B. (1993). *The SOLO Taxonomy applied to undergraduate instruction.* Unpublished doctoral dissertation, University of Alberta.

Lehman, D.R., Lempert, R.O., & Nisbett, R.E. (1988). The effects of graduate training on reasoning: Formal discipline and thinking about every-day events. *American Psychologist, 43,* 431–442.

Marton, F., Dall'Alba, G., & Beaty, E. (1993). Conceptions of learning. *International Journal of Educational Research, 19*(3), 277–300.

Marton, F., & Säljö, R. (1976a). On qualitative differences in learning – I: outcome and process. *British Journal of Educational Psychology, 46,* 4–11.

Marton, F., & Säljö, R. (1976b). On qualitative differences in learning – II: Outcome as a function of the learner's conception of the task. *British Journal of Educational Psychology, 46*, 115–127.

Marton, F., & Säljö, R. (1984). Approaches to learning. In F. Marton, D. Hounsell, & Entwistle (Eds.), *The experience of learning*. Edinburgh: Scottish Academic Press.

Marton, F., Watkins, D., & Tang, C. (1997). Discontinuities and continuities in the experience of learning: An interview study of high-school students in Hong Kong. *Learning and Instruction, 7*(1), 21–24.

McKeachie, W.J., Pintrich, P.R, Lin Y.G., & Smith, D.A.F. (1990). *Teaching and learning in the college classroom* (2nd ed.). University of Michigan: National Center for Research to Improve Postsecondary Teaching and Learning.

Nickerson, R.S. (1989). New directions in educational assessment. *Educational Researcher, 18*(9), 3–7.

Norris, S.P. (1989). Can we test validly for critical thinking? *Educational Researcher, 18*(9), 21–26.

Prosser, M. T., & Millar, R. (1989). The 'How and What' of learning physics: A phenomenographic study. *European Journal of Psychology of Education, 4*, 513–528.

Prosser, M., & Trigwell, K. (1991). Student evaluations of teaching and courses: Student learning approaches and outcomes as criteria of validity. *Contemporary Educational Psychology, 16*, 269–301.

Ramsden, P. (1988). Studying learning: improving teaching. In P. Ramsden (Ed.), *Improving learning: New perspectives*. London: Kogan Page.

Ramsden, P. (1992). *Learning to teach in higher education*. London: Routledge.

Samuelowicz, K., & Bain, J.D. (1992). Conceptions of teaching held by teachers. *Higher Education, 24*, 93–112.

Tang, C., & Biggs, J. (1995). Letter to a friend: Assessing conceptual change in professional development. *Research and Development in Higher Education, 18*, 698–703.

Trigwell, K., & Prosser, M. (1990). Using student learning outcome measures in the evaluation of teaching. *Research and Development in Higher Education, 13*, 390–397.

Trigwell, K., & Prosser, M. (1991). Relating approaches to study and quality of learning outcomes at the course level. *British Journal of Educational Psychology, 61*, 265–275.

Van Rossum, E.J., & Schenk, S.M. (1984). The relationship between learning conception, study strategy and learning outcome. *British Journal of Educational Psychology, 54*, 73–83.

Watkins, D. (1983). Depth of processing and the quality of learning outcomes. *Instructional Science, 12,* 49–58.

Watson, J.M., Campbell, K.J., & Collis, K.F. (1993). Multimodal functioning in understanding fractions. *Journal of Mathematical Behavior, 12,* 45–62.

# CHAPTER 10

# Teaching for Improved Learning in Small Classes

*Barry Dart*

## INTRODUCTION

For some years now Biggs has been adapting Dunkin and Biddle's (1974) presage-process-product model. This adapted model, commonly referred to as the 3P model, is used to describe student learning. It allows a consideration of the relations between what academic teachers do and think, what students do and think, and the nature of student learning outcomes. In its latest form (Biggs, 1993) it not only represents a linear movement from presage to process to product, but also interactions between these components forming an integrated system, a system in equilibrium. This systems feature, in which any change to one part will affect the rest, provides direction for intervention at the micro-system within which the academic teacher is primarily concerned, that is, the classroom. This chapter reports a study in a core unit in educational psychology for a postgraduate pre-service teacher training course at a large Australian metropolitan university. Deliberate changes are introduced in the teaching context (presage); their effects on students' perceptions (presage), how they go about learning (process) and the outcomes of that learning (product) are described.

## BACKGROUND TO THE STUDY

Students in pre-service teacher education programs bring with them considerable informal knowledge of learning and teaching processes and of psychological concepts related to classroom learning and teaching. A 'conduit' metaphor (Iran-Nejad, 1990) frequently underlies common conceptions of learning, that is, somehow or other knowledge is transferred from some outside source into the learner's head. In these conceptions learners are assumed to be more or less passive receptors of knowledge. However, recent conceptions of learning emphasise that learners actively construct knowledge for themselves by forming their own representations of the material to be learned, selecting information they perceive to be relevant, and interpreting this on the basis of their present knowledge and needs (Shuell, 1993). In this view, learners assume more active and interactive roles (Dart & Clarke, 1991; King, 1993; Prawat & Floden, 1994; Zell & Malacinski, 1994).

Knowledge falls into three main kinds: declarative (knowing that), procedural (knowing how), and conditional (knowing when and why) (Marzano et al., 1988). A formidable challenge for teacher educators is to have students link, both 'naive' and 'informed', declarative, procedural, and conditional knowledge: that is knowing what to do, how to do it, and why it should be done, from an informed perspective. Naive represents little or no evidence of a theoretical knowledge base and/or is without relational understanding of theoretical concepts. Informed represents evidence of theoretical knowledge and relational understanding of theoretical concepts. It is therefore important for academic teachers (lecturers) to synthesise the experiences, content knowledge, and reflective activity of student teachers so that they compose these constructs more effectively and more quickly.

## INFLUENCES ON TERTIARY STUDENTS' LEARNING

Recent research on student learning has focused on relationships between students' approaches to learning, their perceptions of their learning environments, their personal characteristics, and their learning outcomes (Biggs, 1991; Dart, 1994a; Dart & Clarke, 1991, 1992; N. Entwistle, 1987; N. Entwistle & A. Enwistle, 1991; A. Entwistle & N. Enwistle, 1992; Marton & Säljö, 1984; Prosser & Millar, 1989; Ramsden, 1992; Ramsden & Entwistle, 1981; Trigwell & Prosser, 1991a, 1991b). If students approach their learning with an intention to reproduce the material being studied through using routinised procedures (surface approach) then low quality outcomes result (Biggs, 1989; Marton & Säljö, 1984; Prosser & Millar, 1989;

Trigwell & Prosser, 1991a, 1991b). These outcomes may include: 'missing the point' of the material, learning that is fragmented and its relationship with new situations remains unrecognised, and misconceptions that remain unchallenged (Bain, 1994). On the other hand, if students seek meaning in and understanding of the material being studied through engaging it in ways that elaborate and transform it (deep approach), higher quality outcomes result (Biggs, 1989; Marton & Säljö, 1984; Prosser & Millar, 1989; Trigwell & Prosser, 1991a, 1991b). Outcomes in this instance may include relationally-structured knowledge which is integrated with the necessary procedures to apply it, misconceptions that have been rectified, and knowledge that can be adapted and applied in new situations (Bain, 1994). A third approach, achieving, is exemplified by an intention to excel using highly organised learning processes.

The central place of the learning environment and the personal characteristics of the learner in influencing whether students adopt deep or surface approaches to learning is emphasised in recent research and writings in higher education (Biggs, 1993; Dart, 1994a; Dart & Clarke, 1991, 1992; Entwistle, 1987; Ramsden, 1984, 1992; Ramsden & Entwistle, 1981). These studies have shown that (i) factors present in the learning context such as good teaching, openness to students, freedom in learning, teaching methods, assessment methods, vocational relevance, appropriate workload, 'press for understanding', and (ii) personal characteristics such as intentions for learning, perceived self-ability and locus of control orientation, influence how students go about their learning.

## STUDENTS' CONCEPTIONS AND APPROACHES TO LEARNING

There has been increasing interest and research in recent years in students' views of learning. This has resulted in findings that students' conceptions of learning are related to ways in which they go about their learning, as well as the quality of their learning outcomes (Marton, 1988; Prosser & Millar, 1989; Van Rossum & Schenk, 1984; Trigwell & Prosser, 1991b).

Biggs (1994) identifies two 'outlooks' on learning which he labels 'quantitative' and 'qualitative'. The quantitative perspective proposes that learning is about acquisition and accumulation of content, the more you 'know' the better the learner you are. On the other hand, the qualitative perspective proposes that learning is concerned with meaning-making and developing understanding through relating new material to what is already known.

Säljö (1979) and Marton, Dall'Alba and Beaty (1993) identified frameworks in which conceptions of learning were arranged hierarchically. The first five levels are similar for both frameworks, that is:

1  Increasing one's knowledge.
2  Memorising and reproducing.
3  Applying.
4  Understanding.
5  Seeing something in a different way.

Marton et al. (1993) included a sixth level, which is an existential extension of the fifth level:

6  Changing as a person.

Examination of what these conceptions embody indicates that in both hierarchies, levels 1, 2, and 3 can be loosely considered as representative of a quantitative outlook, and levels 4, 5 and 6 somewhat indicative of a qualitative outlook. This reduction of conceptions into two categories, 'reproducing' (levels 1, 2 and 3) and 'constructive' (levels 4 and 5), was employed by Van Rossum and Schenk (1984) who found that students who reported using a surface approach to learning held a 'reproductive' conception of learning, whereas those using a deep approach held a 'constructive' conception of learning.

## ACADEMIC TEACHERS' CONCEPTIONS AND APPROACHES TO TEACHING

It has been claimed that the conceptions of, or orientations to, teaching that academic teachers hold may be an important influence affecting the quality of student learning (Kember & Gow, 1994; Prosser, Trigwell, & Taylor, 1994; Samuelowicz & Bain, 1992). This influence was expected to result from the effects that conceptions of teaching would have on teaching methods employed, learning activities and tasks used, and assessment requirements. However, there has been little research in the area of academic teachers' conceptions of teaching and learning (Kember & Gow, 1994; Prosser, Trigwell & Taylor, 1994; Samuelowicz & Bain, 1992).

There is agreement that the varying conceptions can be simplified into broader categories of 'teacher-centred' versus 'student-centred' or 'knowledge transmission' versus 'learning facilitation'. One extreme in each continuum reflects a quantitative 'outlook' on teaching (transmission), whereas the other extreme in each represents a qualitative 'outlook' (construction).

Kember and Gow (1994) examined the relationship between lecturers' conceptions of teaching and students' approaches to learning in 15 departments in two institutions of higher education in Hong Kong. They claimed that their results indicate a relationship between lecturers' orientations to teaching and the quality of student learning. In departments where learning facilitation prevails, surface approaches to learning are discouraged, whereas in departments where the emphasis is on knowledge transmission, deep approaches are deterred.

Recent research with first year university Chemistry and Physics teachers (Prosser, Trigwell & Taylor, 1994) focused on their conceptions of learning and teaching. Findings indicated that conceptions of learning involving accumulation and acquisition of information and knowledge are related to conceptions of teaching which are teacher-centred and imply the transmission of knowledge. On the other hand, conceptions that learning involves the development of personal meaning through conceptual development and change are related to beliefs that teaching is student-centred or entails learning facilitation.

Samuelowicz and Bain (1992) analysed interviews with 13 academic teachers which resulted in the identification of five levels of conceptions of teaching (ordered, not hierarchical). Further analysis of these conceptions manifested five dimensions that allowed for comparison of these conceptions in terms of teacher- or learner-centredness. Similar results to Prosser, Trigwell and Taylor (1994) are reported on the relationships between conceptions of teaching and the degree of teacher-/learner-centredness.

The relationships between teaching approach and student learning were investigated by Sheppard and Gilbert (1991) who found that teachers who taught in ways designed to develop and/or change their students' conceptions of the material being studied through the use of discussion and other student-centred strategies were more likely to have students who employed a deep approach.

## FOCUS OF STUDY

The purposes of this study were to (i) improve the ways in which tertiary education students in small classes engage in learning by focusing on their conceptions of and intentions for learning; (ii) enable students to recognise their own relevant ideas and beliefs, evaluate these ideas and beliefs in terms of what is to be learned and how this learning is intended to occur, and decide whether or not to reconstruct their ideas and beliefs; and (iii) improve the quality of their learning through helping them to develop relational understanding of the material in the course, that is, understanding characterised by connecting or linking new knowledge with their prior knowledge (c.f. Biggs & Collis, 1989).

As a result, it was expected that students would demonstrate positive outcomes from the program including theoretically-informed declarative, procedural, and conditional knowledge of the teaching/learning process, which would be organised in a way that would allow them to apply this knowledge effectively.

The aims were to be achieved by helping them to become aware of and understand their psychological processes when learning, by causing them to focus on their own learning experiences. To this end they were provided with opportunities to take greater responsibility for their own learning, as well as to learn and apply appropriate cognitive and metacognitive strategies associated with a deep or transformative approach to learning. The intention was that they would be more self-regulated and reflective in their learning. The importance of metacognition, reflection and the acceptance of self-responsibility for this approach to learning is propounded by Biggs (1988), Biggs and Moore (1993) and Dart (1994a). From a constructivist viewpoint, learners must have control over their own learning, as the responsibility for learning and meaning-making rests with individual learners. Underlying the aims of this unit was the belief that if you want to become a good teacher then you need to know how students learn: if you want to know how students learn you first need to know how you learn yourself.

To facilitate the organisation of their knowledge of the teaching/learning process, continual emphasis was given to the need for relational understanding through making connections: connections between aspects of the new material, connections between the new material and their prior knowledge, and connections between their naive beliefs and informed knowledge.

Many of these learning experiences and opportunities were provided in a small group (collaborative learning group, n = 3) context in which students discussed, shared their understandings, and examined and evaluated their own and others' beliefs. Numerous writers stress the importance of social interaction in facilitating changes in understanding (for example, Baird, 1991; Jonassen, 1994; King, 1993; Prawat & Floden, 1994). According to Resnick (1987), peer collaboration is essential to the learning process, as learners construct meaning and understanding through active participation and sharing of knowledge. Likewise, Brown (1988) states that a change in understanding is more likely to occur through social interactive approaches that require learners to explain, elaborate and debate with others. Within these learning groups in this unit, learners have the opportunity to recognise, evaluate and, if they decide so, transform their understandings.

Thus, the approach to teaching was based on constructivist learning theory and reflected a conception of teaching representing level 2 (teaching as an activity aimed at changing students' conceptions or understanding of the world) in Samuelowicz and Bain's (1992) classification; a learning facilitation orientation according to Kember and Gow (1994); and approach E (a student-focused strategy aimed at students changing their conceptions) in Prosser, Trigwell and Taylor's (1994) categorisation. As such, the approach to teaching was based on and extended earlier research by the writer (Dart & Clarke, 1991).

## ORIGIN OF THE PROGRAM

As a consequence of the earlier teaching program (Dart & Clarke, 1991) in which students demonstrated increases in deep motive, achieving strategy, deep approach, and deep achieving approach to learning, it was decided to vary some of the learning experiences provided in that program, as well as measure the quality of learning outcomes. The reasons for these changes were simple: further experience had indicated that some learning activities could be improved to support the move to self-direction in learning more adequately and so provide structure for those students requiring it. As well, there were no measures of learning outcomes included in the earlier study and it was believed that some qualitative measures of learning outcomes would enhance this study.

In accordance with the stated conception of teaching underlying the teaching approach, teaching/learning strategies, learning tasks and activities and assessment items were developed that were congruent with this conception of teaching and concomitant goals of learning.

## OUTLINE OF THE PROGRAM

### INITIAL MEETING

Pre-unit data (as described later) were collected immediately the group had formed. On the completion of this, general introductions in which the teacher and students gave their names and talked briefly about themselves, both personally and professionally, and there followed a brief discussion of what Psychology, and more specifically Educational Psychology, involved.

Students were then informed of the objectives for the unit, the teaching approach adopted for the unit and the rationale for these. In particular, the functions and importance of the collaborative learning group were emphasised.

The content of the unit that all students were to study was then identified: Learning (theories of learning, models of learning, and learning strategies); Motivation; Classroom Management; Learning Styles; and Teacher Expectation Effects. The content may seem limited for a one semester unit of study. However, to foster understanding (which may require confronting powerful prior knowledge which could interfere with the learning experiences provided) requires time to engage in what Baird (1991, p. 102) described as 'the constructivist processes of recognition, evaluation, and possible reconstruction of personal views' which encompass reflection and metacognition. Furthermore, Bain (1994) asserted that for the development of transformative understanding the curriculum needs to 'be stripped', that is, 'to enable students to "wrestle with ideas" over a sustained period, the syllabus must be reduced to a few essential generative topics' (Bain, 1994, p. 19). Previous experience of the writer supports these assertions (Dart & Clarke, 1991).

The two assessment items for the unit – a 'teaching episode' (seminar) within the student's collaborative learning group (defined later,

40 per cent), and a negotiated learning contract (discussed later in the paper, 60 per cent) – were explained and discussed in detail with the students as were the relationships of these items with the learning objectives and teaching approach for the unit.

Students were then asked to reflect on what they believed learning entailed, and how they had engaged in learning in the subjects studied in their undergraduate degrees and why. They were then asked to write their responses and join with some other student and share and discuss these responses. The exercise was repeated by two groups combining and following the same procedure. When this was completed a whole class discussion ensued. Many of the students reported holding quantitative conceptions of learning, using surface approaches to learning and beliefs that these had been sufficient for them to succeed in their previous learning. These were contrasted with how students were expected to go about learning in this unit, and the objectives and rationale for the program were discussed again.

At the end of the initial meeting session, students were given a reading task which they were to prepare for discussion in the next session. They were asked to try to get to know other group members during the week so that collaborative learning groups could be formed at the beginning of the next session.

## LEARNING EXPERIENCES AND TEACHING STRATEGIES

The focus of the learning experiences is the collaborative learning group, usually made up of three students who have elected to work with each other in the unit. Normally, the first part of each meeting period is organised around these learning groups. It is emphasised in the first session and during the semester that learning is an active process and requires students to take responsibility for their own learning (with the support of the teacher and their learning group partners). What is important is that 'opposing views become alternatives to be explored rather than competitors to be eliminated' (Roby, 1988, p. 173). To this end, 'conceptual exploration' is stressed rather than 'personal confrontation'.

In the collaborative learning group discussions in this program, students discuss their understandings of and share their responses to questions (both teacher and student generated) relating to assigned readings or other allied material. In these discussions, students are encouraged to examine, explain, and apply concepts and their understandings generally to the teaching/learning context, and specifically to their teaching areas. As well, in this collaborative process, students might share their writings, concept maps, and other examples of their generated knowledge.

Other activities that take place within the learning group include the analysis of case studies developed by themselves and previous students from their practice teaching experiences, and role-plays relating to teaching/learning activities such as classroom management episodes.

To help them in their collaborative learning endeavours students are introduced to strategies that are useful for their understanding, examining, evaluating, explaining, and applying activities. These include activities that require them to read with purpose: identifying main ideas, writing summaries, and drawing mind-maps and concept maps.

Students are also given experience in Guided Reciprocal Peer Questioning (King, 1993), a constructivist, interactive learning method that helps them actively process material. Students are provided with a range of generic question stems to use as a guide for developing their own specific questions relating to the material being studied. Subsequent to this self-questioning phase of the process, students ask each other questions in their learning group and take turns answering each other's questions and discuss these responses. Constructing specific questions requires students to identify relevant concepts in the material, elaborate on them, and think about how these concepts relate to each other as well as to their prior knowledge. Responding to others' questions promotes further active learning.

The teacher's role in these learning group activities is to help identify students' beliefs, guide them in this approach to learning (which is a new experience for many of them), and work with them to master impediments to understanding. This is achieved through facilitating student-student interaction, using reflective feedback to enhance the nature of the discussion, and providing critical feedback related to students' contributions. As mentioned earlier, relational understanding is emphasised through connecting new and existing knowledge.

Following the learning group activities is a whole class discussion and debate. In this, learning group experiences are shared with the whole group, and further examining, explaining, and applying of the material under discussion (and related material) occurs, this time in a wider context. The teacher feeds in material considered relevant to that under discussion where necessary, and uses similar sorts of teaching strategies as used in the learning group activities. The role of the teacher is to frame stimulus questions that enable students to: identify relevant naive and informed knowledge, consider alternative perspectives and their effects, and examine and evaluate the opinions and beliefs put forward by other class members and themselves. At the end of the session, expectations regarding learning tasks and activities for the next session are given.

Students are usually referred to journal articles or material from textbooks to be read before the next session. However, a structured approach to this pre-reading is taken. There were some variations in these activities. One required pre-reading and then responding to teacher generated questions (requiring understanding and application). The students' written responses were then discussed in the learning group at the next session. Another activity required pre-reading and students to generate their own questions relating to the material, followed by discussion of these questions in the learning group at the next session. A third variant involved pre-reading and each group responding to a different question developed by the teacher. Members of each group discussed their responses to their question and presented these to the whole class. In all instances for these activities, whole class discussion followed as usual.

## ASSESSMENT

As mentioned earlier, there were two assessment items.

### 1. Teaching episode (40 per cent)

Each member of a group 'teaches' the other students in the group about some topic relevant to the teaching/learning process. These teaching episodes occur towards the end of semester and usually students take one hour for their presentation. The importance of peer group teaching experiences for a variety of reasons (including the promotion of reflection, metacognition, and reconstruction) is documented in McKeachie, Pintrich, Lin and Smith (1986) and Biggs and Moore (1993).

The group may decide to teach about a particular topic, such as Motivation or Inclusive Education, in which case each member selects some aspect of the 'theme' to teach. Otherwise, individual group members may elect to teach a particular topic of personal interest. The format is similar to that used previously by the writer (Dart & Clarke, 1991). Each group prepares a statement indicating what each group is going to teach. If they are teaching a particular theme, then it will include group objectives for the activity. On the other hand, if they are teaching different topics, it will include individual objectives for each episode. As they are to evaluate each other's teaching as well as their own, the statement includes agreed upon criteria for this assessment, together with standards of performance to facilitate this evaluation. A written report including preparation notes, notes of lesson, resources, group members' evaluations, as well as self-evaluation, is required one week later.

## 2. Learning contract (60 per cent)

The effectiveness of contract learning in promoting student autonomy in learning, a sense of ownership, and intrinsic motivation, all characteristics of a deep approach to learning (Biggs & Moore, 1993; Ramsden, 1992), has been established by Dart and Clarke (1991), Knowles (1986) and Tomkins and McGraw (1988). The use of contract learning is to help students control their learning experiences to meet their own interests and needs, and so become more self-directed.

The contract specifies their intended learning goals, the learning activities they will engage in to reach these goals, and the evidence they will provide of attaining their goals. The importance of starting early in developing their contracts is stressed, and students are encouraged to submit them as early as possible so as to allow for renegotiation if needed. The only constraint on the learning contract is that it must relate to the teaching/learning process.

The method of assessing their contract work is given at the initial meeting, and is focused on in following sessions until students understand clearly what is required. The product is assessed qualitatively using a procedure based on Biggs (1992) developed from the Structure of Observed Learning Outcomes (SOLO) taxonomy (Biggs & Collis, 1982), a measure of the level of complexity of structure of knowledge. This scheme identifies five categories of learning, ranging from: 'irrelevant or incorrect (prestructural), through increasing use of relevant data (uni- and multistructural), integration of data into an appropriate relationship (relational), to generalisations and applications well beyond the call of duty (extended abstract)' (Biggs, 1992, p. 4).

There are three levels within each category; the level can be illustrated minimally, adequately, or very well. This type of assessment provides not only summative information, but also serves a diagnostic function in indicating to students at what stage their learning is.

This form of assessment relates to one of the expected outcomes of the program, viz. the knowledge of the teaching/learning process gained would be organised in such a way that it would be able to be applied effectively, that is, the knowledge would be connected through relational understanding.

Students are provided with examples of written work at each level to help familiarise them with what is required. Writing activities in their learning group require students to attempt to structure responses at the relational level. These responses are shared with other group members and students evaluate the structure of the response using the SOLO categories. They then discuss these evaluations. These activities provide them with useful experiences which help relational understanding to be expressed.

Even though other studies in higher education have reported measuring the quality of student learning using a procedure based on the SOLO taxonomy, they have either studied qualitative differences in outcomes on specific academic tasks (Van Rossum & Schenk, 1984; Watkins, 1983), or differences in students' descriptions of what their course of study was about (Trigwell & Prosser, 1991a, 1991b). Exceptions to these include Boulton-Lewis and Dart (1994) and Tang (Chapter 5 in this volume) which qualitatively assessed student assignments based on course content. In addition, Boulton-Lewis (1995, Chapter 9 in this volume) has described the use of the SOLO Taxonomy for helping develop and assess learning.

## METHOD

### SAMPLE

The students in the program were enrolled in the Post Graduate Diploma of Education (Secondary Teaching) in 1993 in the Faculty of Education at the Queensland University of Technology. They were members of a class studying educational psychology taught by the writer. There were 22 students for whom there is complete data.

Fourteen were female and eight were male; 12 were aged less than 25 years, seven were between 25 and 30 years, and three were older than 30 years.

DATA COLLECTION PROCEDURES AND VARIABLES

Since the interest was in changes that may have occurred as a result of the program, information was collected at the beginning and end of the first semester. At the initial meeting of the class, students completed the pre-test measures before any other activities took place. Students completed open-ended statements relating to their beliefs about learning, as well as two quantitative questionnaires; the first measuring how they usually went about their learning, and the other asking them to indicate how they preferred their classroom learning environment to be structured. These measures were administered again at the end of the semester. However, on this occasion the first quantitative measure required students to indicate how they typically learnt in this unit and the second asked them to evaluate the classroom environment as experienced during the semester.

### Organisation of knowledge of learning (SOLO)
Unstructured data on what students believed learning was and how they acquired those beliefs were obtained from open-ended statements. Furthermore, students were asked to consider how they went about learning, what factors they felt influenced their learning, and how they knew that they had learnt something in formulating their responses.

### Level of conception of learning (Conception)
The responses to the open-ended statements were also utilised to obtain some indication of conceptions of learning that were held by students.

### Approach to study (Approach)
Students' orientations to learning were measured using Biggs' (1987) Study Process Questionnaire (SPQ). The SPQ is a comprehensive measure of study processes. There are six subscales: three measure students' motives for studying (surface, deep and achieving), the

other three measure the learning strategies that students use (surface, deep and achieving). The corresponding subscales for motive and strategy can be combined to produce a score representing a surface approach, deep approach and achieving approach. Items are rated on a 5 point Likert scale (5 = always or almost always true of me, 1 = never or only rarely true of me). Reliability coefficients for the subscales are reported in Biggs (1987), as are studies indicating construct validity of the scale.

### Perceptions of the classroom learning environment (Environment)
Students responded to a questionnaire developed to measure their perceptions of the classroom learning environment from a constructivist perspective (Dart, 1994b). This questionnaire has three subscales: Autonomy, Collaboration and Responsibility. Two forms of the questionnaire were developed: one to measure students' preferred learning environment, and administered at the beginning of semester; the other to measure students' perceived experiences of the learning environment in this unit, and administered at the end of semester. Students responded on a 5 point Likert scale (5 = very often, 1 = never). Reliability coefficients for the two forms, preferred and perceived, and validation procedures are reported in Dart (1994b). One reason for using this questionnaire was to obtain information at the beginning of the semester that would inform the teacher of individual preferences, and so could be used to vary the amount of support students required in the program.

### Interviews
Seven students volunteered to be interviewed to give their impressions of the program, as well as more detailed accounts of their learning, their perceptions of teaching practices and the relationship between teaching and learning. These interviews were conducted by a research assistant and were audiotaped. They provided qualitative data to supplement the quantitative data.

### Student evaluation of teaching
Students were also given a standard Student Evaluation of Teaching Questionnaire used in the University to complete on the last day of semester. The questionnaire was administered by one of the students and students responded anonymously. The questionnaire is standard to the extent that all such questionnaires at this University include seven items which are the same: six are general items

relating to teaching (rated on a 5 point Likert scale, 1 = disagree strongly to 5 = agree strongly), and the seventh requires students to give an overall rating of the lecturer's teaching (rated on a 7 point Likert scale, 1 = very poor to 7 = excellent). Lecturers are free to choose another 10 items to be included in the questionnaire. These are selected from numerous items representing various elements of teaching, such as teaching, assessment, student learning, organisational skills, and lecturer-student relationships (also rated on a 5 point Likert scale, 1 = disagree strongly, 5 = agree strongly). The optional 10 items in this questionnaire represented teaching, assessment, and course material. The 10 items that were selected for this section were chosen on the basis that they best reflected the aims of the unit. These items are presented in Table 10.1.

The purpose of including this information is not to reflect on the relative merits of the writer as a teacher, but rather to indicate students' perceptions of various aspects of the program, which are reflected particularly by the selected items representing teaching, assessment, and course material.

## ANALYSIS

Data analysis of the Approach variables was carried out using SPSS Release 4.1. Since pre- and post-test data were collected to measure change, a repeated measures design, the procedure used was to carry out a multivariate analysis of variance (MANOVA) to test for the within-subject effect of Time. If such an effect exists, the MANOVA provides the confidence that univariate measures are operating at the pre-scribed level of $p = 0.05$. Similarly, the Environment variables were analysed using MANOVA to determine if there were differences between what students preferred and what they perceived they experienced. In both cases of Approach and Environment variables, scores for each subscale were transformed to a 5 point scale for ease of interpretation.

Student responses to the open-ended statements, pre- and post-, were analysed by a research assistant and the writer separately, using a procedure developed by Boulton-Lewis (1992, 1994) which is based on the SOLO taxonomy (Biggs & Collis, 1982). Each student's response was classified into one of the five SOLO categories. There was total agreement between the two sets of categorisations.

Likewise, each response, pre- and post-, was identified as representing a particular level of conception of learning using the

TABLE 10.1    Student evaluation of teaching questionnaire

| Item | Mean |
|------|------|
| **General teaching** | |
| 1.   The lecturer makes clear what I need to do to be successful in this unit. | 4.32 |
| 2.   The lecturer is well organized and prepared for classes. | 4.73 |
| 3.   The lecturer structures the unit content in ways which assist my learning. | 4.64 |
| 4.   The lecturer provides feedback which is constructive and helpful. | 4.09 |
| 5.   The lecturer shows genuine concern for student progress and needs. | 4.27 |
| 6.   The lecturer presents the unit clearly. | 4.73 |
| **Overall rating of lecturer** | |
| 7.   Overall, how would you rate the teaching of this lecturer in this unit? | 6.14 |
| **Selected teaching** | |
| 8.   The lecturer teaches at a level understood by students. | 4.73 |
| 9.   The lecturer motivates me to work independently. | 4.18 |
| 10.  The lecturer develops a class atmosphere conducive to learning. | 4.59 |
| 11.  The lecturer allows me to develop my own ideas. | 4.32 |
| 12.  The lecturer has good rapport with students. | 4.77 |
| **Assessment** | |
| 13.  The lecturer makes assessment requirements clear. | 4.05 |
| 14.  The assignments set by the lecturer are useful learning experiences. | 4.68 |
| **Course material** | |
| 15.  The lecturer seems well-informed on the material presented. | 4.86 |
| 16.  The lecturer relates course material to real life situations. | 4.45 |
| 17.  The lecturer helps me to understand relationships between topics and ideas. | 4.36 |

hierarchy of Marton, Dall'Alba, and Beaty (1993) discussed earlier. This framework indicates at which level within a hierarchy of conceptions a particular response best fits. Again, there was complete agreement between the writer and the research assistant.

Both SOLO and Conception variables were analysed using the Wilcoxon matched-pairs signed-ranks test accessed through NPAR tests within SPSS Release 4.1. This tests to see if there are any differences between the pre- and post- measures of the variables being tested within the one population, taking into account the size of the differences.

Transcripts of students' interviews were content analysed to determine relevant material about the program and their learning that would enrich the quantitative data.

Means for each section of the Student Evaluation of Teaching questionnaire were calculated.

## RESULTS

### APPROACH

MANOVA results indicated that there was an overall multivariate effect for Time (Hotellings = 1.31, F = .3.5, df = 6,16, p = .021). Univariate statistics showed a significant effect for Time for achieving motive (F = 10.49, p = 0.004) and for achieving strategy (F = 22.57, p = .000). In both instances there were significant decreases in mean values (achieving motive: pre- = 3.56, post- = 3.10; achieving strategy: pre- = 3.83, post- = 3.23). Effect sizes were calculated for these differences. They were respectively − 0.68 and 1.06. According to Cohen (1969), these can be considered as representing large differences. There were slight increases in means from pre- to post- for deep motive (3.52→3.75), deep strategy (4.19→4.25), and surface strategy (2.44→2.53), and a slight decrease for surface motive (2.73→2.67).

### ENVIRONMENT

MANOVA results for these variables showed an overall multivariate effect for Time also (Hotellings = 1.29, F = 8.2, df = 3,19, p = .001). Univariate tests identified a significant difference for autonomy (F = 26.36, p = .000). The mean for preferred autonomy (at the beginning of semester) being 3.30, and that for perceived autonomy (experienced during the semester and measured at the end) being 4.27. The effect size for this change was large, 1.41. The means for preferred and experienced collaboration differed slightly (3.63 vs 3.79), as did those for responsibility (4.21 vs 4.25).

### SOLO

Results of the Wilcoxon test indicated a significant change in SOLO category from the beginning to the end of semester (z = −2.67, p = .008). No student's SOLO category changed to a less complex category; 13 students' categories remained the same; however, nine students' categories increased. One student's knowledge of learning was in the relational category prior to the commencement of the program, whereas at the end of semester another eight students' knowledge of learning was judged to be in the relational category. The other students' knowledge of learning reflected the multistructural category.

## CONCEPTION

There was no significant change in levels of conception of learning. Four students' levels decreased, eight remained the same, and 10 increased. If the levels of conceptions of learning are modified in a similar fashion to that used by Van Rossum and Schenk (1984) (that is, the first three levels are combined to form a 'reproductive' conception of learning, while the remaining three levels are combined to form a 'constructive' conception of learning), then at the end of the program 17 students had a 'constructive' conception and five had a 'reproductive' conception.

## EVALUATION OF TEACHING

The mean for the six items representing general teaching characteristics was 4.46; the mean for selected items representing teaching was 4.52; the mean for assessment items was 4.36; and the mean for course material items was 4.56. The overall mean for the rating of the lecturer (on a 7 point scale ) was 6.14.

## ASSESSMENT BASED ON SOLO

As stated earlier, students' performances on their learning contract assignment were assessed using a procedure based on the SOLO taxonomy. Twelve students' work was evaluated as being in the relational category, nine as being in the multistructural category, and one as being unistructural.

Similar to the significant change in SOLO category from the beginning of semester to the end of semester (evidenced in responses to open-ended statements on learning), there was significant change in pre-program SOLO category and assessment SOLO category. Two students' assessment SOLO category was less than their pre-program SOLO category, seven students' categories remained the same, and 13 increased their assessment category over their pre-program category ($z = -2.50$, $p = .013$).

OTHER INCIDENTAL RESULTS

Crosstabs were carried out to examine the joint distribution of level of complexity of structure of knowledge of learning (SOLO) and level of conception of learning (Conception). The result for the pre-measures was not significant, however that for the post-measures was significant ($x^2 = 4.28$, $df = 1$, $p = .038$). Results indicated that as Conception changed from reproductive to constructive, SOLO level increased. For those students holding reproductive conceptions, five were at the multistructural level and none at the relational level. However, for those holding constructive conceptions, eight were at the multistructural level and nine were at the relational level. The value of the phi coefficient, which measures the extent of association between SOLO and Conception, was 0.45 which has an approximate significance of .034.

The joint distribution of students' level of conception of learning at the end of the program (Conception) and assessment SOLO category was also examined using Crosstabs. Results showed that students having constructive conceptions of learning demonstrated better quality in their learning as evidenced by more complex structuring of their knowledge ($x^2 = 8.8$, df = 1, p = .003).

For students holding reproductive conceptions, one had an assignment SOLO at the unistructural level and four were at the multistructural level. In the case of the other students holding constructive conceptions, five had an assessment SOLO category at the multistructural level and 12 were at the relational level. The level of association between Conception at the end of the semester and assessment SOLO category was phi = 0.65 (p = .009).

**DISCUSSION**

The results reported above suggest that essentially the program achieved what it set out to do. Although there was no significant change for surface and deep motives and strategies, there was significant decrease in achieving motive and strategy. That is, students were less competitive in their learning as a result of the learning experiences provided in the course. This most likely resulted from their learning activities in the collaborative learning groups. The means for deep motive and strategy were initially high (particularly for deep strategy), and even though there were slight increases, it is most likely that a 'ceiling' effect was operating here, that is, there was little scope for significant increases. Similarly for surface motive and strategy, means were initially low so maybe a 'cellar' effect operated for them, that is, there was little capacity for significant decreases. Overall, the predominant approach to learning was deep or transformative.

Evidence for students getting in touch with their ideas and beliefs relating to the teaching/learning process, evaluating these, and restructuring them when considered necessary, is provided by a consideration of their changes in conception of learning. Even though there was no significant change in pre- to post-conceptions for the class as a whole, that 10 students' levels of conception increased and 17 students reported having a 'constructive' construction at the end of the program provides a strong message that the program is operating satisfactorily in this regard. The relationship between students' level of conception of learning and level of complexity of structure of knowledge of learning is important as it suggests that teaching aimed deliberately at changing one or other of these constructs is likely to lead to a change in the other. As well, the association between post-conceptions and assessment SOLO category provides evidence that quality in learning (in terms of more complex knowledge structures) is related to what students believe learning to be.

Support for improvement in the quality of learning through the development of relational understanding is supplied in a number of instances. Firstly, there was significant change during the program in students' understanding of the complexity of the learning process, as evidenced in their responses to the open-ended statements. Secondly, evaluation of students' learning contract assignments at the end of semester placed 12 of them in the relational category of the SOLO taxonomy. Finally, when students' pre-program responses to the open-ended statements are compared with their assignments at the end of the program there is significant change in SOLO category.

Student responses to the preferred and experienced environment measure indicate that for collaboration and responsibility 'what they got was what they wanted'. However, for autonomy, they reported experiencing more autonomy than they stated they preferred (at the beginning of the program). The degree of autonomy provided is confirmed by examining responses to two items (items 9 and 11, Table 10.1) in the student evaluation of teaching questionnaire.

The means for these items are respectively 4.18 and 4.32, indicating students agreed that they were motivated to work independently and that they were allowed to develop their own perspectives on the material addressed. That there were no written comments accompanying these evaluations or statements made in the interviews criticising the degree of autonomy provided suggests that students accepted the freedom in learning provided. In fact, there were comments or statements affirming this freedom. For example:

> I got a lot out of this subject because I was able to determine my own learning and assessment.

> I was a lot more motivated in this course than others, because I had a lot more freedom.

Results from the student evaluation of teaching questionnaire suggest that students approved the approach to teaching; believed the material of the course was relevant and that they were helped in forming connections within it and with their previous knowledge; and the assessment items were suitable learning experiences.

Confirmation that the program was useful in facilitating students' linking of declarative, procedural and conditional knowledge of the teaching/learning process is provided by their practice teaching results for the year. Students are rated on a 7 point scale by their supervising teachers (7 = outstanding, 1 = very weak). Three students received a 7 (outstanding), fifteen a 6 (excellent), three a 4 (competent), and one student withdrew during the final practice school period.

Other units in the course obviously contributed to these positive practice teaching evaluations and it is not suggested they were solely the result of learning experiences in this unit. However, because of this unit's focus on the teaching/learning process, some influence can be claimed.

Supplementary evidence to support the above findings is provided by some of the comments in the student evaluations and interviews. These comments are organised into categories for ease of reading:

## OVERALL PROGRAM

> I actually felt I learnt something through this program. I felt comfortable in giving my own ideas.

The subject was very good in that I am now more aware of my own thinking processes and how they relate to my actions.

The information was relevant and will be useful, it will not just be kept in a folder.

Teaching teachers to learn is so beneficial. I had never really reflected on my own learning for years.

It encouraged us to draw upon our own ideas, and helped me to change my mind and not to acquire somebody else's ideas.

I've found that I am able to discuss more easily. I never was a very discussive type but now I do talk about things a lot more, especially relating to the course, and I now have a more informed perspective.

I really think a lot of it sunk in because I was frantically interested in what I was studying and I could see how it could be applied.

The group was good because it allowed you to discuss and thrash through issues and come to a point, where you could concisely state, or think in your head, 'well, I have all this information, this is what I think as a result'.

## ASSESSMENT

The assessment was clear and relevant. Initially, the learning contract seemed too unstructured for me, I guess this was the result of 'spoon feeding' in high school.

The assessment structure was relevant and exciting and fostered intrinsic motivation.

The learning contract was an excellent learning experience.

I really loved the assignment I did, I really enjoyed researching it and writing it.

Possibly the most appealing comment, in relation to the program, came from a student discussing practice school experiences:

The thing I found most disheartening, if not of least help, was the lack of opportunity, or difficulty in applying the type of metalearning experiences that in the program are shown to lead to better learning outcomes. The aspects of the course concerning social learning and group work, along with the self-awareness (from the student's point of view) that extend 'knowing' to encompass the living entity of 'learning', had filled me with enthusiasm for the kind of teaching I had not experienced as a student before, but would have liked to have at least had a taste of.

Although aware of the hard work required to introduce this type of learning process, the actual experience of being in a classroom that stunk of Rote, Rote, and more Rote, and even more disturbingly had teachers and students relaxing in its comforting arms, brought me down to a very hard realistic earth from the romance of the university classroom.

Nevertheless, believe it or not, I now ache for the class I can call my own, because although I respect the supervising teachers I had during my Prac, I am quite sure there is a better way. Without this course I doubt I would have this appreciation.

## CONCLUSION

Results reported in this study imply that quality of learning outcomes may be improved through the provision of a learning environment characterised by learning activities and teaching strategies designed to promote student control of their own learning, qualitative perspectives on learning, constructivist approaches to learning, and relational understanding of material engaged. Increased complexity in structure of knowledge of the teaching/learning process also resulted from the teaching/learning strategies described in this program, and practice school teaching results provided evidence of how effectively students related declarative, procedural, and conditional knowledge of this process. That is, there is evidence of a positive relationship between conception of teaching, teaching approach, conceptions of learning and student learning outcomes.

Although there were no significant increases in the use of deep or transformative approaches to learning (they were initially high and remained so), the quality of learning outcomes, as well as the structure of knowledge of the teaching/learning process and conceptions of learning of the students were reflective of those described in the literature as representative of students adopting a deep or transformative approach to their learning.

The learning environment as perceived by the students is one in which the teacher provided a high degree of autonomy, moderate opportunities for collaboration, and many opportunities to accept responsibility for one's own learning. As well, students perceived the assessment to be highly relevant, the teacher to have provided highly relevant material and facilitated relational understanding of it, and the teaching to have promoted a high degree of independence and positive interpersonal relationships. Although limited by the items selected in the measures used in this study, the characteristics mentioned above provide powerful directions for developing learning environments for fostering meaningful learning.

In part, this program may be seen to directly address the plea of Trigwell and Prosser (1991b) that 'Teachers need to explicitly help students focus on the structure of the course as a whole while it is being taught' (p. 274). The results indicate that if this is done, positive learning outcomes eventuate.

### References

Bain, J. (1994). *Understanding by learning or learning by understanding: How shall we teach?* Inaugural lecture presented at Griffith University.

Baird, J. (1991). Individual and group reflection as a basis for teacher development. In P. Hughes (Ed.), *Teachers' professional development.* Melbourne: Australian Council for Educational Research.

Biggs, J. (1987). *Student approaches to learning and studying.* Melbourne: Australian Council for Educational Research.

Biggs, J. (1988). The role of metacognition in enhancing learning. *Australian Journal of Education,* 127–138.

Biggs, J. (1989). Approaches to the enhancement of tertiary teaching. *Higher Education Research and Development,* 8, 7–25.

Biggs, J. (1991). Approaches to learning in secondary and tertiary students in Hong Kong: Some comparative studies. *Educational Research Journal,* 6, 27–39.

Biggs, J. (1992). A qualitative approach to grading students. *HERDSA News,* 14(3), 3–6.

Biggs, J. (1993). From theory to practice: A cognitive systems approach. *Higher Education Research and Development,* 12(1), 73–85.

Biggs, J. (1994). Student learning research and theory: Where do we currently stand? In G. Gibbs (Ed.), *Improving student learning: Theory and practice.* Oxford: OCSD.

Biggs, J., & Collis, K. (1982). *Evaluating the quality of learning: The SOLO taxonomy*. New York: Academic Press.

Biggs. J., & Collis, K. (1989). Towards a model of school-based curriculum development and assessment: Using the SOLO taxonomy. *Australian Journal of Education, 33*, 149–161.

Biggs, J., & Moore, P. (1993). *The process of learning* (3rd ed.). New York: Prentice Hall.

Boulton-Lewis, G. (1992). The SOLO taxonomy and levels of knowledge of learning. *Research and Development in Higher Education, 15*, 482–489.

Boulton-Lewis, G. (1994). Tertiary students' knowledge of their own learning and a SOLO taxonomy. *Higher Education, 28*, 387–402.

Boulton-Lewis, G. (1995). The SOLO taxonomy as a means of shaping and assessing learning in higher education. *Higher Education Research and Development, 14*(2), 43–154.

Boulton-Lewis, G., & Dart, B. C. (1994). assessing students' knowledge of learning: A comparison of data collection methods. In G. Gibbs (Ed.), *Improving student learning: Theory and practice*. Oxford: Oxford Centre for Staff Development.

Brown, A. (1988). Motivation to learn and understand: On taking charge of one's own learning. *Cognition and Instruction, 5*, 311–322.

Cohen, J. (1969). *Statistical power analysis for the behavioral sciences*. New York: Academic Press.

Dart, B.C. (1994a). A goal-mediational model of personal and environmental influences on tertiary students' strategy use. *Higher Education, 28*, 453–470.

Dart, B.C. (1994b). *Measuring constructivist learning environments in tertiary education*. Paper published electronically in the proceedings of the annual conference of the Australian Association for Research in Education, Newcastle.

Dart, B.C., & Clarke, J.A. (1991). Helping students become better learners: A case study in teacher education. *Higher Education, 22*, 317–335.

Dart, B.C., & Clarke, J.A. (1992). *Learning and learning environments*. Paper presented at the annual conference of the Higher Education Research and Development Society of Australasia, Churchill Campus, Monash University.

Dunkin, M., & Biddle, B. (1974). *The study of teaching*. New York: Holt, Rinehart & Winston.

Entwistle, A., & Entwistle, N. (1992). Experiences of understanding in revising for degree examinations. *Learning and Instruction, 2*, 1–22.

Entwistle, N. (1987). *Understanding classroom learning*. London: Hodder and Stoughton.

Entwistle, N., & Entwistle, A. (1991). Contrasting forms of understanding for degree examinations: The student experience and its implications. *Higher Education, 22,* 205–227.

Iran-Nejad, A. (1990). Active and dynamic self-regulation of learning processes. *Review of Educational Research, 60,* 573–602.

Jonassen, D. (1994). Toward a constructivist design model. *Educational Technology, 34*(4), 34–37.

Kember, D., & Gow, L. (1994). Orientations to teaching and their effect on the quality of student learning. *Journal of Higher Education, 65*(1), 58–74.

King, A. (1993). From sage on the stage to guide on the side. *College Teaching, 41*(1), 30–35.

Knowles, M. (1986). *Using learning contracts.* San Francisco: Jossey-Bass.

Marton, F. (1988). Describing and improving learning. In R. Schmeck (Ed.), *Learning strategies and learning styles.* New York: Plenum Press.

Marton, F., Dall'Alba, G., & Beaty, E. (1993). Conceptions of learning. *International Journal of Educational Research, 19*(3), 277–300.

Marton, F., & Säljö', R. (1984). Approaches to learning. In F. Marton, D. Hounsell, & N. Entwistle (Eds.), *The experience of learning.* Edinburgh: Scottish Academic Press.

Marzano, R., Brandth, R., Hughes, C., Jones, B., Pressersen, B., Rankin, Suhor, C. (1988). *Dimensions of thinking.* Alexandria, Vir.: Association for Supervision and Curriculum Development.

McKeachie, W., Pintrich, P., Lin, Y-G., & Smith, D. (1986). *Teaching and learning in the college classroom.* University of Michigan: National Center for Research to Improve Postsecondary Teaching and Learning.

Prawat, R., & Floden, R. (1994). Philosophical perspectives on constructivist views of learning. *Educational Psychology, 29*(1), 37–48.

Prosser, M., & Millar, R. (1989). The 'how' and 'what' of learning physics: A phenomenographic study. *European Journal of Psychology and Education, 4,* 513–528.

Prosser, M., Trigwell, K., & Taylor, P. (1994). A phenomenographic study of academics' conceptions of science learning and teaching. *Learning and Instruction, 4*(3), 217–231.

Ramsden, P. (1984). The context of learning. In F. Marton, D. Hounsell, & N. Entwistle (Eds.), *The experience of learning.* Edinburgh: Scottish Academic Press.

Ramsden, P. (1992). *Learning to teach in higher education.* London: Routledge.

Ramsden, P., & Entwistle, N. (1981). Effects of academic departments on students' approaches to studying. *British Journal of Educational Psychology, 51,* 367–383.

Resnick, L. (1987). Learning in school and out. *Educational Researcher,* *16,* 13–20.

Roby, T. (1988). Models of discussion. In J. Dillon (Ed.), *Questioning and discussion: A multidisciplinary study.* Norwood, NJ: Ablex.

Säljö, R. (1979). Learning About Learning. *Higher Education, 8,* 443–451.

Samuelowicz, K., & Bain, J. (1992). Conceptions of teaching held by academic teachers. *Higher Education, 24,* 93–111.

Sheppard, C., & Gilbert, J. (1991). Course design, teaching method and student epistemology. *Higher Education, 22,* 229–249.

Shuell, T. (1993). Toward an integrated theory of teaching and learning. *Educational Psychologist, 28*(4), 291–311.

Tompkins, C., & McGraw, M-J. (1988). The negotiated learning contract. In D. Boud (Ed.), *Developing student autonomy in learning* (2nd ed.). London: Kogan Page.

Trigwell, K., & Prosser, M. (1991a). Improving the quality of student learning: The influence of learning context and student approaches to learning on learning outcomes. *Higher Education, 22,* 251–266.

Trigwell, K., & Prosser, M. (1991b). Relating approaches to study and quality of learning outcomes at the course level. *British Journal of Educational Psychology, 61,* 265–275.

Van Rossum, E., & Schenk, S. (1984). The relationship between learning conception, study strategy and learning outcome. *British Journal of Educational Psychology, 54,* 73–83.

Watkins, D. (1983). Depth of processing and the quality of learning outcomes. *Instructional Science, 12,* 49–58.

Zell, P., & Malacinski, G. (1994). Impediments to developing collaborative learning strategies: The input vs output conflict. *Journal of Science Education and Technology, 3*(2), 107–114.

# CHAPTER 11

# Teaching in Higher Education

*Michael Prosser and*

*Keith Trigwell*

## INTRODUCTION

In this chapter, we first review the earlier chapters in terms of the presage-process-product model of student learning, and in so doing we move the focus back to teaching in higher education by extracting some of the implications for higher education teachers. In the second part, we introduce a model of teaching and learning which goes beyond the original linear-causal and more recent systems presage-process-product model.

The chapters of this book have, in addressing the topics of quality in higher education, models of student learning, cross-cultural issues in learning, constructive alignment, the use of heuristics and instruments such as the SOLO taxonomy and the Study Process Questionnaire, acknowledged and celebrated the substantial contribution that John Biggs has made to the discipline of higher education. That this book is essentially focused on higher education alone is testament to the substance of his work, as he is perhaps better known internationally for his contributions in other areas of education in collaboration with John Kirby and others.

This chapter continues that celebration, by focusing on an area which has been of interest to us for over 10 years: The study, and improvement, of teaching and learning in higher education. Our interest in John's work was initially through the presage-process-product model of learning which gives teachers a practical model for developing their teaching, as it builds on research in student learning to demonstrate the relations between what teachers do and think, what students do and think, and the quality of the student learning outcomes. Our version of that model is shown in Figure 11.1. More recently, as a natural extension of his work on student learning, John began to publish on issues in teaching in higher education, and the conjunction of our interests with his has led to many fruitful developments, some of which are included in this chapter.

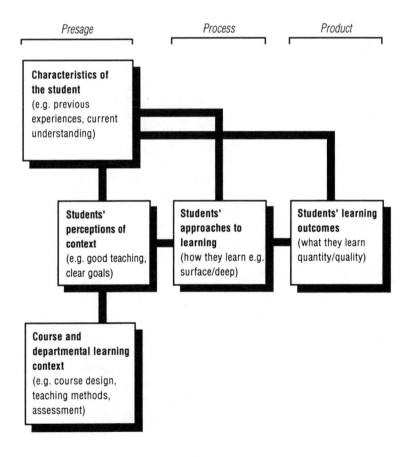

FIGURE 11.1    Presage-process-product model of student learning

## THE PRESAGE-PROCESS-PRODUCT MODEL AND UNIVERSITY TEACHING

The simplicity of the presage-process-product model is one of the reasons it is so valuable as a teaching development aid. Of even greater value is the way it relates what teachers do with what students do. There would be few teachers in higher education who, if asked to focus on the learning of their students, would not wish the quality of that outcome to be high. The presage-process-product model illustrates how teachers may think through the consequences of their teaching actions for their student learning outcomes. The empirical support for this aspect of the model is well documented in the chapters in this book.

The presage-process-product model describes a relation between the approaches students take to their learning and the quality of that learning outcome. This aspect of the model is supported by numerous empirical studies, including those mentioned by Entwistle (Chapter 4) and Tang (Chapter 5) in this volume. Those studies suggest that students who adopt a deep approach to learning are more likely to be the students who produce higher quality learning outcomes. Students' approaches to learning are in turn related to their perceptions of their learning environment, and those perceptions are a function of the teaching/learning environment and their prior experiences. Some environments, and some prior experiences are more likely to lead to students adopting deeper approaches to learning than others. Again these associations are supported by empirical studies, and suggest that what teachers do in establishing the teaching-learning environment is related to the quality of their students' learning outcomes.

The chapters in this book address aspects of research that relate directly and indirectly to the whole and/or to parts of the presage-process-product model. In the Preface, the editors note that the model is the theme that draws the chapters of the book together, making it a book rather than a collection of unrelated papers. The argument proceeds logically from the way teachers think about and design their courses to the way their students approach their studies and, finally, the quality of their students' learning outcomes. However, like the current 'systems' version of the presage-process-product model (Biggs, 1993) the argument cannot be sustained within a linear approach, and the content in the various chapters is not restricted to any one of the presage, process or product areas, nor to relations between any two. All authors, like all teachers, would acknowledge that their aim is to contribute to knowledge that may lead to improvement of the quality of learning. Some (Marton, Dart, Boulton-Lewis, Tang) have done this explicitly and have included all three components of the model.

We have, in reviewing these chapters, decided to begin with those that explicitly address all three components of the model. Two of the chapters within this group are quite different to the other chapters in that they are closely associated with, but represent considerable departures from, the work of John Biggs. We have decided to leave one of these, Chapter 8 by Ference Marton, until last, as the point of departure that he takes is closely associated with the direction of our own developments of John's work, and it forms a link between the present analysis and our description of a way ahead in the second half of this chapter.

The other chapter which departs significantly from the Biggs approach is by Erik Meyer (Chapter 3). In addressing the need for models and analytical procedures that are sufficiently sophisticated to accommodate the complexity of student learning, he focuses on the point that each student experiences teaching and learning in a different way, and that this has implications for teaching which are not addressed in many of the current (general) models. He notes that student perceptions of the context of teaching and learning, the way they approach their learning, and the outcomes of those approaches vary between individuals in the same context, as well as between contexts. The implications for teaching of the consideration of this departure are profound. Individual variation has been given little consideration in the improvement of teaching and learning and yet the variation within a group can be as great as the variation between groups (see also Trigwell, Hazel & Prosser, 1996). This point is also explored further in the second part of this chapter.

Three other chapters (Boulton-Lewis, Chapter 9; Dart, Chapter 10; Tang, Chapter 5) each embrace presage, process and product factors but the emphases they each take raise different implications for teaching.

Gillian Boulton-Lewis reviews the research in each of the presage, process and product areas that has used the SOLO taxonomy developed by Biggs and Collis (1982). The versatility of this heuristic device for all forms of research, including teaching action research, is well illustrated. Good teaching involves reflection on the processes and consequences of teaching. This chapter highlights the value of the instruments of Biggs in evaluation, reflection and the development of teaching practice. It describes the SOLO taxonomy as being of use in finding out what students know and believe about their own learning; in assessing entering knowledge in a discipline; in presenting examples and models of structural organisation of content in a discipline area; in shaping learning through assessment; in illustrating acceptable levels of outcome; and finally, in assessing the quality of learning outcomes.

Barry Dart uses the presage, process and product factors in the presage-process-product model to help structure the analysis and interpretation of data from a study designed to observe the effects on student learning of changes to teaching. He concludes that the quality of student learning may be improved through teachers providing a learning environment characterised by learning activities and teaching strategies designed to promote (a) student control of their own learning, (b) learning as a qualitative change in understanding, (c) constructivist approaches to learning, and (d) a relational, as distinct from a multistructural, understanding of the material.

Catherine Tang, in describing her study of the reactions of students to a learning scenario in which they find themselves, uses the presage-process-product associations in the presage-process-product model to help structure her explanation of her results. She also introduces the concept of constructive alignment (Biggs, 1996) which is based on the notion that the course objectives, the teaching context, and the assessment tasks should all address the same student learning-related cognitive activities. She notes that this alignment was not present in the context studied, and that the students compensated for the lack of supportive teaching in this area by forming collaborative learning groups.

Tang concludes with implications for teaching by noting that as a part of normal teaching, the presage variables should be given due consideration in 'that the objectives of assessment by assignment should be clearly defined, along with the assessment criteria used, and the procedural knowledge necessary in preparing for the assignment.' This step back to the presage variables, from the process and product variables, came from her observations of the approach students took (a collaborative learning approach) and the learning outcomes (a better performance from those who used that approach) in the context of a specific learning environment.

The balance between the design of a learning environment, students' perceptions of that environment, and their approach to learning is a very delicate one. In a study of the relations of these three variables in two Physics courses and two Biology courses, we observed a breakdown of the association between perceptions and approaches in one of the Physics courses (Trigwell, Hazel & Prosser, 1996). An analysis of the course material and an interview with the lecturer suggested that the course would be likely to afford a deep approach to learning. Student responses to a version of the Course Experience Questionnaire also indicated that they perceived the context as intended by the lecturer. However, self-reports of their approaches to learning suggested that they were not able to match the expectations of the lecturer in responding to assessment questions that really tested their understanding. Many reported that they had adopted more of a surface approach. The difficulty in preparing a suitable learning context may have been overcome in this case (as in the case reported by Tang) by incorporating more of the other presage dimension – student characteristics. The conclusion from the study was that there is a fine line between challenging students through processes such as those proposed by Dart, or through constructive alignment, and over-extending them.

Presage variables are treated in more detail in the first Part of the book. Chapter 1 by Kember and Chapter 2 by Martin and Ramsden each address the role of teacher thinking, but they do so from quite different perspectives. Kember focuses on teachers' conceptions of teaching and the association between these conceptions and student learning, while Martin and Ramsden focus on the object of study – how teachers conceive of and constitute what it is that students will be asked to learn.

Elaine Martin and Paul Ramsden report that in their sample of six teachers there were four qualitatively different ways in which the object of study in creative writing was constituted by the teachers. They found that the way that teachers constitute the object of study is related to the way students approach their learning. This result, though not unexpected, is new. It serves to remind us when we are striving to improve student learning that while our current focus may be on how teachers teach, we cannot ignore what it is that they teach, or how they constitute what they teach.

There are also implications for the evaluation of teaching in these results. Martin and Ramsden found that all their interviewees were highly rated as teachers by their students, but an analysis of what they were asking of their students showed considerably qualitative differences. These teachers were constituting qualitatively different objects of study for their students – with some objects of study clearly being superior to others. And yet, as often occurs, if student rating of teaching is used as the sole indicator of teaching quality, all these teachers would be rated equally highly.

David Kember raises the issues of the importance of challenging teachers' beliefs about teaching and learning when engaged in academic development programs. His message is based on an association between the ways teachers think about teaching, their approach to teaching and the approaches to learning of their students. In making this case he discusses his own work using the academic department as the unit of analysis. Our own most recent studies, which show that qualitatively different approaches to teaching are associated with qualitatively different approaches to learning, provide further confirmation of this fundamentally important relation (Trigwell, Prosser & Lyons, 1997).

Our study made use of a teaching approach inventory derived from interviews with staff, and a modification of the Study Process Questionnaire of Biggs. Over 2000 science students, who adopt significantly deeper approaches to learning than a similar number of their colleagues, were found to be taught by staff who adopt approaches to teaching that are significantly more oriented towards students and to changing their conceptions. Conversely, in classes where teachers describe their approach to teaching as having a focus on what *they* do and on transmitting knowledge, students are more likely to report that they adopt a surface approach to the learning of that subject (Trigwell, Prosser & Lyons, 1997). These conclusions are derived from analyses at both the class level and for individual students, and so confirm and extend the work reported by Kember. Together with the numerous studies that show correlations between students' deeper approaches to learning and higher quality learning outcomes, these results demonstrate the importance of attempts to improve the quality of student learning by encouraging teaching of a higher quality. In this context, high quality teaching is that with a conceptual change/student-focus approach rather than an information transmission/teacher-focus approach.

The second Part of the book focuses on the learning process. As an instrument to monitor the processes or approaches students are adopting to learning at a general level, the Study Process Questionnaire (SPQ) developed by Biggs has been thoroughly tested, has been proved reliable and valid, and is widely used. In our own studies, we have adapted the SPQ for use at the topic level (photosynthesis and electricity and magnetism) with good results. We have also used a shortened version in an exercise with academic staff to demonstrate to them that they prefer their students to adopt a deep approach to learning, rather than the more surface oriented approach that most teachers suspect their students adopt (Prosser & Trigwell, forthcoming). David Watkins has, for many years, been subjecting SPQ results from both his own studies and the studies of others to tests of reliability and construct validity. In Chapter 6 he assesses the appropriateness of using the SPQ in non-Western cultures, for understanding student learning and for staff development. He concludes that it can validly be used in these situations and thus for evaluating teaching effectiveness. He notes, however, that cross-cultural comparisons are less justifiable, and that modifications of the SPQ may be needed in some contexts.

Chapters 4 and 7 are concerned with the relations between the way students go about learning (the learning process) and the outcome of that approach (the learning product). In both of these chapters the emphasis is on the product (learning outcomes), but both also illustrate the power of the presage-process-product model in the 'systems' form in which the factors are interdependent.

Noel Entwistle, along with John Biggs and Ference Marton, was one of the pioneers of the student learning research 'school'. In Chapter 4 he reviews the previous research work on relations between students' approach to learning and their learning outcome, specifically the relations between a deep approach to learning and understanding. He concludes (like Meyer, Chapter 3, with whom he has worked on other relations described in the presage-process-product model) that most of the previous work in this area has not accommodated the complexity of the situation in which learning occurs. While Meyer presented the case that we have not taken sufficient account of individual differences, Entwistle argues that it is in describing the processes and outcomes of learning that we fall short. From interviews with students on examination revision strategies, he describes five contrasting forms of understanding which range from a process of absorbing facts, details etc. without consideration of structure, to developing their own understanding which transcends examination requirements.

He also introduces the idea of knowledge objects (Entwistle & Marton, 1994) based upon descriptions of student experiences of understanding as having some internal form and structure. The two ideas – forms of understanding and knowledge objects – illustrate the richness with which a product of learning can be described. Entwistle concludes that being able to explain the way understandings are developed, elaborated, rehearsed and converted into explanations should help lecturers build more effective organising principles into their planning of lectures, and their development of supporting materials.

Unlike the knowledge object described by Entwistle and Marton, the SOLO taxonomy is a decontextualised way of describing the structure of students' learning. John Hattie and Nola Purdie (Chapter 7) demonstrate the usefulness of this feature of the SOLO taxonomy in measures of the quality of student learning. In an overview which complements the description of the broader applications of SOLO by Boulton-Lewis in this volume, they focus on SOLO as an underpinning for the development of criterion-referenced assessment systems. Using such a model as the basis for teaching development is similar to the approach adopted in this chapter. It illustrates the power of the presage-process-product model by showing how shifts in thinking from student learning outcomes to teaching development are supported. They conclude their chapter by noting that there is tangible evidence of the capacity of the SOLO model to inform the practice of educators at all levels of student learning.

As we noted earlier, we have left Chapter 8 by Ference Marton until last because it contains the most significant point of departure from most of the work described in this volume. In addressing quality in higher education, Marton's chapter touches on most of the implications for teaching included in the brief summaries above. The point of departure, which involves a different way of thinking about student learning, results in two further implications for teaching which are not included in the summaries. In the next few paragraphs we exemplify the implications for teaching of Marton's chapter, and then in the next part of this chapter we use a perspective somewhat similar to Marton's to outline our thoughts on a way ahead for studies of teaching and learning in higher education.

Ference Marton describes how the experience of variation and relevance to the learner can constitute two elements of a high quality teaching-learning context. He writes

> By becoming aware of other ways of understanding a certain phenomenon, our own understanding becomes visible to us and appears exactly as *a* way of understanding. In this way it becomes much easier to change, and develop, our way of understanding that phenomenon. When teachers become aware of the students' ways of understanding of what *they* (the students) take for granted, they become aware of what *they* (the teachers) have taken for granted – and should not take for granted.

He is suggesting that teachers use variation of thought (to expose the ways in which learners are thinking) and use these ideas as the content in education, and adopt a focus on the taken-for-granted aspects of different phenomena in, or aspects of, the surrounding world. The goal of learning must appear to the learner as relevant.

In a recent article (Prosser & Trigwell, 1997) we have shown how these elements can be built into the design of teaching development workshops for staff teaching in higher education. The workshop activities are structured to help the participants see variation within the teacher's and learner's experience as a way of helping them examine their own experience and change their way of seeing and understanding teaching. The activities also set the experience in a context where staff can see the connections between teaching and learning such that the goal of changing teaching to improve student learning appears to the teacher as relevant.

The aims of the programs are to change teacher's conceptions of, and approaches to, teaching. This is approached in two ways – through variation and through relevance. The first approach involves developing among teaching staff an awareness of the variation in teachers' experience of teaching, and the second approach involves generating discussion of teaching intentions and strategies and how these are likely to relate to the way students approach their learning. It is supported by the relations represented in the presage-process-product model (Figure 11.1) which show that the quality of the student learning outcome is related to the students' approach to learning, their perceptions of the learning context and the lecturers' perceptions of the departmental context. Teachers who recognise the variation in approaches to teaching are guided through this series of relations to the conclusion that some approaches to teaching are more likely to lead to desired student learning outcomes than others.

## A WAY AHEAD

Having briefly reviewed earlier chapters structured in terms of Biggs' presage-process-product models of learning and teaching, we wish to turn our focus to an input-process-outcomes model of teaching and learning which goes beyond the original presage-process-product and the systems oriented models of teaching and learning. In particular, we wish to take a more experiential perspective on such models, and raise some issues about the experiential outcomes of teaching. In doing so, we wish to illustrate how we are attempting to build upon, and further develop, several of the key ideas developed by John Biggs during his very productive and creative career.

### Inputs-processes-outcomes of learning and teaching

In a 1978 paper Biggs first proposed a way of structuring the factors associated with the inputs-processes-outcomes of student learning in terms of a presage-process-product model. That model was described in linear-causal terms with the direction of flow from the presage to the process and then to the product factors (Biggs, 1978). In 1989 he proposed a similar model for teaching. In that model the products of teaching were students approaches to and outcomes of learning. This model was again a linear-causal model with the direction of flow from presage to process to product factors (Biggs, 1989). More recently he reconstituted the presage-process-product model from a linear-causal model to a fully interactive systems model in which, while there was a general flow from presage to process to product, there was also a continuous interaction between each of the parts of the model (Biggs, 1993).

Recently we have argued also for a further reconstitution and restructuring of the model, to explain better the results of research and provide issues and concerns for practice. We wish to reconstitute the model as a way of describing the temporal structure of individual students' and teachers' awareness of their individual acts of teaching and learning (Trigwell & Prosser, 1997). The main practical issue to emerge from this analysis is that teachers and individual students in the same classroom do not experience the same world. We wish also to restructure the model of teaching, with a focus on the teachers' awareness of their outcomes of teaching rather than students' learning approaches and outcomes being the product (Prosser, Martin, Ramsden, Trigwell & Entwistle, 1997). We believe that the way teachers understand the subject matter they are teaching is fundamentally related to the way they approach their teaching and consequently to the way their students approach their learning (see Martin & Ramsden, Chapter 2 in this volume).

## Reconceptualising the presage-process-product models of teaching and learning: Conscious awareness of individual acts of learning and teaching

How do individual learners and teachers experience individual acts of learning and teaching? How are the inputs-processes-outcomes of learning and teaching constituted in learners' and teachers' awareness of individual acts of learning and teaching?

In our 1997 paper we describe the structure of four examples each of individual acts of teaching and learning (Trigwell & Prosser, 1997). Our main point is that the presage-process-product factors are simultaneously but successively present in conscious awareness in any act of teaching and learning, and that in any act one or more of the factors may be more to the fore than the other factors. We also argue that learners and teachers are present in situations in classrooms which afford a variety of approaches to learning and teaching, and that the approach adopted by the learner or the teacher fundamentally depends on their awareness of the situation. Our conceptualisation of the presage-process-product model describes the moment to moment relationship between the cognising individual student or teacher and the situation in which the students or teachers find themselves.

Let us take one example each of learning and teaching from the 1997 paper. A student whose prior experience of learning of the topic being taught has been of limiting conceptions of learning and surface approaches to study finds himself or herself in a situation which is designed to afford a deep approach to study. Given the student's prior experience, he or she is likely to focus on, or be aware of, those aspects of the situation which do not afford a deep approach. Consequently the student is likely to adopt a surface approach and have a low quality learning outcome. On the other hand, a student whose prior experience has been of sophisticated conceptions of learning and deep approaches to study is more likely to focus on those aspects of the situation which are designed to afford a deep approach. That student is likely to adopt a deep approach and have high quality learning outcomes. This is consistent with the qualitative and quantitative research being conducted from within the student learning research perspective.

This is just the situation previously described by one of us (Prosser, 1993). The example used was of two students attending the same set of lectures. The lectures were designed to afford a deep approach, attempting to get students to focus on developing their conceptual understanding by using active teaching and learning methods within the lecture theatre. In interviews about their experience of these lectures, one of the students focused on those aspects of the lecture which did not afford a deep approach – for example, direct transmission of information – while the other focused on those aspects designed to afford a deep approach – for example, small group discussion of misconceptions. The former student adopted a surface approach, resulting in low quality learning outcomes, while the latter adopted a deep approach, resulting in high quality learning outcomes. These two cases represent good illustrative examples of our reconceptualised model.

Turning now to teachers and teaching, our reconceptualised model allows for similar descriptions of teaching. A teacher whose prior experience of teaching has been of limiting conceptions of teaching and information transmission/teacher-focused approaches to teaching finds himself or herself in a situation affording a conceptual change/student-focused approach to teaching. That teacher is likely to focus on, or be aware of, those aspects of the situation which do not afford a conceptual change/student-focused approach to teaching. Consequently, the teacher is likely to adopt an information transmission/teacher-focused approach, which may result in lower quality teaching outcomes. On the other hand, a teacher whose previous experience has been of more sophisticated conceptions of teaching and of conceptual change/student-focused approaches to teaching is more likely to focus on the aspects of the situation affording a conceptual change/student-focused approach to teaching and to adopt such an approach, resulting in higher quality teaching outcomes. This is consistent with the qualitative and quantitative research on teaching being conducted from within the student learning research perspective, although much more research needs to be done.

We will illustrate this with an example from our own research on teaching from the student learning perspective (Prosser, Trigwell & Taylor, 1994; Trigwell, Prosser & Taylor, 1994). In the study reported in these two papers, part of the sample consisted of several teachers teaching in parallel streams in a large first year university science course. They were teaching the same syllabus to the same sorts of students with the same examination in the same lecture theatres. Yet their approaches to teaching varied between the information transmission/teacher-focused approach and the conceptual change/student-focused approach. The approach adopted by individual teachers was consistent with their conceptions of teaching. As well, the teachers who adopted the information transmission/ teacher-focused approach seemed to be focusing on class size aspects of the teaching situation – with class sizes being too large – while the teachers who adopted conceptual change/student-focused approaches to teaching classes of a similar size and in a similar situation had little or no focus on the size of the class.

So what are the implications of reconceptualising the presage-process-product model in this way? Such a reconceptualisation suggests that presage factors such as prior conceptions are not independently constituted from process factors such as approaches. That is, in every act of teaching and learning, conceptions, perceptions, approaches and outcomes are being continually reconstituted in relation to each other. For instance, at every moment an outcome is being reconstituted as an input to the next moment. The presage-process-product factors are simultaneously present in awareness. Learners' and teachers' actions are characterised by the interaction between the simultaneous awareness of the presage-process-product factors and the situation within which they are constituted. This is particularly clear in the learning and teaching of the physical sciences and mathematics where prior understanding of the subject matter being taught is fundamentally and continuously related to their awareness of the learning situation, their approaches to study in that situation and to the simultaneous outcomes in that situation. We believe that this is one way of explaining the fundamental importance of understanding of the subject matter in any teaching and learning situation – an importance which is often not given due attention.

### Restructuring the presage-process-product model: Experiential outcomes of teaching

In the previous section we have described a way of reconceptualising the presage-process-product model which helps us understand the relations between the qualitative variation in conceptions, approaches and outcomes of people finding themselves in the same or very similar situations; situations which on the surface would be expected to evoke similar conceptions, approaches and outcomes. We now wish to focus on one aspect of the presage-process-product model of teaching of John Biggs – again related to understanding of the subject matter – and argue for a restructuring of the model.

In the Biggs model, the outcomes of teaching were conceptualised as being students' approaches to, and outcomes of, learning. That is, while the presage and process factors related to the teachers and their experiences of teaching, the product factors related to students and their experiences of learning. While the students' experiences are undoubtedly very important outcomes of teaching, we would argue that there are experiential outcomes of teaching from the teachers' perspective which are fundamentally related to how they approach their teaching and perceive their teaching context. Such outcomes should be an important aspect of the structure of the model.

Our proposed restructure extends the inputs, processes and outcomes included in the Biggs (1989) model by including teachers' prior understanding of subject matter and the understanding of the subject matter that teachers intend students to develop (the intended object of study for their students) among the presage factors, and teachers' post-understanding of subject matter and the objects of study they constituted for their students in their classrooms among the product factors. So while the inputs and processes of the Biggs model related to the teachers and their experiences of teaching, the outcomes related to the learners and their experiences of learning. Our focus is to conceive of the outcomes in terms of the teachers' experiences of the outcomes, and not the students' experiences of those outcomes. But how can we conceptualise the outcomes of teaching from this perspective in ways which are able to be researched and analysed?

Recent research on student learning outcomes has moved away from investigating understandings of specific concepts and ideas to documenting the qualitative variation in the nature and extent of students' understanding of whole topics and disciplines (Crawford, Gordon, Nicholas & Prosser, 1994; Prosser, Walker & Millar, 1996). In interviews with students about their experience of understanding whole topics, Entwistle and Entwistle (1991, 1992) described this variation in terms of contrasting 'forms of understanding' which involved variations in the breadth, depth, and structure of their understandings. But in describing their understandings, some students seem to go beyond describing it in terms of breadth, depth and structure to describing feelings of connectedness, coherence and confidence in explaining the knowledge they were studying. This highly structured form of understanding was experienced almost as a 'quasi-sensory', tightly organised entity. This deeper level of understanding was termed a 'knowledge object' (Entwistle & Marton, 1994; Entwistle, Chapter 4 in this volume).

While that research has focused on students and students' understanding of the subject matter they are learning, we propose that such concepts can be used to help investigate teachers and their understanding of the subject matter they are teaching, as well as changes in that understanding as a result of teaching the subject matter. We propose to draw upon the concepts of forms of understanding and knowledge objects in developing our descriptions of teachers' understanding of the subject matter they are teaching.

Our knowledge and understanding of student learning has been advanced enormously by focusing on the variation in the way they understand and structure the key concepts they are studying. We believe that our knowledge and understanding of teaching, from a student learning perspective, will similarly be advanced by focusing on the variation in teachers' understanding of the subject matter they are teaching, and including such factors as teachers' understanding of their subject matter in restructured presage-process-product models of teaching and learning. The relations between teachers' understanding of subject matter, the way they approach their teaching, and their perceptions of teaching and learning contexts and situations, and how these factors relate to the quality and experience of students and their learning represents, for us, the next major development for our understanding of teaching and learning in higher education.

## CONCLUSIONS

In this chapter we have attempted to do two things. In the first part we have tried to summarise and analyse the previous chapters in terms of a heuristic model which John Biggs has played a large part in developing. In the process, by describing the implications for teaching in the content of each chapter, we have illustrated one of the more significant uses of the presage-process-product model of learning.

In the second part of this chapter we have tried to show how we are building on and extending the work for which John Biggs has successfully laid the foundations over several years. In our previous work we have drawn upon and used many of his ideas. We have used the SOLO taxonomy to help us analyse the way students conceive of, and understand, what their courses are about. We have used the Study Process Questionnaire and modifications of it to investigate the way in which students approach their studies. We have drawn upon the intention-strategy structure of the Study Process Questionnaire to help us constitute the categories of description for teachers' approaches to teaching, and again used it to structure our Approaches to Teaching Inventory. Finally, we have used the Biggs presage-process-product models of teaching and learning as a heuristic to help us structure our research and interpret its findings.

Of most importance, however, has been John's continued friendship and encouragement for us and our work over many years. We very fondly remember trudging behind John over many hills in Hong Kong during a study leave in 1992. We can only aspire to remain as open to new ideas and new ways of thinking about teaching and learning as John has done.

We believe that the contents of this volume, and the authors represented in it, highlight the very significant and pioneering role that John Biggs has played in the student learning research movement over the last 20 years or so. The range of authors and their institutional affiliation signify to the fact that John has influenced the work of leading researchers on both sides of the Atlantic Ocean and all around the Pacific Ocean. His recent work on constructive alignment suggests that he is still very active, and we await his next publications on teaching and learning with great anticipation.

## References

Biggs, J.B. (1978). Individual and group differences in study processes. *British Journal of Educational Psychology, 48,* 266–279.

Biggs, J.B. (1989). Approaches to the enhancement of university teaching. *Higher Education Research and Development, 8,* 7–26.

Biggs, J.B. (1993). From theory to practice: A cognitive systems approach. *Higher Education Research and Development, 12,* 73–86.

Biggs, J.B. (1996). Enhancing teaching through constructive alignment. *Higher Education, 32,* 347–364.

Biggs, J.B., & Collis, K.F. (1982). *Evaluating the quality of learning: The SOLO taxonomy.* New York: Academic Press

Crawford, K., Gordon, S., Nicholas, J., & Prosser, M. (1994). Conceptions of mathematics and how it is learned: The perspective of students entering university. *Learning and Instruction, 4,* 331–345.

Entwistle, A.C., & Entwistle, N.J. (1992). Experiences of understanding in revising for degree examinations. *Learning and Instruction, 2,* 1–22.

Entwistle, N.J., & Entwistle, A.C. (1991). Contrasting forms of understanding for degree examinations: student experience and its implications. *Higher Education, 22,* 205–227.

Entwistle, N.J., & Marton, F. (1994). Knowledge objects: Understanding constituted through intensive academic study. *British Journal of Educational Psychology, 64,* 161–178.

Prosser, M. (1993). Phenomenography and the principles and practices of learning. *Higher Education Research and Development, 12,* 21–32.

Prosser, M., Martin, E., Ramsden, P., Trigwell, K., & Entwistle, N.J. (1997). Application for Australian Research Council grant, La Trobe University.

Prosser, M., & Trigwell, K. (1997). Using phenomenography in the design of programs for teachers in higher education. *Higher Education Research and Development, 16*, 41–54.

Prosser, M., & Trigwell, K. (in press). *Learning & teaching in higher education.* Open University Press.

Prosser, M., Trigwell, K., & Taylor, P. (1994). A phenomenographic study of academics' conceptions of science teaching and learning. *Learning and Instruction, 4*, 217–231.

Prosser, M., Walker, P., & Millar, R. (1996). Differences in students' perceptions of learning physics. *Physics Education, 31*, 43–48.

Trigwell, K., Hazel, E., & Prosser, M. (1996). Perceptions of the learning environment and approaches to learning university science at the topic level. *Research and Development in Higher Education, 19*, 921–926.

Trigwell, K., & Prosser, M. (1997). Towards an understanding of individual acts of teaching and learning. *Higher Education Research and Development, 16*, 241–252.

Trigwell, K., Prosser, M., & Lyons, F. (1997). *Defining good teaching: Relations between teachers' approaches to teaching and student learning.* Paper presented at the 7th Conference of the European Association for Research in Learning and Instruction. Athens, August, 1997.

Trigwell, K., Prosser, M., & Taylor, P. (1994). Qualitative differences in approaches to teaching first year university science courses. *Higher Education, 27*, 74–84.

# Index